Managing Services

Managing Services

Challenges and Innovations

Edited by Kathryn Haynes and Irena Grugulis

OXFORD
UNIVERSITY PRESS

Great Clarendon Street, Oxford, OX2 6DP,
United Kingdom

Oxford University Press is a department of the University of Oxford.
It furthers the University's objective of excellence in research, scholarship,
and education by publishing worldwide. Oxford is a registered trade mark of
Oxford University Press in the UK and in certain other countries

© Oxford University Press 2014

The moral rights of the authors have been asserted

First Edition published in 2014

Impression: 1

Published in the United States of America by Oxford University Press
198 Madison Avenue, New York, NY 10016, United States of America

British Library Cataloguing in Publication Data

Data available

Library of Congress Control Number: 2013940188

ISBN 978–0–19–969608–6

Printed and bound in Great Britain by
CPI Group (UK) Ltd, Croydon, CR0 4YY

Links to third party websites are provided by Oxford in good faith and
for information only. Oxford disclaims any responsibility for the materials
contained in any third party website referenced in this work.

Preface

In the second five-year period of the ESRC/EPSRC of the Advanced Institute of Management (AIM) research initiative, we appointed three cohorts of academics to two-year mid-career fellowships in three specified domains: innovation, services, and management practices.

This book covers the research and conclusions from the second of these cohorts that relate to the area of services from a range of perspectives. As befits the overall AIM agenda, however, it also includes some contributions from other cohorts of AIM Fellows and indeed the Deputy Director of AIM as well.

The overall field of services has expanded and extended in both practice and research at a rapid rate over the last several years, which has resulted in a plethora of developments and innovations. At the macro-level, it is now widely recognized that service activities as well as service-based organizations account for a large proportion of overall economic activity in developed economies such as the UK, while at the micro-level it is now common to consider service components in a wide range of transactions between supplier and user.

The collection of chapters in this book covers a series of insights and frameworks that provide us with an opportunity to appreciate scholarly work, which explores current aspects of this burgeoning field. As with all research in the overall field of management, we also have to balance general insights alongside the specific context and detail of the phenomenon we are studying. So not only do we look for useful general conclusions but also for specific insights.

I trust this book will provide both of these to those who read it and at the same time they will both enjoy and be somewhat challenged by it.

Robin Wensley

Acknowledgements

The editors and authors would like to acknowledge the support of the Advanced Institute of Management (AIM), particularly Robin Wensley and Andy Neely, in facilitating and encouraging this book. Also grateful thanks to the ESRC for funding the research projects on which this book is based.

ESRC Research award references are as follows: Giuliana Battisti—RES-331-27-0039; Irena Grugulis—RES-331-27-0038; Kathryn Haynes—RES-331-27-0022A; Irene Ng—RES-331-27-0024; Joe O'Mahoney—RES-331-27-0071; Katy Mason—RES-331-27-0049; Ammon Salter—RES-331-25-3010; Martin Spring—RES-331-27-0036; and Bruce Tether—RES-331-25-3008.

Contents

Contents

List of Figures

List of Tables

Notes on the Contributors

Luis Araujo is Professor of Industrial Marketing at Lancaster University Management School. His research is broadly related to how and why industrial firms form different types of exchange relationships, and engage in particular types of market practices. Recent publications include *Reconnecting Marketing to Markets* (Oxford University Press) co-edited with John Finch and Hans Kjellberg.

Giuliana Battisti is a Professor of the Economics of Innovation at Warwick Business School and an Advanced Institute of Management Fellow in Services. Her research focuses on the economics of innovation and innovation performance measurement. Her research findings have appeared in *Research Policy*, *Oxford Economic Papers*, *British Journal of Management*, *International Journal of Industrial Organisation*, etc. She is vice-chair of the Business and Industrial Statistics section of the Royal Statistical Society and co-chair of the British Network of Industrial Economists.

Yogesh K. Dwivedi is a Professor of Information Management in the Swansea University Business School in the UK. He obtained his PhD and MSc in Information Systems from Brunel University, UK. He has co-authored several papers that have appeared in international referred journals such as *CACM, DATA BASE, EJIS, ISJ, JIT*, and *JORS*. He is Associate Editor of *EJIS*, Assistant Editor of *TGPPP*, Senior Editor of *JECR* and member of the editorial board/review board of several journals.

Irena Grugulis is the Professor of Work and Skills at Leeds University Business School, an ESRC/AIM Services Fellow and an associate fellow of SKOPE. Her principal research interests are in the area of skills. Recent projects have focussed on the creative industries, particularly film and TV production and digital games and her research has been funded by the ESRC, EPSRC, and the EU. She is the Joint Editor in Chief of *Work, Employment and Society*.

Kathryn Haynes holds the Northern Society Chair in Accounting at Newcastle University Business School, UK. Kathryn is a Chartered Accountant and Fellow of the Institute of Chartered Accountants in England and Wales (ICAEW). Kathryn is also a Fellow of the Advanced Institute of Management Research (AIM), funded by the ESRC, where she was Lead Fellow of the Services research cohort. She is a co-facilitator of the Gender Equality Working Group of the UN Principles of Responsible Management Education.

Adrian T.H. Kuah is Senior Faculty at James Cook University Australia. Previously, he was the MBA Director at Nottingham Business School and Director of UG Business Studies at Bradford University School of Management. His research focuses on competitiveness, financial services, and regional development. He holds a PhD from the Manchester Business School, MBA from Strathclyde Business School and ITP from SDA Bocconi. Adrian is a Fellow of the Chartered Management Institute and an AIM Scholar.

Cristiana R. Lages is an Associate Professor of Marketing at Henley Business School, University of Reading and an Advanced Institute of Management Scholar. She holds a PhD in Marketing from the University of Warwick (UK). Her current research interests include: creativity in services; service recovery strategies and performance; eWOM; as well as export performance. Her publications have appeared in the *Journal of Business Research, Journal of Service Research, Journal of International Marketing, European Journal of Marketing*, and *International Marketing Review*, among others.

Katy Mason is a Reader in Marketing and Management at Lancaster University, and an AIM Management Practice Fellow. Katy's research focuses on how managers make and shape markets and the market devices used to enrol and mobilize others across organizational boundaries. Her interest in offshoring and outsourcing business services comes from working to understand how people organize and practise new ways of working in new markets. Katy's work has been published in *Journal of Management Studies, Industrial Marketing Management, Long Range Planning*, and *Journal of Marketing Management*. AIM Fellowship Grant [RES-331-27-0049].

Andy Neely is the Royal Academy of Engineering Professor of Complex Services at the University of Cambridge and Director of the Cambridge Service Alliance. He is widely recognized for his work on the servitization of manufacturing, as well as his work on performance measurement. Previously he has held appointments at Cranfield University, London Business School, and Nottingham University. He was Deputy Director of AIM Research—the UK's management research initiative—from 2003 until 2012.

Irene C.L. Ng is the Professor of Marketing and Service Systems and Director of the International Institute of Product and Service Innovation (IIPSI) at WMG, University of Warwick. Her research lies in the transdisciplinary understanding of *value*, as well as new business models and value co-creation in complex service systems. Irene is one of six UK Advanced Institute of Management (AIM) research Services Fellows and was the ESRC/NIHR Placement Fellow and Academic Advisor of the Cambridge University Health Partners.

Joe O'Mahoney is a senior lecturer at Cardiff University. He writes on critical realism, management consultancy, and identity theory. In his previous life, he was Head of Business Analysis at Three and founded a small manufacturing company. His work in this volume is the result of a Fellowship with the Advanced Institute of Management.

Ammon Salter is Professor in Technology and Innovation Management at Imperial College Business School. He holds a first degree in Political Science from the Concordia University in Canada and a doctorate from the Science Policy Research Unit (SPRU) at the University of Sussex. His main research interest concerns the management of technological innovation, including examining how organizations can harness external networks to help them innovate more successfully. From 2005 to 2007 Ammon Salter was a Ghoshal Fellow of the ESRC's Advanced Institute of Management (AIM).

Laura A. Smith is an Associate Research Fellow and doctoral candidate at the University of Exeter Business School. Her research interests include service science, servitization, and customer value in B2B services. Laura has worked on a programme of research with defence organizations and equipment manufacturers in the UK and overseas resulting in a number of publications on the creation of value-in-use in service systems and its implications for provider organizations.

Martin Spring is Professor of Operations Management in the Department of Management Science, Lancaster University Management School, and an AIM Services Fellow. His research interests are in business-to-business services, business model innovation, and operations strategy. He has published in a variety of journals, including *International Journal of Operations and Production Management* and *Industrial Marketing Management*. He recently advised the UK Government's Foresight unit on future manufacturing business models. ESRC Grant number RES-331-27-0036.

Bruce S. Tether is Professor of Innovation Management and Strategy at Manchester Business School. He holds a first degree in geography and a doctorate from the Science Policy Research Unit (SPRU) at the University of Sussex. His main research interests concern service innovation, innovation in services (especially among professional services firms), and design-based innovation. From 2005 to 2007, Bruce Tether was a Ghoshal Fellow of the ESRC's Advanced Institute of Management (AIM), and his research was supported by the ESRC funded AIM Targeted Initiative on Innovation.

Stephen L. Vargo is a Shidler Distinguished Professor and Professor of Marketing at the University of Hawai'i at Manoa. He has held visiting positions at the University of Cambridge, University of Warwick, Karlstad University, the University of Maryland, and the University of Auckland. He has published in leading journals including the *Journal of Marketing*, *Journal of the Academy of Marketing Science*, and *Journal of Service Research*. He has also received the Harold H. Maynard Award and the AMA/Sheth Foundation Award for his contributions to marketing.

1

Managing Services and the Service Sector: An Introduction

Irena Grugulis and Kathryn Haynes

Until fairly recently the service sector barely merited mention as an 'also ran' in studies of national economies, organizations, and organizing. A nation's prosperity was measured in terms of the productive industries (the very phrase is revealing) that manufactured tangible goods, studies of organizations concentrated on how these might be created more efficiently, and workplace research was effectively confined to the men (and very occasionally women) employed in manufacturing. Operations management (OM) scholars were an exception to this general rule since from the earliest they have taken an interest in certain parts of the service sector and studied transport links, and the logistics of railways, postal services, and distribution networks but, for the most part, management academics would have agreed with Adam Smith (1776/2005: 270) when he wrote:

> There is one sort of labour which adds to the value of the subject on which it is bestowed; there is another which has no such effect. The former as it produces a value, may be called productive, the latter, unproductive labour....Thus the labour of a manufacturer adds generally to the value of the materials which he works upon, that of his own maintenance, and of his master's profit. The labour of a menial servant, on the contrary, adds to the value of nothing....A man grows rich by employing a multitude of manufacturers; he grows poor by employing a multitude of menial servants.

Manufacturing and the other productive industries created goods that could be traded and so could be classified as wealth creating. Services on the other hand, a broad category that encompassed the sovereign, the civil service, academics, puppeteers, opera-dancers, clergymen, and buffoons (among many others) might deserve respect or cause amusement but they certainly did not create wealth. Rather, they were what wealth was spent on (but only after various productive workers had been taken care of).

Today few people would question the service sector's role in economic growth, nor its capacity for providing employment. Indeed, in the developed world, it is the service sector that employs the greatest number of people, contributes the most to GDP and attracts most attention from commentators, although the associated problems of measurement are widely acknowledged and gauging service sector productivity raises far more difficulties than that of manufacturing. In 2010, the World Bank published figures for 138 countries on the proportion of value-added GDP attributable to the service sector. Of these, only thirty-six countries owed less than half of their value added to the service sector and even in those thirty-six countries the service sector was a significant contributor to the economy since only seventeen had earned less than 40% of value added from it and only two less than 30% (see http://data.worldbank.org/indicator/NV.SRV.TETC.ZS).

The service sector is where most people in the developed world are employed. It also attracts a considerable amount of government interest as most 'knowledge'-based jobs and professional jobs are situated in the service sector, making it the powerhouse of the 'knowledge economy'. As a result, when commentators attempt to predict the future for work and national economies they tends to focus on the service sector as prosperous futures are seen in terms of knowledge work. Technological aficionados also see the future as service-based with the rise of e-Services shifting the way we communicate, enjoy music or film, and shop, through the likes of Facebook, Amazon, and E-Bay. Does this activity, employment, and value added disprove Adam Smith's analysis?

What Adam Smith failed to appreciate of course, was that it is possible to view service sector businesses from different standpoints. A pub, restaurant, or café may indeed be where many people *spend* their money but these are also from the perspective of the publican, restaurateur, and coffee-shop owner, the places where money is *made*. Service labour is not unproductive, in the sense that money cannot be made from it, simply because it has no tangible outputs.

This is not to argue that the intangibility of service sector goods do not generate some concerns. It is difficult to establish quality in the service sector or assess productivity. Some headway has been made in this regard but the most robust figures are taken from transport and distribution where activities are more tangible and more susceptible to measurement (Broadberry 2006). The dot.com bubble and the Banking Crisis in the first decade of the twenty-first century raised questions about both the regulation of, and the fragility of, service sector organizations. Clearly, the same could be said of many other markets, as well as of money itself. There have been bubbles of inflated prices followed by crashes in housing, tulips, and gold, so tangibility is no defence. Even if the service sector is more vulnerable than manufacturing this is an aspect of economic life that most countries must learn to deal with, as, for the near future at least, the economies of the developed world will be based on services.

Because of this, unsurprisingly, there is a positive tsunami of interest in services and the service sector. They are now the subject of extensive research, dedicated books and journals, detailed studies, and theoretical innovations. The service sector was also, between 2008 and 2011, the focus of the Economic and Social Research Council's Advanced Institute of Management (AIM) initiative. AIM was designed to foster and promote the best in British management research and, as part of its remit, it funded six cohorts of AIM Fellows, including one dedicated to the service sector. These Service Fellows were Giuliana Battisti, Kate Blackmon, Irena Grugulis, Kathryn Haynes, Irene Ng, and Martin Spring. We were all mid-career academics and, between us, we covered the areas of marketing, OM, economics, accounting, and employment. We all had very different perspectives on what the service sector was, whether it existed at all and why it was important. Details of our individual research projects can be found on the AIM website at http://www.aimresearch.org/ and details of the findings together with many of the publications, which resulted from the work are accessible on the Economic and Social Research Council's website at http://www.esrc.ac.uk/. In addition to these individual research projects, we also met regularly as a cohort, updated each other on the progress of our fieldwork, engaged with and challenged each other's ideas. This book is a product of those meetings. Some of the chapters include material from the fieldwork we conducted during our fellowships but its primary aim is not to report the detail of individual studies but to provide a broad overview of the many different perspectives on the service sector. In this venture, we were fortunate enough to be joined by some AIM Fellows from other cohorts who had also been working on the service sector and we are very grateful that Joe O'Mahoney and Katy Mason (Management Practices Fellows) and Bruce Tether (Ghoshal Fellow) were able to share their work with us. In addition, there are contributors beyond the AIM cohorts who have added significantly to the book, including AIM scholars, Yogesh Dwivedi, Christiana R. Lages, and Adrian Kuah; AIM Visiting International Fellow, Steve Vargo; and other collaborators Luis Araujo, Ammon Salter, and Laura A. Smith. We are grateful for their contributions. Finally, we are pleased that the AIM directors, Robin Wensley and Andy Neely, were also able to contribute to the book.

An Overview of Chapters

Chapter 2 continues and develops our initial discussion of the challenges of defining and measuring services and the service sector. Battisti, Dwivedi, Kuah, and Lages discuss the nature of services and the diverse conceptualizations, which may comprise the term, together with how they are classified and measured by governments and businesses themselves. They suggest that measuring services is not an easy task as services are highly heterogeneous, with some national statistical instruments such as Standard Industrial Classifications (SIC codes) inappropriate for measuring services and failing to capture the increasing servitization of manufacturing. Service activities play a key role in enhancing productivity and competitiveness and to be fully understood they need to be considered along the various dimensions of services.

In Chapter 3, Spring brings an OM perspective to the discussion and considers the way services have been treated in OM research. It is an extremely wide-ranging chapter. In it he considers the blurring lines between manufacturing and service, and the multitude of hybrid organizations and the privatization of the state, before going on to explore services through the customer, process, and supply chain. The implications of technology and IT for service OM are reviewed, together with new business models such as systems integration, servitization, and procuring complex performance.

Grugulis provides a review of employment in the service sector in Chapter 4. The sector is significant in employment terms, accounting for over 80% of jobs in both the USA and the UK and it is also diverse. Grugulis describes the principal focus of much service sector research, considering the nature of the customer and the triangular relationship between managers, customers, and workers but argues that these capture only part of the diversity of the service sector. Instead, she offers a new way of classifying service work with five different categories: customer facing, high touch service sector work; 'traditional' work; work in the creative industries; knowledge work and public sector service work. She then concludes with a discussion of 'soft' skills.

In Chapter 5, Haynes focuses on the professional services sector, characterized by recent social and demographic shifts in the workforce in which more women are entering professional services. Haynes examines the role of the professions in providing professional services, the role and influence of professional services firms, the nature of professional service work, and relationships with clients, in conjunction with concepts of gender and diversity. She examines whether, and how, professional services limit their membership through closure regimes based on the traditional nature of professionals and professionalism. The main focus of the discussion is on how gender in the professional services context acts as a form of social closure caused by the need to have appropriate social and physical capital. However, the chapter also considers other forms of social closure, based on class and race among other factors, which also may interact with each other, drawing out implications for equality within professional services firms and potential for further research.

O'Mahoney continues the professional services theme in Chapter 6, presenting his research on management innovation in the consulting sector. O'Mahoney argues that, while many studies of innovation provide a micro-level analysis, it is at the macro- or meso-level that the relationship between agency and a changing structural environment is enacted. Drawing from research in the sector, informed by a critical realist perspective, he seeks to explain how and why management innovation is changing in the consulting industry, through factors such as increased competition, the need to differentiate, the growth of procurement by clients, and pressure to reduce risk.

In Chapter 7, Neely argues that although the servitization of manufacturing is not a new phenomenon, it remains an important area to explore due to three broad challenges facing society: the changing structure of the global economy; new technological innovations; and demographic, social and environmental pressures. The chapter offers a framework for thinking about servitization, identifying five options that firms appear to be pursuing, and integrating them with society's grand challenges. Services have a large role to play in addressing and tackling these problems, enabling creativity and innovation.

Ng, Vargo, and Smith offer a way to reconceptualize all organizations in Chapter 8. They argue that previous accounts of organization have followed a goods-dominant logic, prioritizing the ownership of tangible goods. By contrast, service-dominant logic focuses on value creation rather than ownership. This means that firms can be redesigned to provide better service to customers, that design can be a collaborative process shared between customers and suppliers, and that traditional functional divides can be broken down.

In Chapter 9, Salter and Tether consider both the level and nature of innovation in services. Noting the diversity of the sector, and implications of this for innovation, they classify firms as traditional, systemic, and professional services. Traditional firms tend to be small, with high failure and turnover rates, many lacking the capacity to innovate. Systems services are much larger and highly specialized often involving extensive use of sophisticated technologies (as, for example, in the airline industry). However, size can also impede innovation here and new ways of working are often introduced by launching new firms. Professional services firms are characterized by high levels of professionally qualified staff (see Haynes, Chapter 5 in this book) and are often very innovative. Salter and Tether go on to review the different types of innovation that may be found in the service sector and observe that product, process, and organizational innovation often move in tandem.

In Chapter 10, Spring, Araujo, and Mason outline some of the treatments of offshore outsourcing found within different areas of management literature and argue that an approach based on the 'modularity theory of the firm' can shed helpful light on the complexities of offshore outsourcing practice. They review the nature of modularity; its cost structures and standards to evaluate how readily this approach, with its roots in product-based industries, might be applied to services. While modular approaches will make service activities more readily accessible from other firms, the modularity theory of the firm also suggests that in varying degrees, these interfaces are never 'frictionless' or cost-free, and hence that firms must work to become expert at managing them.

Chapter 11 returns to the theme of service-dominant logic to investigate the challenges of a service system for value co-creation. Smith and Ng provide a review and comparative analysis of three published cases in the defence industry considered as service systems for co-created outcomes. As a result, six challenges of a service system for value co-creation are summarized: determination challenge; measurement challenge; revenue challenge; context challenge; resource challenge; and skills challenge. They argue that co-creation of value is gaining a prominent role in our understanding of service systems.

The book as a whole is wide ranging. It covers the service sector from the perspective of economists, OM, marketing, employment, professional work, and servitization. We hope that this breadth will help it to contribute to academic study of the service sector and facilitate its introduction to the mainstream of work and organizations.

References

Broadberry, S. (2006). *Market Services and the Productivity Race 1850–2000: British performance in international perspective*. Cambridge: Cambridge University Press.
Smith, A. (1776/2005). *The Wealth of Nations*. Hazelton, PA: Pennsylvania State University, PA.

2

Service Measurement and Definition: Challenges and Limitations

Giuliana Battisti, Yogesh K. Dwivedi, Adrian T.H. Kuah,
and Cristiana R. Lages

Introduction

In recent years, there has been significant growth in the contribution of services to the economy of developed nations. In the UK, the service sector is a major contributor to the country's economic prosperity. However, despite the importance of the service economy, there has been a delay in the collection of data. The challenges relating to the definition and classification of services alongside the measurement of their performance raise a number of important issues yet to be addressed adequately. This has partly contributed to a delay in the development of public policies aimed at sustaining the growth of services.

In this chapter, we try to shed some light on the conceptualization of services and service performance measurement and on those issues that would benefit from further attention especially by academics and policy makers. Our aim is to present some stylized facts and to highlight limitations and advancements in our understanding of the nature of services, the associated statistics, and performance measures. We conclude by emphasizing the need to revisit the basics to ensure that the contribution of services to economic competitiveness and more in general to the UK economy is properly measured and maximized.

The Nature of Services

Competitive pressure and low-cost production inputs from developing countries are leading firms in developed economies to adopt competitive strategies such as outsourcing or repositioning within the production chain. Indeed, the Cox Review of Creativity in Business to the HM Treasury in 2005 suggests that firms should add value to the final product (whether good or service) rather than merely focus on cost minimizing strategies. The servitization of manufacturing (Neely 2009, 2010) provides direct evidence of one such strategy, whereby manufacturing companies increasingly offer complementary services, or directly incorporate services into their final products, e.g. provision of financial services or product insurance to the purchase of the manufacturing good (see Chapters 3 and 7, this volume). In some cases, companies have totally repositioned themselves in areas of higher value. IBM, for example, has become a supplier of 'computing and business services' rather than being a computer manufacturer. Services have become increasingly important indeed. Moreover, manufacturing-based companies are not the only providers and users of services. Pure service firms constitute a large share of the service economy.

It can be argued that the provision of services is nothing new. Services have played a major role in the Industrial Revolution (e.g. financial services) and hence contributed to the long-run growth. What is new is that in recent years an increasing number of manufacturing firms worldwide have embarked on service-based strategies to increase their sales. Today, services account for well over 70% of the EU economic activity and a similar, very substantial proportion of UK employment and value added. The rapid growth of service employment brings about the need to understand, promote, and sustain the growth of the service economy. However, there are major obstacles to this, including: lack of standard definition and classification of services; problems in measuring service performance; protecting, sustaining, and measuring innovation in services, which is reflected in the lack of clear (standard) guiding policies to encourage and promote the growth of services. Until recently, most of the research and policy remained focused on traditional manufacturing activities. Innovation policies primarily remained based on the model of technological innovation generation such as R&D and patents and these only recently seem to be slowly changing to being scarcely applicable to many services. As a result, a number of projects at both national and international levels have been launched to understand better the nature of service activities and to identify the role government might play in promoting a broad range of innovative activities in sustaining a service driven economy.

One of the difficulties in classifying and measuring services is caused by the non-capital intensive nature of services. Services are also heterogeneous in nature and intangible (Lovelock 1983; Silvestro *et al.* 1992; Stell and Donoho 1996). Complexity and heterogeneity of services is also added by the role of technology and consumer/user power in the innovation process such as in the case of knowledge intensive business services (KIBS) and R&D intensive innovation leader versus 'non-R&D and non-technology' intensive services that involve low skills services or that involve only indirectly new technologies, e.g. service innovation derived (for example by the combination of existing services and technologies but perceived as value adding by final users) (European Commission 2007). As a result, different policy and management experts define and classify services differently. Some refer to the nature of the service provided such as the quantity, time, and space dimension of pure services, e.g. intermediation services and contact services (see Melvin 1990; Haskel 2007). Others consider service as a product (Thomas 1978; Lovelock 1983) or complement to a good (Judd 1964; Lovelock 1983), others regard services as a sector (Miozzo and Soete 2001) or services as different types of economic activities ranging from pure to hybrid forms (Neely 2009). Boundaries are even less clear when distinguishing services from manufacturing in standard industrial classifications (SICs) of economic activities. IKEA, for example, is a home furnishing company. The group has a fully integrated supply chain, including its own industrial groups and suppliers (Swedwood and Swedspan) with 20,000 co-workers and 46 production units in 14 countries. In 2010, the IKEA Group had 127,000 co-workers, a total of 280 stores in 26 countries and 1074 suppliers in 55 countries (see The IKEA Group Annual Report 2010). Although the IKEA Group works in four areas (range; strategy and product development; production; supply and retail) the volume of its main activity is such that the group is now classified as a service company in Swedish national statistics, i.e. SIC 5712: furniture store. The fact that companies such as IKEA, the world's biggest home furniture company, are now classified in their home country (Sweden) as a service firm suggests that wrapping tangible goods in services is having an increasingly significant impact and is clearly the main economic activity of the group. However, services offered by most manufacturing firms often go undetected by current statistics. For example, according to the UK fourth Community Innovation Survey (2005), 41.2% of the 16,445 firms in the sample were classified as production manufacturing (based upon the SIC of main economic activity) with the remaining 58.8% firms being classified as service companies. Furthermore, of all the services introduced, 31% of them were introduced by manufacturing companies, 37.7% of the new goods were introduced by companies classified as service firms and about 44% of firms that introduced a new service[1] also introduced a new good. This suggests that the SIC classification underestimates the contribution of services to final output and that there exist important complementarities in the production and provision of goods and services. Clearly, a number of hybrid firms that offer both goods and services are present. However, even if the hybrid classification was introduced, it would be difficult (if not impossible) for many companies to separate the (production) process and the operations management from the final product (Bryson 2010). This difficulty is also reflected in the separation of the stream of revenue derived from the service provision versus the tangible product (Neely 2009). The qualitative, rather than the quantitative aspect of services can become a crucial issue such as in the extent to which prices reflect the qualitative aspect of service delivery quality satisfaction.

The fact that goods and services are often offered jointly would suggest that an integrated approach would be better than a targeted approach aimed at only one of the two products. This should lead to a rethink of services in industrial statistics and whether a separation of services from tangible goods provision would be possible, desirable, or necessary given the generic and broad nature of product offering (Smith 2010).

Nevertheless, why is it important to define and classify services? Without clarity of definition in times of growing importance, it is difficult to develop instruments for service performance measurement and to support this important economic activity. If there is an agreement or common view on what a service is, then it could be appropriate to create and validate a service-specific performance measurement for the firm and appropriate policy tools for policy makers.

Defining and Classifying Services

Traditionally, a service is described as a 'deed, act or performance' (Berry 1980; Lovelock 1983) but this definition can be too vague and limited in today's context. The various views of what services 'are' and 'do' pose challenges. It is both useful and pertinent to have more clarity in terms of existing definitions and classifications to understand and measure them. We report below some of these definitions—showing few but quite diverse views on services (see Table 2.1(a) and 2.1(b)).

One early conceptualization defined services as being primarily delivered with equipment or through people (Thomas 1978). This forms the basis for classifying services into two categories. The first category is 'equipment-based services', which includes automated services (e.g. car wash), monitored by unskilled operators (e.g. movie theatre) and operated by skilled personnel (e.g. airline) (Thomas 1978). The second category is people-based services, which include unskilled labour (e.g. lawn carers), skilled labour (e.g. mechanics), and professionals (e.g. lawyers) (Thomas 1978).

Another conceptualization is based on the intensity of contact and degree of separation between production and consumption (Judd 1964; Lovelock 1983). Services can be classified based on the type of goods they are integrated with. This includes categories such as rented goods services, owned goods services (e.g. repair or improvement of goods owned by customers), and non-goods services (e.g. personal experiences) (Judd 1964; Lovelock 1983).

Table 2.1(a) Classification and definition of service(s) as a product and/or as an economic activity

	Classification and definition
Neely (2009)	Based on services as complement to a final good: • Integration-oriented product–service systems • Product-oriented product–service systems • Service-oriented product–service systems • Use oriented product–service systems • Result oriented product–service systems Service categories: (a) Design and development services; (b) Systems and solutions; (c) Retail and distribution services; (d) Maintenance and support services; (e) Installation and implementation services; (f) Financial services; (g) Property and real estate; (h) Consulting and operating services; (i) Procurement services; (j) Leasing services and (k) Transportation and trucking services
Stell and Donoho (1996)	Based on consumer perspective on level of perceived risk and purchase efforts and consumer involvement: • Convenience services • Preference services • Shopping services • Speciality services
Melvin (1990)	Based on time and space separation: • Intermediation services • Contact services
Lovelock (1983)	Based on the nature of service and the direct recipient of the service: • Services directed at people's bodies • Services directed at people's minds • Services directed at goods and other physical possessions • Services directed at intangible assets
Thomas (1978)	Based on medium of delivery: • Primarily equipment based • Primarily people based
Chase (1978)	Based on degree of separation between consumption and production • High contact • Low contact
Judd (1964)	Based on integration of services with three types of goods: • Rented goods services • Own goods services • Non-goods services

Table 2.1(b) Classification and definition of service(s) as a core sector/economic activity

Miozzo and Soete (2001)	• Supplier dominated: personal services (e.g. restaurants, beauty) and public and social services (e.g. health, education) • Scale-intensive physical networks (transport and wholesale) • Information networks (finance, insurance, and communications) • Specialized suppliers/science based (software and specialized business services)
Neely (2010)	• Pure manufacturing • Pure service • Hybrid
Standard Industrial Classification (SIC; e.g. 2007)	• Services: wholesale and retail trade, hotels and restaurants, transport, storage and communication, finance and banking; and real estate, renting, and business activities such as consultancy and research firms • Manufacturing

The main criticism of this classification is that the third category 'non-goods services' is still too broad for many modern day services such as insurance, banking, legal advice, and accounting (Lovelock 1983: 11).

The nature of service actions and the type of recipients are two other ways to characterize services (Lovelock 1983). By using these two factors, services can be divided into four categories. First, services directed at people's bodies, which include healthcare, beauty salons, exercise clinics, restaurants, and hair-cutting. Second, those services directed at people's minds, for example, education, broadcasting, information services, theatres, and museums. Within the third category are those directed at goods and other physical possessions, for example, freight transportation, industrial equipment repair and maintenance, laundry and dry cleaning, landscaping and lawn care, and veterinary care. The fourth category involves services directed at intangible assets, including banking, legal services, insurance, and accounting (Lovelock 1983).

Another approach classifies services in terms of time and space separation in production and consumption (Melvin 1990; Haskel 2007). A service that overcomes the time or space separation between consumers and producers is termed an intermediation service. This includes services such as transport, retailing, and some financial services. The second type of service is contact services and includes haircuts, education, and medical and financial advice (Melvin 1990; Haskel 2007). Contact services could be further classified in two categories as high and low contact services (Chase 1978; Lovelock 1983). This classification is based on the premise that it is difficult to control product variability in high contact services. Owing to greater involvement of customers in the service process, they exert a higher degree of influence on timing of demand and service features. The examples of high contact services include healthcare, hotels, and restaurants and low contact services include the postal service and wholesaling (Chase 1978; Lovelock 1983).

Services can exist in a pure form, or they can be integrated within tangible goods (a satellite navigator), or can be offered alongside the final goods such as financial or insurance services. Neely (2010) identified 12 different types of such services as either hybrid or pure forms. Building upon the level of integration of service into the manufactured good provides another classification of product–service systems: product, service, use, result, and integration oriented (Neely 2009).

The classification of services as an economic activity is also diverse. A number of taxonomies of services have been proposed. Complex taxonomies of services can be found based, for example, upon linkages with manufacturing and other services sectors and that distinguish among supplier dominated, scale intensive physical networks, information networks, specialized suppliers and science-based sectors (Miozzo and Soete 2001). Other classifications are based upon the tangible and intangible nature of the final product such as the broad classification into manufacturing and services, very often criticized for being too restrictive. More refined classifications of services are provided by the Standard Industrial Classification (SIC) of economic activities used in official national statistics. The latter classifies manufacturing, public services activities, and business services into 16 subsections. Among business services, it includes wholesale and retail trade, hotels and restaurants, transport, storage and communication, finance and banking; and real estate, renting, and business activities such as consultancy and research firms (see ONS 2007). Many government reports and research agencies use the SIC classifications to further differentiate business services into high skills, R&D intensive high-value business services (also known as KIBS)[2] from low skills services with limited or no use of technology (see also Chapter 4 this volume for a full discussion of skills requirements). Examples of the former are environmental testing and professional services while examples of the latter are cleaning services and call centres. SIC is often criticized for being unrepresentative as it is based exclusively on the main economic activity and production technology used in the provision of the main product. As a result SIC may not capture the complexity of services derived from the professions (for a discussion of the nature of professional services see Chapter 5 this volume). The SIC classification is often criticized for underestimating services nested within capital goods and alternative definitions based upon 'pure manufacturer', 'pure services', and 'servitized' manufacturers have been provided (Neely 2010). Based upon the value co-creation views, the service dominant logic of marketing argues that service(s) is any final output delivery of any tangible or intangible good (Vargo and Lusch 2004a,b, see also Chapters 8 and 11 this volume). This horizontal approach to services clearly rules out any issues about standard classification of economic activity.

The above represents a few of several definitions and classifications of services. Their heterogeneity clearly reflects the nature of services and suggests that any encompassing methodological approach should start with revisiting the fundamentals, rather than adopting a closed view.

Performance Measurement of Services

The methodological approaches to service performance measurements tend to be skewed, depending on whether economic outputs or subjective customer experiences are captured. This complexity is justified by the inseparability, heterogeneity, and intangibility nature of services (Fisk *et al.* 1993; Kotler 2003). There are, however, some fundamental issues that need to be resolved.

First, financial reports and national statistics do often under-report the service component of a product. Product–process–service distinction may be cumbersome. It may be difficult to isolate and quantify how much service there is in any given product. With few exceptions, the breakdown of the value of services (e.g. the stream of revenue derived from the service provided alongside the final good) is not reported separately in firm's accounts. Thus, while many national statistics do report output of the service sector, service provision of many hybrid companies (whose main activity is classified as manufacturing) is captured badly, if at all. Consequently, while manufacturing outputs can be exaggerated, service output is often under-reported (Neely 2010). This issue is quite important for countries such as the US where about 58% of US firms with 'production' as the main economic activity (based upon the manufacturing SIC code) do increasingly offer supporting services (Neely 2010).

Heterogeneity exists in service output measurements depending on whether the service is offered by the private or public sector. For example, in public sector health and education services, output is often measured through ranking exercises based on relative qualitative measures such as waiting time or level of attainment (see for example De Wette *et al.* 2010). In contrast, private sector output is usually measured by quantitative measures such as overall revenue.

While an accounting quantitative approach may be appropriate as it avoids any ambiguity in measurement, it also has its limitations. One would think that price would be able to capture the value[3] of services and accurately reflect the quality and cost of the service. But that happens only in perfectly competitive markets. As a result, its value often remains hidden in the final output price along with any potential mark up because of different market power (Griffith *et al.* 2003) and that is irrespective of whether the final service is offered in isolation or jointly with other goods or services. A further complication is that prices may not only provide an inaccurate reflection of 'quality' due to the market structure and market power, but also of the input costs such as land and capital, which differ due to taxes, technology, and geography (Reynolds *et al.* 2005).

Last, revenue measurement of service performance does not explicitly include the measurement of intangible benefits such as overall quality of the service, service provider's speed of response to customers' requests, service provider's empathy with the customer, and range (small versus large) of services offered. As a result, several non-standard accounting measures, based on subjective assessment, have been implemented. The most widely used form of service performance measurement is based on the consumers' perception of the quality of service offered by the service provider (see Cronin and Taylor 1992). That would be based on aspects such as tangibility, reliability, responsiveness, assurance, and empathy (e.g. Parasuraman *et al.* 1988). An alternative would be to assess service performance based on employees' behaviour in serving and helping customers, i.e. service delivery (e.g. Liao and Chuang 2004; Ray *et al.* 2004; Storey and Hull 2010). A more balanced measurement of service performance would take into account three aspects: customer evaluation of the quality of the service provided by the service unit; an organization's own evaluation of the quality of the service provided by the service unit; and ability to retain stakeholders over time (Ray *et al.* 2004). Some studies have emphasized two levels of analysis in service performance measurement, i.e. the organization and individual levels (Liao and Chuang 2004). At the organizational level, emphasis is on the influence of managerial actions and service climate (Schneider 1990) on service performance at the store level (e.g. Johnson 1996; Schneider *et al.* 1998; Borucki and Burke 1999). At the individual level, emphasis is on the impact of employees' personalities on their performance (among others Barrick and Mount 1991; Frei and McDaniel 1998).

In summary, a variety of performance measures are available specific to the nature of the service provided, whether a financial or public service. Some are objective but might ignore the quality aspects and broader welfare implication of the service offered. Others are subjective or mixed or stratified across levels of responsibility and therefore more difficult to standardize across the variety of services. Whether it is a measure of revenue or a customer experience, or an assessment of the quality of the delivery, measuring service performance may need a completely new rethinking along the lines of modern organization of economic activities, and that of services as an economic activity that creates value to a firm or a market.

Discussion and Conclusion

In recent years, there has been significant growth in the contribution that services make to the economic output of developed nations. Since 1970, the service sector's contribution to the economic output of the UK has grown from 53% to 73% while the manufacturing sector has declined from 33% to 16% (source: Office for National Statistics). Similar figures are shown for the EU where services account for about 70% of EU economic activity. The increase in importance of services is partly due to greater numbers of manufacturing companies offering services, either alongside or incorporated into their final products. As a result, the need to define and classify services, to understand and measure service performance, assumes a greater significance.

Despite the rapid growth of the service economy, to date there is no consensus neither on a standard definition and classification of services nor on the best way to measure service performance. There has been a substantial delay also in the collection of statistics for services and in the development of policies of relevance to business services. Advancements are clearly constrained by the various difficulties encountered with the conceptualization of services. More research is clearly needed in this direction.

Measuring services is not an easy task. Services are highly heterogeneous. There is frequently no product–process distinction and requirement for heterogeneous skills (see Chapter 4, this volume). In their current format, statistical instruments such as the SIC are not appropriate to deal with services. Despite the increasing servitization of manufacturing, the financial records of businesses rarely incorporate the service aspect of a good in their books. As a result, service output is often under-reported and most official national statistics fail to capture the increasing servitization of manufacturing.

Measuring services performance can be taken from either the employee or customer perspectives, but also in terms of their intangibles or their economic value. There is a clear need for a refinement of survey instruments to capture these, as well as a need for a greater accounting of manufacturing–service interaction in industrial classification.

Although it might be argued that it is not necessary to distinguish a service from a tangible good, as the boundary between them is increasingly blurred (see Chapter 3, this volume), there is a clear need for a more diverse array of survey and statistical instruments, as well as a greater accountability of manufacturing–service interaction in industrial classifications. Clearly, a rethinking of the fundamentals of classifications along the lines of industrial organization and economic activities in the modern era is needed.

The diversity of definitions of services and their performance measures reflects the difficulties associated with the conceptualization of services. The variety of service offerings raises questions as to whether the service economy is subject to market failures and whether, as a result, it requires government intervention. If this was the case, another question would address which policy instruments are the best for supporting the growth of the service economy (see Chapter 9 this volume).

The challenges relating to the definition, classification, and measurement of services raise a number of important policy issues yet to be addressed adequately. For example, with regards to policy discussion, exploring how the UK can drive growth more effectively though innovation in (high and low skills) services is almost completely neglected with the focus tending to remain on high-tech manufacturing. There is a clear need to change this.

Indeed, services present unique challenges. They are characterized by a relatively short life cycle and can be imitated by competitors in a very short time. While in some cases that can be desirable (as standardization can increase diffusion), in others that can make it difficult for firms to sustain high rates of competitive performance in the long run. R&D incentives and intellectual property protection are the most commonly used government policy tools in support of innovative activities. However, most services innovation does not take place in formal R&D laboratories. In many cases, the applicability of intellectual property rights is quite limited. That suggests the need to rethink strategies and policies not only designed to sustain the UK science base, but that stimulate the development of systems and applications to foster better and competitive service provision.

Some authors see services as any value creation or co-creation activity associated with the final delivery of any tangible good or service, irrespective of whether outsourced or internally produced (see Chapters 8 and 11, this volume). This view encompasses the various forms of service offerings and would favour horizontal rather than vertical policies supporting and promoting service innovation across service sectors and offerings. Service activities play a key role in enhancing productivity and competitiveness and to be fully understood they need to be considered along the various dimensions of services.

Services are a major contributor to UK economic prosperity. The issues arising in this chapter, regarding existing approaches to the classification and measurement of services and service innovation and performance, highlight serious deficiencies in current approaches. Only by focusing on these issues, and addressing them, the contribution of services to the UK economy and to the UK economic competitiveness may be maximized.

Notes

1. SIC is a widespread tool used internationally in official national statistics to classify companies at detailed levels of disaggregation based upon their main economic activity. This classification promotes uniformity of definition over time and across countries (ONS 2007). SIC was first issued by the United Nations in 1948 and is revised periodically to include emergent and new industries. For the UK, the

current SIC includes 16 subsections, 60 divisions, 222 groups, 503 classes, and 253 subclasses.

2. The definition of knowledge intensive business services was first introduced in 1995 in a report to the European Commission by Miles *et al.* (1995).

3. This represents a form of value creation or value added in the value–price–cost (VPC) model (Hoopes *et al.* 2003; Hoopes and Madsen 2008; Leiblein and Madsen 2009). According to this view, the firm can either attract buyers due to the better surplus associated with its good or service (V-P) or make a higher profit (P-C) or both (Leiblein and Madsen 2009).

References

Barrick, M.R. and Mount, M.K. (1991). The big five personality dimensions and job performance: a meta-analysis. *Personnel Psychology*, **44**, 1–26.

Berry, L.L. (1980). Services marketing is different. *Business*, **30**(3), 24–29.

Borucki, C.C. and Burke, M.J. (1999). An examination of service-related antecedents to retail store performance. *Journal of Organizational Behavior*, **20**(6), 943–962.

Bryson, J.R. (2010) Service innovation and manufacturing innovation: bundling and blending services and products in hybrid production systems to produce hybrid products. In: *The Handbook of Innovation and Services: a multi-disciplinary perspective*, Gallouj, F. and Djellal, F. (Ed.), pp. 679–701. Cheltenham: Edward Elgar Publishing.

Chase, R.B. (1978). Where does the customer fit in a service operation? *Harvard Business Review*, **56**, 137–142.

Cronin, J.J. Jr, and Taylor, S.A. (1992). Measuring service quality: a reexamination and extension. *Journal of Marketing*, **56**, 55–66.

De Wette, K., Thanassoulis, E., Simpson, G., Battisti, G., and Charlesworth-May, A. (2010). Assessing pupil and school performance by non-parametric and parametric techniques. *Journal of the Operational Research Society*, **61**, 1224–1237.

European Commission (2007). Towards a European strategy in support of innovation in services: challenges and key issues for future action. Commission Staff Working Document SEC (2007) 1059.

Fisk, R.P., Brown, S.W., and Bitner, M.J. (1993). Tracking the evolution of the services marketing literature. *Journal of Retailing*, **69**, 61–103.

Frei, R.L. and McDaniel, M.A. (1998). Validity of customer service measures in personnel selection: a review of criterion and construct evidence. *Human Performance*, **11**, 1–27.

Griffith, R., Harrison, R., Haskel, J., and Sako, M. (2003). The UK productivity gap and the importance of the service sector, *AIM Briefing Note*, Available at [http://www.aimresearch.org/uploads/File/Publications/Academic%20 Publications%202/The_UK_Productivity_Gap_&_The_Importance_Of_The_ Service_Sectors.pdf].

Haskel, J. (2007). Measuring innovation and productivity in a knowledge-based service economy. *Economic & Labour Market Review*, **1**(7), 27–31.

Hoopes, D.G. and Madsen, T.L. (2008). A capability-based view of competitive heterogeneity. *Industrial and Corporate Change*, **17**(3), 393–426.

Hoopes, D.G., Madsen, T.L., and Walker, G. (2003). Guest editors' introduction to the special issue: Why is there a resource-based view? Toward a theory of competitive heterogeneity. *Strategic Management Journal*, **24**, 889–902.

Johnson, J.W. (1996). Linking employee perceptions of service climate to customer satisfaction. *Personnel Psychology*, **49**(4), 831–851.

Judd, R.C. (1964). The case for redefining services. *Journal of Marketing*, **28**, 58–59.

Kotler, P. (2003). *Marketing Management,* 11th edn. Upper Saddle River, NJ: Prentice Hall.

Leiblein, M.J. and Madsen, T.L. (2009). Unbundling competitive heterogeneity: incentive structures and capability influences on technological innovation. *Strategic Management Journal*, **30**(7), 711–735.

Liao, H. and Chuang, A. (2004). A multilevel investigation of factors influencing employee service performance and customer outcomes. *The Academy of Management Journal*, **47**, 41–58.

Lovelock, C.H. (1983). Classifying services to gain strategic marketing insights. *Journal of Marketing*, **47**(3), 9–20.

Melvin, J. (1990). Time and space in economic analysis. *Canadian Journal of Economics*, **23**(4), 725–747.

Miles, I., Kastrinos, N., Flanagan, K., Bilderbeek, R., Hertog, B., Huntink, W., and Bouman, M. (1995). Knowledge-intensive business services: users, carriers and sources of innovation. European Innovation Monitoring System (EIMS). EIMS Publication No. 15.

Miozzo, M. and Soete, L. (2001). Internationalization of services: a technological perspective. *Technological Forecasting and Social Change*, **67**, 159–185.

Neely, A. (2008). Exploring the financial consequences of the servitization of manufacturing. *Operations Management Research*, **1**(2), 1–50.

Neely, A. (2010). The servitization of manufacturing: how do we track global developments? Paper presented at the workshop 'Innovation and firm performance in services: are we measuring them correctly?' Held at Nottingham University Business School. [www.aimresearch.org/index.php?mact=CGCalenda r,cntnt01,default,0&cntnt01event_id=118&cntnt01display=event&cntnt01retur nid=61"].

Office for National Statistics. (2007). UK Standard Industrial Classification of Economic Activities 2007 (SIC 2007), by Prosser, L. pp. 1–246.

Parasuraman, A., Zeithaml, V.A., and Berry, L.L. (1988). SERVQUAL: a multiple-item scale for measuring consumer perceptions of service quality. *Journal of Retailing*, **64**, 12–40.

Reynolds, J., Howard, E., Dragun, D., Rosewell, B., and Ormerod, P. (2005). Assessing the productivity of the UK retail sector. *International Review of Retail, Distribution and Consumer Research*, **15**, 237–280.

Schneider, B. (1990). The climate for service: an application of the climate construct. *Organizational Climate and Culture*. San Francisco: Jossey Bass.

Schneider, B., White, S.S., and Paul, M.C. (1998). Linking service climate and customer perceptions of service quality: test of a causal model. *Journal of Applied Psychology*, **83**(2), 150–163.

Silvestro, R., Fitzgerald, L., and Johnston, R. (1992). Towards a classification of service processes. *International Journal of Service Industry Management*, **3**(3), 62–75.

Smith, K. (2010). Services, innovation and growth: current policy challenges. Paper presented at the workshop 'Innovation and firm performance in services: Are we measuring them correctly?' Held at Nottingham University Business School. [http://www.aimresearch.org/index.php?mact=CGCalendar,cntnt01,default,0&cntnt01event_id=118&cntnt01display=event&cntnt01returnid=61].

Stell, R. and Donoho, C.L. (1996). Classifying services from a consumer perspective. *Journal of Services Marketing*, **10**(6), 33–44.

Storey, C. and Hull, F.M. (2010). Service development success: a contingent approach by knowledge strategy. *Journal of Service Management*, **21**(2), 140–161.

Thomas, D.R.E. (1978). Strategy is different in service businesses. *Harvard Business Review*, **56**, 158–165.

Vargo, S.L. and Lusch, R.F. (2004a). Evolving to a new dominant logic for marketing. *Journal of Marketing*, **68**, 1–17.

Vargo, S.L. and Lusch, R.F. (2004b). The four services marketing myths: remnants from a manufacturing model. *Journal of Service Research*, **6**(4), 324–335.

3

The Shifting Terrain of Service Operations Management

Martin Spring

Introduction

This chapter presents an idiosyncratic review of the treatment of services in operations management (OM) from someone not instinctively attracted—or at least no more than any other customer—to the study of such service OM staples as queues in hotel lobbies or the time taken to serve a meal on an aeroplane. In that sense, then, I am not a 'service junkie' (Chase 1996). When I board a flight, my professional antennae are raised not by the way I am greeted by the flight attendants, but by speculating about the contractual relationship between the airline and the firm providing baggage handling services, and by the processes that ensure that the engine hanging on the wing operates satisfactorily.

Part of my antipathy has been rooted in the tendency of the vast majority of service OM work to be based in mass services. We all like to be treated as individuals, and some of the work at the more cynical end of service OM can appear to be about firms covering a standard process with a thin veneer of superficial personalization, in the interest of productivity. Of course, productivity is important: work by researchers involved with the Advanced Institute of Management (AIM) Research initiative in the UK has indeed drawn attention to the relatively low productivity of UK service businesses (Griffith *et al.* 2003), and productivity in services has been an abiding concern in OM research. For example, in two papers developing a strategic perspective on the design of service processes, the leading US OM scholar Roger Schmenner (1986, 2004) argues that successful service firms conform to his own 'theory of swift even flow' (Schmenner and Swink 1998). The data are compelling: his selected firms have used service standardization, process automation, and scale to deliver higher sales per employee and growth than the average for their industry sector. The 'production line approach to service' (Levitt 1972) seems to work. Schmenner's research therefore raises the question of the role of OM. Is the sole objective to eliminate variation and increase throughput? Once all traces of individuality have been eliminated, is the OM's job done, and can we then move on?

The aim of this chapter is to use this rather personal stepping-off point to examine more generally what has changed in services OM in recent years and whether these changes have been developments in theory, reflections of changes in the empirical world, or both. The main question I will address is whether the emerging topics in the service OM literature really are saying something new, or are merely re-stating some core OM concerns in new terms and in a new context. I begin with an overview of some indicative changes in services OM, in both theory and practice, and a brief discussion of the enduring question of the definition of services. I then provide, for the benefit of the non-OM reader, a very brief outline of some of the key concerns of the OM discipline. The rest of the chapter is then devoted to a review of what seem to me some of the most active and interesting areas of development in services OM research.

What's New? Has Service Operations Management Changed?

Service Operations Management: Some Trends in the Discipline

The purpose of much of the chapter is to discuss some specific recent trends in the way services have been treated within the OM discipline. However, in this short section, I'd like to make some brief observations about the broader patterns, before these later sections look at some of the emerging themes a little more closely. This will be a brief and selective review of some issues that seem important to me: fuller accounts of the development of service OM can be found in a number of excellent review papers (e.g. Johnston 1999; Roth and Menor 2003).

First, the amount of research effort devoted to services has grown. As Slack *et al.* (2004) noted almost ten years ago, however, this growth has been rather patchy and still leaves services grossly under-researched relative to manufacturing, bearing in mind the economic domination of the 'service sector' (broadly interpreted) in developed economies. Nevertheless, a casual look at leading academic OM conferences in Europe and the United States shows service OM to be playing an increasingly important role and, for example, both EurOMA (Europe) and Production and Operations Management Society

(USA) have established special service OM colleges in the past few years. The framing of service OM work has generally shifted from a concern with 'service sectors'—banking and insurance, professional services, education, health, and hospitality management, to give some examples—to a concern with service or services as such. Healthcare is perhaps an exception, in that there continue to be tracks and research groups devoted to this sector. This shift is also reflected in a very small but significant way in the renaming, in 2009, of *The International Journal of Service Industry Management* as *The Journal of Service Management*. According to the Editors:

> As economies across the world have become more service orientated, so does the importance of studying and understanding all aspects of managing service. These new managerial challenges include traditional service organizations not only in hospitality and retail but also in information, engineering, health care, consulting, government, not-for-profits, and services in manufacturing companies. All require new knowledge, skills and abilities in the emerging science of service which can be found within the journal. (Emerald website)

Whether framed as sector-specific or generic service research, the empirical settings studied and written about in practice have been critical to the conceptual development of the discipline. A combination of factors has led to an overwhelming emphasis on large-scale business-to-consumer (B2C) services. First, as Levitt (1972) was quick to note, we are victims of outdated taxonomies derived from national accounting statistics and SIC classifications (see Chapter 2, this volume), which have determined what constitutes the 'service sector', and this has influenced the focus of service OM research. Second, for many OM researchers with an operations research (OR) background, the high volume of B2C settings means quantitative data, and therefore susceptibility to modelling. Third, the teaching of services OM can readily draw on the experiences of students by being grounded in B2C examples and cases—all to the good in some ways, but this emphasis may spill over into the shaping of the research agenda.

My own shift to service is symptomatic of a wider shift in the OM discipline. Furthermore, in my case, as in others, it is more than simply giving in to the decline in significance of manufacturing in developed economies and joining other OM people studying 'the service sector' as typically interpreted (i.e. phenomena such as hotel reception desks). Something else is happening: indeed, many things are happening. In 'small m' manufacturing (Hayes 1992)—that part of OM concerned with running production facilities to make things—many of the basic issues of production planning and control have been heavily researched. Although practical implementation of the solutions may still be uneven, the basic concepts and models are well established and, from an academic standpoint, all but the most arcane (and, harsher critics than I might suggest, pointless) theoretical problems of production planning and control have been solved. The once-novel practices of TQM, JIT, SPC, ERP, SCM[1], and lean manufacturing have been confronted, studied, and integrated within the corpus of teaching and research in manufacturing OM. While there are still many badly run factories, poorly implemented initiatives, and dysfunctional supply relationships, in the vanguard of practice and research other concerns are coming to the top of the agenda.

The Definition of Services in Operations Management

In the previous section, I suggested that there has been a shift from studying service sectors to studying services as such. That is not to say that there hasn't always been a concern with some of the fundamental questions: above all, what makes a service a service, and what the implications of that might be. Other chapters explore the thorny question of defining services at some length, but it is perhaps useful here briefly to outline some of the most influential OM discussions of this question. The Harvard Business School introduced its first course on managing service operations in 1972, based on 'the hypothesis that the tasks of managing service firms differ significantly enough from those of manufacturing firms to justify separate (or at least special) treatment' (Sasser *et al.* 1978: ix). The defining characteristics of services Sasser and his colleagues identified were intangibility, heterogeneity, simultaneity, and perishability (IHIP), and these were considered to 'make the management tasks of service executives different from their counterparts in manufacturing firms' (Sasser *et al.* 1978: 15). In some treatments, 'simultaneity' has become 'inseparability' and the set of characteristics hence known as 'IHIP'. These have endured as fundamental precepts of service OM teaching (Fitzsimmons and Fitzsimmons 2008) and of how most OM faculty view service operations (Nie and Kellogg 1999).

Alternative views have been presented intermittently over forty or more years. Judd (1964), albeit from a marketing standpoint, proposed 'non-ownership' as an important defining characteristic: this has lately been re-emphasized by Lovelock and Gummesson (2004), and incorporated into reappraisals of operations strategy (Spring and Araujo 2009). Scott Sampson (Sampson and Froehle 2006) has also been critical of the IHIP characteristics, and argues that the defining characteristic of services is that 'the customer provides significant inputs into the production process' (Sampson and Froehle 2006: 331), where the input might be themselves, their possessions, or their information. Sampson's recent empirical studies (Sampson 2011) have shown that, while OM academics are still enthusiastic about IHIP, the practitioners and consumers he studied find the customer input definition a more compelling way to capture what is special about 'services'. This debate has considerable implications for many of the specific areas of service OM research discussed later in the chapter.

The Changing Empirical World and its Effect on Service Operations Management

It is a truism that we live in a world where services are increasingly important in both developed and developing economies. But it is worth pausing to reflect on how and why this is the case, as some of these empirical developments have rather specific effects on the service OM research agenda. Here, I consider the changing location and form of what we could conveniently call 'manufacturing', the more general issue of offshoring and outsourcing (which is examined in much more detail in Chapter 10), some issues related to the changing role of consumers, and the changing boundaries between the private and public sector, which has been an important driver of change in at least some developed economies.

For a variety of reasons, the business of making things has significantly shifted location—most obviously to China. So, from a Western European or North American perspective, although manufacturing OM is still on the agenda, it is increasingly concerned with understanding the relationship between business activities located in the West and the manufacturing capacity and capabilities accessed in other parts of the world, often in other firms. Although this might, in principle, be framed simply as a matter of international purchasing, it is very different from the world envisioned in the (rather limited) international purchasing literature (Monczka and Trent 1992; Trent and Monczka 2003), which typically sees a core, higher-value manufacturing activity in a 'home' location and peripheral purchasing of components and materials being globally dispersed. It is much more likely than it was ten years ago that 'manufacturing' firms in developed economies will outsource all of their material conversion and assembly activities, sometimes to contract manufacturers who integrate the whole production and supply process, and sometimes to multiple providers. Either way, managing this requires an understanding of manufacturing OM concepts, as it is more like managing an external manufacturing capacity than simply purchasing 'inputs' (cf. Axelsson *et al.* 2005: 4). This is not to say that it does not represent a change from an exclusively internal focus for manufacturing managers. As Parker and Anderson (2002) explain very tellingly in their discussion of the transition of roles in Hewlett-Packard as they outsourced detailed design and manufacturing, managers needed to know 'operations management 101', but also be sophisticated project managers and persuaders to bring new products to market by mobilizing actors across organizational boundaries. Furthermore, the skills and capabilities that are being accessed globally are increasingly expanding into 'Big M' manufacturing (Hayes 1992); in other words, they are extending beyond merely running a facility to make things, and into new product development, managing the entire supply chain and even more fundamentally, R&D (Manning *et al.* 2008).

In this 'unbundling' process (Sako 2006), other corporate functions that overlap with operations have been offshored, outsourced, or both: these include the design, provision and support of IT, engineering design services, routine diagnostic testing, cost accounting and so on. All in all, from the supply side, it is increasingly difficult to separate manufacturing from services, when activities that would have been integrated into the 'self-sufficient' manufacturing facility are increasingly dispersed, organizationally and geographically, and the 'core' process of making things is increasingly outsourced and procured as something rather like a service, i.e. contract manufacturing (Arruñada and Vázquez 2006).

So, manufacturing isn't what it was, and this raises many new research questions that blur the empirical distinction between production and service OM. At the consumer end of the process, we find more blurring. Affordable availability of the more basic requirements of life is a problem that, compared to, say, the 1970s, has been solved in developed economies. For whatever combination of reasons takes your economic and political fancy—the restless need of capital to create novelty (Harvey 1989), the desire of consumers for distinction (Bourdieu 1984), and the potential of technological innovation to provide new benefits, commercial attention has shifted to emerging service–product combination offerings such as mobile telephony, web-centred personal computing, subscription-based satellite TV, and the like. There is also a generation of consumers who, for example, given the availability of pre-prepared salads, wouldn't dream of trimming and washing a lettuce for themselves, but are quite happy to act as stores clerk, warehouse operative, van driver, and assembler in respect of their IKEA furniture. [The latter phenomenon calls to mind Gershuny and Miles' emphasis on the 'self-service' aspect of the 'new service economy' almost thirty years ago (Gershuny and Miles 1983).] See also Peter Hill on DIY and GDP (Hill 1979).) The boundary between the commercial and the domestic sphere is fluid, fascinating, and under-researched.

The privatization of the state—certainly from a UK and European perspective—has led to the dismantling of nationalized industries such as coal, energy, transportation, and many of the administrative functions of government such as vehicle licensing and the provision of social security benefits (cf. Walsh 1995). The fact that many of these services are carried out in the private sector and, perhaps, the very fact of the change, has drawn attention to them as subjects of study and targets of redesign and improvement for the operations managers responsible for them[2]. Recent extra pressure on public expenditure has heightened interest in innovation in these services. It is none the less striking that very little service OM research is or has been conducted in the public sector. Even if its importance has diminished with privatization and outsourcing, it still constitutes a large proportion of many developed economies' GDPs and employment[3].

For the Non-operations Management Reader

In a book such as this, there is a danger of running ahead with an argument that too quickly becomes preoccupied with the hair-splitting that goes on in any academic discipline (Abbott 2001) and that would only be of interest to those inside the discipline, or even subdiscipline, on which it centres. Even if that temptation is avoided or at least attenuated, there is also a danger that the discussion won't mean much to those outside the discipline unless they are provided with a little background. That is what I would like to provide here: as such, OM readers may wish to skip this section (although they will probably be among the keenest readers, so that they can then take issue with my sweeping summary).

OM is about designing, running, and improving the systems that make products and deliver services. It has its roots in analysis at the level of the workshop, facility, or firm: it is increasingly concerned with inter-facility and inter-organizational systems (which some might call supply chains or networks). Its roots also lie in manufacturing, and, over the past thirty or forty years, it has tentatively extended its reach into the study of services. Certainly in the past thirty years,[4] the starting point of OM is that activities in production, service, and even in support functions such as accounting are framed as processes, which carry out transformation of inputs (materials, customers, information) into outputs (products and services) for the benefit of customers. The classic OM analysis is concerned with the determination of the efficient use of scarce resources through the planning and control of capacity and production to achieve required production or service delivery objectives. The work of Skinner (1969, 1974) on manufacturing strategy argued that OM had been too pre-occupied with tactical methods and cost reduction and that operations could compete strategically on other performance criteria such as flexibility or very high quality. Hayes and Wheelwright (1979, 1984) formalized this and laid the foundations of manufacturing strategy, which became the most active research stream in the discipline for the next fifteen years or more (Pilkington and Meredith 2008). Arguably, Hayes and Wheelwright's 1984 book established the framework for many of today's OM texts and courses. The basic message was:

- operations are an important competitive weapon and need to be managed strategically

- operations cannot be exceptionally good at everything and managers need to make a 'trade-off'—to design and run operations to compete primarily on one or two of the following criteria: quality, delivery, flexibility, or cost

- the focus on certain criteria will determine design decisions regarding structure (e.g. process technology) and infrastructure (e.g. planning and control systems)

- these decisions are closely aligned with the demand that operations try to satisfy: high volume/low variety (e.g. a chlorine production plant) or low volume/high variety (e.g. a university chemistry lab).

Since this basic framework was set out, OM research and practice has devoted considerable attention to various waves of process improvement methods such TQM, BPR[5] and lean. Supply chain management—the study of inter-organizational operations—has been an extremely active area, and OM researchers have increasingly turned their attention to new product/ service development. Various computer-based approaches to process control and production planning—CIM,[6] material requirments planning, enterprise resource planning—have also generated considerable interest. Despite all this and more besides, and despite the very significant practical improvements in real-life operations that mean that levels of efficiency *and* quality *and* delivery have improved, the basic frameworks for making choices about the design of operations endure. In other words, even though the operations that produce the Nissan Micra and the BMW 7 Series are much better on all criteria than they would have been twenty-five years ago, they are still deliberately and significantly different to one another. The trade-off endures.

The Emerging Research Agenda

The empirical and theoretical changes sketched out in earlier sections have given rise to new streams of activity in service OM. Partly this has been brought about by 'late entrants' such as me, coming from a background in manufacturing, finding some of the things they have always been interested in now falling under the ambit of service OM. Relatively complex manufacturing, supplying B2B markets, has always entailed activities that look like services, and these have become more explicitly accepted as such by the OM community. But there is also substantive change in the division of labour between firms, in the framing of activities, and in the business models used in B2B markets. Completely new empirical developments (e.g. the web) have given rise to wholly new domains of investigation.

In this section, I want to discuss a number of these streams of activity in service OM research and practice. To some extent, they are presented by way of a summary of what is going on in OM. But I also want to suggest that there is a good deal of continuity as well as change in what we see. As discussed over many decades (Fuchs 1968; Petit 1985; Giarini and Services World Forum (Association) 1987; Gadrey and Gallouj 2002), as well as by earlier AIM research (Griffith *et al.* 2003) (see also Chapter 2, this volume), there is an enduring concern about the low productivity of services compared to manufacturing. Service activities have consistently been seen as difficult to scale up from the idiosyncrasies of the unique, one-to-one encounter. The problem of service productivity, then, is one of service *scalability*: I suggest that many of the developments discussed in the rest of this chapter are attempts to tackle that problem. Although they take different forms, many of the areas of work I discuss are concerned with shifting the trade-off while taking account of the competitive positioning of operations (Clark 1996; Slack and Da Silveira 2001). Putting it another way, this aspect of OM is about standardizing processes and reducing unit cost *where, when and to an extent consistent with the operation's competitive position*, and that is what many of the approaches discussed here are intended to do. However, some of the new research areas I discuss go beyond mere productivity. These are concerned with innovation (see also Chapters 6 and 9), with finding new sources of value, rather than new ways to reduce cost. This is in some ways part of a general trend across OM, not just in service OM. But the particular characteristics of services—that they necessarily involve connections between operations and their customers—provide especially rich opportunities for innovation that is rooted in operations, not left to other functions such as marketing and R&D.

To provide some structure to the discussion, I will examine service OM research topics grouped as follows: customer, process, and supply chain. I will also outline service OM themes related to innovation, more specifically the impact of information technology (IT), studies of the new service development (NSD) process, and some of the changing organizational forms and business models associated with service OM. In many ways, the second cluster, associated with innovation, intersects with the first. Of course, all these groupings are rough organizing schemes rather than suggestions of hard and fast categories of research activity.

The Customer

The role of the customer has been a theme throughout the service OM literature, albeit, I suggest, one that has been treated in a rather static manner, which in turn results from empirical domains that much of the service OM work was conducted in. In hotels, shopping malls, theme parks, restaurants, and airlines, the role of the consumer (for the customer was usually a consumer) was fairly well defined and stable, and so the OM analysis centred on service quality (at the B2C interface), queues, details of the design of frontline service jobs, and so on. Two of the 'IHIP' characteristics mentioned earlier—intangibility, heterogeneity, inseparability, and perishability—loom large in the approach to analysing the role of the customer. The first is heterogeneity. Services are difficult to manage, we are told, because of the differences between customers. The second is inseparability. Production and consumption occur simultaneously: this means that the customer cannot inspect services before consumption, and operations have to have capacity available at the time when the customer wants to be served. (Always, the implicit or explicit comparison is with manufacturing.) As well as presenting an operation's constraint, the presence of the customer in the archetypal B2C service presented an opportunity—to use customers to do some of the work. Accordingly, they were analysed as 'human resources' (Bowen 1986) or 'employees' (Johnston 1989), who needed careful recruitment, selection, training, and motivation. To the extent that the customers could serve themselves, the operation was scalable.

As already mentioned, Gershuny and Miles (1983) made many prescient observations in their vision of 'the new service economy', one of which was the possibility of a growth of 'self-service'. And it is indeed the case that the relationship between, and the respective roles of the service provider and the customer has been one of the most active areas of review and re-thinking in service OM and, in related and overlapping ways, service marketing. As outlined already, early conceptions tended to see the customer as being 'employed' to take part in a process that was very much the service provider's (Bowen 1986), while simultaneously being a source of (unwelcome) variation, both as an 'employee' and as a customer (Larsson and Bowen 1989). [It is notable that Bowen (1986) is particularly concerned with the 'on-site' customer.] Part of this conceptualization arose from the empirical domain of much of the research. Various strands of work in OM, service management, and strategic management then came to present a rather freer and more generative conceptualization of the relationship between the service provider and the customer. One of these strands is the work of Normann and Ramirez (Normann 1991, 2001; Normann and Ramirez 1993; Ramirez 1999), which in various ways breaks with the conception of a linear sequence of value-adding activities derived—and, they would argue, over-extended—from the model of the mass production assembly line and the linear supply chains of early industrialization. They suggest that our conception should shift to 'value constellations', emphasizing mutual, horizontal, and complementary connections as much, if not more, than unidirectional, vertical, and exclusive ones. Similar ideas have been treated elsewhere as 'value networks' (Basole and Rouse 2008) or 'ecosystems' (Basole 2009; Gawer 2009).

Even if retaining a fairly linear conception of the relationship between the service provider and the customer, it has been emphasized, particularly by Sampson (Sampson 2000; Sampson and Froehle 2006), that a defining characteristic of services is that customers provide significant inputs to the process. With its roots in marketing, but with something to say to OM, the service-dominant logic of Vargo and Lusch (2004, 2008) emphasizes the co-creation of value between provider and customer (see Chapters 8 and 11, this volume). Although presenting a different emphasis and interpretation, Grönroos (2008) is also at pains to explore the precise role of the customers in creating value for themselves, using the resources provided by the supplier. The provider's role is to 'facilitate customer value creation by providing the value foundation required' (Grönroos 2008: 305) and it is therefore important for the service provider to understand in depth how the 'value foundation' plays its role in the customer's practices.[7] If this is so, what is the OM task? The operation no longer 'transforms customers' as per the transformation process model that forms part of the first chapter of many OM texts; rather, it provides 'value foundations'. Staying with the Scandinavian perspective a little longer, Richard Normann uses the term 'offering' to identify something very much akin to Grönroos's 'value foundation': offerings are 'artefacts designed to more effectively enable and organize value co-production. They are agents created by agents' (Normann 2001: 114). Importantly, the offering contains some 'frozen' knowledge—which may well be embodied in a physical product—but also a 'code' (2001: 119) for learning—learning by the customer about how to use it to create value in different and new ways, which may impossible for the provider to anticipate fully.

While the concept of the offering opens up the role of the customer in value creation, it might be said that there is still a somewhat linear logic—the offering is released into the world and the customer is empowered to make new value by using it in her own practices. In business-to-business (B2B) services, we are often concerned with enduring interactions (Axelsson and Wynstra 2002, Chapter 5; Wynstra et al. 2006) and these lead not only to co-production of value, but also to co-design and periodic redesign of the offering. In my own work with Kostas Selviaridis on third-party logistics, for example (Selviaridis and Spring 2010), although the basic building blocks of the service activity were resources such as warehouses and vehicles, how these building blocks were combined to provide logistics services in a changing context was the subject of frequent, interactive design of the service offering. In both business and consumer settings, lateral, peer-to-peer, and complementary interactions are increasingly important. For example, social media offerings such as Facebook exist to provide a platform for peer-to-peer interaction, and draw in advertisers and other actors. Such arrangements are more akin to Normann and Ramirez's 'value constellations' (Normann and Ramirez 1993) than to linear supplier–customer dyadic interactions: hence, the role of the customer in relation to other customers as well as in relation to the supplier—and indeed in developing the offering (e.g. setting up a group on a social networking site) as well as using it—all become part of the service provider's management challenge.

The Process

In this section, I want to discuss two areas of research that concentrate on the service provider's process. Although by definition we cannot ignore the customer altogether, these approaches do emphasize what goes on inside the service provider's operation rather than the interaction with the customer: in some sense, that is their aim. One is lean services, the application of lean approaches to service settings. The second is service modularity—again, adapting a way of thinking developed in manufacturing to a service setting.

Lean Services

'Lean', as we OM people know, is a term that arose from the International Motor Vehicle Programme, a global comparative study of car manufacturing based at MIT since 1979. John Krafcik, then a postgraduate student at MIT, is credited with first using the term 'lean', to describe the approach of the Toyota joint venture NUMMI assembly plant:

> ...is 'lean' because it uses less of everything compared to mass production—half the human effort in the factory, half the manufacturing space, half the investment in tools, half the engineering hours to develop a product in half the time.
>
> Also, it requires less than half the needed inventory on site, results in many fewer defects, and produces a greater and ever growing variety of products. (Krafcik 1988)

According to Holweg (2007), the term 'lean' was introduced as a more positive sounding alternative to the original term, 'fragile', which in its turn, was diametrically opposed to 'buffered'. In a more general sense, this represented the connection of what Thompson (1967) termed the organization's 'buffered technical core' more directly with its business environment.

So—what about lean services? Bowen and Youngdahl (1998) take their cue from Levitt (1972, 1976) in defending and to some degree extending the 'production-line approach to service'. According to them, the main difference drawn between the production-line approach and the lean service approach is the shift from the replacement of human contact and discretion with technology (as in Levitt's discussion of McDonald's) to one centred on empowering employees and allowing them more discretion in their interaction with customers. In their case examples, this is always combined with efforts to standardize and scale up, and in other ways, makes more efficient the back office, non-customer-contact aspects of the operation. This is consistent with one of the principles of Chase's 'customer contact approach': 'Employ traditional efficiency improvement techniques (production control, industrial engineering, etc.) to improve low contact operations' (Chase 1981: 703).

For the most part then, the 'leanness'—in the sense of doing more with less—seems to be in the non-customer-contact parts of the process, what Chase called the 'quasi-manufacturing' part. And studies in lean services since Bowen and Youngdahl have tended to continue in that vein, reporting improvements in the 'technical core', back office processes such as preparation of sales quotations in a manufacturing firm (Buzby *et al.* 2002), insurance policy application processing (Swank 2003), loan application processing (Allway and Corbett 2002), finance office processes in local government (Furterer and Elshennawy 2005), and even preparation and distribution of animal feed in a safari park (Julien and Tjahjono 2009). Although these settings, in the main, might be classified as services by virtue of being in service sectors, the processes studied are clearly amenable to lean approaches as they involve flows, inventory (of paperwork or animal feed, etc.), and, crucially, are insulated from the customer. (Indeed, that is the very purpose of standardized application forms for loans, insurance policies, and the like.) It is no surprise, then, that the authors in these examples conclude that lean approaches can be used in 'service' settings.

Although these translations of lean manufacturing approaches to back office service operations are interesting in their own right, Piercy and Rich (2009) and Staats *et al.* (2011), writing on lean approaches in call centres and software engineering respectively, focus on additional issues. Piercy and Rich emphasize the group problem-solving and continuous improvement aspects of lean, and see that co-located teams can indeed work effectively in this respect in service settings as they do in the typical production facility setting of most studies of lean. Staats *et al.* conclude that many of the philosophies and methods of lean production also apply to knowledge-intensive services, but the less fully specified nature of work elements in knowledge work lead to some limitations on the applicability of the full range of lean methods. Interestingly, both of these studies draw attention to the importance of co-located workgroups in resolving problems and or planning and controlling activities that are less susceptible to *ex ante* specification, suggesting that there are limits to the extent to which lean services can be geographically dispersed.

Modular Services

The last section of Bowen and Youngdahl's (1998) 'lean services' paper suggests the next step in the development after lean service production might be mass customization. This was fashionable in the mid-1990s (Pine 1993; Kotha 1994, 1995) and was seen as a way to break a classic OM trade-off—between customization and cost (also present in the 'advanced manufacturing technology' literature, e.g. Lei and Goldhar 1991). In another paper along the same lines at the time, McLaughlin holds that:

> the ultimate objective [in dealing with variation in service requirements] is the development of mass customization of these services, which involves the configuration of service modules to meet individual needs effectively and efficiently. (McLaughlin 1996: 28)

And, while mass customization as a term has slipped from prominence, the idea of modular services more recently has taken hold. Typically, the approach is to transpose concepts from the well-established literature on modular products to the service domain, to provide variety and flexibility of service offerings while avoiding the need to provide entirely bespoke services for each customer, with attendant increase in cost. Voss and Hsuan (2009) have conceptualized and proposed ways of measuring service modularity, and illustrated this using an example from the cruise line industry, showing how elements of the total service package can, in principle, be reused and recombined to provide different packages, maybe on different ships in a cruise operator's fleet, while still gaining economies of scale in the development of each modular service element. De Blok *et al.* (2010) report on empirical work in the design of modular care services for elderly people, examining how modular design allows reconfiguration of service offerings during delivery, as customers' needs change or become better understood. Service modularity in the sense of Voss and Hsuan can be seen as tackling the problem of scalability in services. Modularity allows, in principle, bespoke offerings to be provided to a large number of customers without sacrificing the benefits of economies of scale. As one of the supposed foundational definitions of services is that there is high variation ('heterogeneity' in IHIP) among customers, this has the potential to address one of the central challenges of service OM, but there is still much to do in developing the concepts and elements of a theory of modular services. For example, where the notions of platforms and interfaces are well understood in relation to products, their transposition to a service setting is far from straightforward.

Services Supply and the Service Supply Chain

Here I want to concentrate on service OM developments associated with the 'upstream' connections between organizations. An important part of this is the purchasing of services. Adopting for the time being a fairly conventional definition, it is widely thought that services are more difficult to buy than products and materials. From a theoretical point of view, this is often associated with their 'intangibility' and 'heterogeneity', which supposedly make the specification and assessment of quality more difficult. Empirically, buyers report that buying services is indeed more difficult (Ellram *et al.* 2007); however, this probably says more about existing processes for and organization of purchasing than about any inherent properties of services. This is also reflected in typical treatments in purchasing and supply texts, where 'purchasing services' is treated as a special case, in one chapter, somewhere near the end of the book. This is a clear legacy of the days when services were more appropriately treated as a residual. Although all kinds of OM is, increasingly, inevitably, inter-organizational (Sinha and Van de Ven 2005; Hayes 2008), the sourcing of services is treated as a special case in research, too, because of the supposed problems services present in specification and assessment of quality. OM writers have drawn on transaction costs and resource-based theories to explain and explore inter-organizational phenomena in general (Holcomb and Hitt 2007; McIvor 2009) and services outsourcing in particular (Ellram *et al.* 2008).

The empirical reality, of course, is that in most developed economies service-based businesses are the main feature, not a sideshow, and that large firms—whether notionally in manufacturing or service sectors—are outsourcing activities that had hitherto been carried out within the vertically integrated firm. This has, as discussed already, led to the outsourcing of relatively simple supporting services such as cleaning and security, more complex but still supporting services such as facilities management, and, increasingly, complex and strategic activities such as the operation of critical materials- and data-processing technologies, as well as design and R&D. Where services are involved, the inter-firm relationships are frequently less obviously linear and 'chain-like' than in manufacturing; for example, a software firm might outsource help-desk services, which are then provided direct to the software firm's end customer. Such 'triads' (Li and Choi 2009) involving the provision of 'component services' (Wynstra *et al.* 2006) set up interesting issues in contracting, quality management, and other areas of OM.

Two of the dominant factors leading to growth in outsourcing are ease and low cost of transportation and of communication. These, combined with the opening up of new markets in China, the former Soviet Union, and elsewhere, have meant that offshoring is increasingly routine, either within the firm or in conjunction with outsourcing. Developments in information and communications technology (Metters and Verma 2008) have made it increasingly feasible to move large amounts of data across the world and therefore to relocate parts of operations involving data transfer, storage, and analysis, particularly the 'routine intellectual labor' (Learner and Storper 2001). Service supply networks, then, are increasingly globally and organizationally dispersed. Research on offshoring and outsourcing in OM has tended to focus on the rationale for change, i.e. whether to outsource and/or offshore particular activities. This to some extent reflects the empirical reality of organizations evaluating newly emerging opportunities, and, I suspect, the theoretical tools that are ready to hand. In other words, if you have a transaction cost economics hammer, everything looks like a make-or-buy nail. By comparison, there has been much less research on the operation and adaptation of what we might call service supply chains, once the basic structure of which organization does what has been determined: indeed, it is only relatively recently that the importance of B2B services as such has been acknowledged by some leading service OM scholars (Johnston 2005). Akkermans and Vos (2003) found something similar to the well-known Forrester Effect (Forrester 1961) in enquiry handling at a telecoms firm; this is an example of a concept from product supply chains being transposed to a service context. Sampson (2000) takes a different approach and seeks to identify supply chain implications of the inherent characteristics of services, suggesting that the provision of an input by the customer makes them both customers and suppliers and, therefore, the supply chains bidirectional. More recent work, although emphasizing the importance of service supply chains, has tended, in fact, to concentrate on services purchasing (e.g. Ellram *et al.* 2007). Much remains to be done in understanding the supply chain and network phenomena arising from extended and dispersed inter-organizational provision of services.

New Information Technologies

The infrastructural technology of the internet has clearly changed the landscape of service supply networks. It has also provided new ways to involve customers 'as employees' through the use of online reservation and ordering systems, internet banking, and so on (Sousa *et al.* 2008), with some of these facilities increasingly being used through mobile computing platforms (e.g. see Buellingen and Woerter 2004). Existing supply chains in some sectors— e.g. music distribution, travel agents, many areas of retailing—have been radically changed or almost eliminated. In many B2B applications, ubiquitous or distributed computing technologies allow new service benefits to be provided. Radio-frequency identification tags on pallets of goods or on other equipment can allow location tracking and precision in transfer of owner-ship [see Lee and Özer (2007) and other papers in the same special issue], and integrated systems for sensing, communication, and analysis allow remote diagnostics and prognostics of various types of capital equipment such as aircraft, trucks, and railway rolling-stock, allowing real-time management of valuable capital assets (Benedettini *et al.* 2009). Such technologies increas-ingly become an important and integral part of more complex service opera-tions; this contrasts with the typical focus in OM on process technologies more obviously concerned with processing flows of materials, information, or customers. In goods supply chains, it is an old dictum that information replaces inventory: here, information reduces reactive maintenance and can allow new insights into more effective ways for the supplier and customer to work together to, once again, shift performance trade-offs.

Of course, all these dispersed, information-intensive service operations require a large amount of data storage, transfer, and analysis capacity. This has given rise to a new multibillion-dollar industry associated with 'cloud computing', the external transfer and storage of data. Various service offer-ings are emerging: public clouds, private clouds, infrastructure-as-a-service, platform-as-a-service, and software-as-a-service. There are intriguing parallels between this and the type of specialization that has occurred over the past twenty years or so in the third-party logistics industry in respect of physi-cal distribution and storage, and this offers an interesting area of empiri-cal research for service OM. More generally, the treatment of IT in OM has mainly been rooted in studies of the application of IT to existing, relatively stable supply chains in mature sectors such as automotive manufacturing and grocery retailing, and has tended to focus on the adoption of large enter-prise systems intended to integrate firms and their processes. Much less evi-dent in research, although very important in practice, is the more *ad hoc* use of multiple IT artefacts that often cross organizational boundaries to pro-vide particular service solutions, maybe for a limited period (Mathiassen and Sørensen 2008).

New Service Development, Organizational Forms, and Business Models

New *product* development (NPD) was brought under the OM umbrella in the mid-1980s, as manufacturing strategy researchers discovered the importance of integrating NPD with manufacturing operations, based in particular on exposure to Japanese manufacturing (Imai *et al.* 1985). Speed of introduc-tion of new products was increasingly important (Stalk 1988) and out of this concern grew a distinctively OM approach to NPD (Wheelwright and Clark 1992), treating NPD as a process to be managed just like any other operations process. By comparison, NSD is very much less researched; within OM there are only a handful of studies (Menor *et al.* 2002; Froehle and Roth 2007; Menor and Roth 2008); other work appears in the product innovation literature, where recent studies have taken the comparison between NSD and NPD as a starting-point (e.g. Ettlie and Rosenthal 2011). Studies in so-called 'experience services' have begun to identify critical, distinctive issues for the development of this type of service, characterized by their engaging with customers in a 'personal, memorable way' (Zomerdijk and Voss 2010: 68). An interesting notion that arises from this work is that experience-centric services are in 'permanent beta testing' (Zomerdijk and Voss 2010: 78), i.e. constantly being redesigned and improved. Although it is perhaps a little early to tell, it seems that there is a willingness to study NSD in its own right, rather than trying to force it into normative stage-gate NPD models (e.g. Cooper 1994).

As well as this emerging interest in the NSD process as such, particular forms of novel service arrangement, especially in B2B settings, are of increasing concern. I will briefly outline three of these, aware that aspects of them are dealt with more fully in other chapters of this book. The three related areas are systems integration, 'servitization', and procuring complex performance (PCP). They all involve the combination of many product and service elements in innovative ways, often in large-scale, technologically sophisticated capital goods settings.

In systems integration (Davies 2003), the emphasis is on the role of particular firms, usually in large-scale capital equipment provision, who specialize in integrating their products and services with those of others to provide 'integrated solutions'. This has at least two important implications for service OM. First, it draws attention to a particular form of the kind of hollowing-out of manufacturing discussed earlier. Systems integrators typically do not do a lot of material conversion themselves, either because they never have, or because they have progressively outsourced it. What remains is a technology-intensive provider of high-value capital goods, most of whose in-house activities look like knowledge-intensive or professional services. In one way or another, such firms manage an external network of hardware and service providers not just as 'suppliers' of inputs, but much more as an extended enterprise. Whether we call it service or not, this is a new form of OM, or at least a form of OM that has become much more commonplace. The second implication is that systems integrators provide more or less inclusive solutions, rather than simply selling a capital good to a customer. That is, they may lease the capital equipment, and provide a complete maintenance and spares service over its lifetime in the field, sometimes sold based on 'performance'. For example, a rail operator might contract for the availability of a certain number of carriages from a supplier, who would be responsible for the provision, repair, and maintenance required to achieve the desired availability. This sees erstwhile manufacturing-centred firms moving from the factory out into the field of use, and providing service operations that were probably once the preserve of its customers.

Servitization continues some of these themes, but there is less emphasis on large-scale capital equipment. Servitization can refer in quite a general way to various combinations of product and service element (Vandermerwe and Rada 1988), or more specifically to the provision of the type of integrated product–service offering discussed here as part of systems integration. The term servitization does not connote large-scale technology-based offerings in the way that systems integration does and is very much concerned with *manufacturing* firms adding services to their offerings. In contrast, some systems integrators are consultancy firms who draw on manufacturing partners, but have no roots in manufacturing themselves. Neely (2008) has studied the aggregate trends in patterns of servitization, showing equivocal results on the supposed financial benefits of servitization (see also Chapter 7, this volume). Others (e.g. Baines *et al.* 2009) have studied the challenges faced by firms undergoing this transformation, and the performance trade-offs involved in shifting to selling performance outcomes rather than products (Kim *et al.* 2007).

Finally, PCP (Caldwell and Howard 2011) looks at the same type of empirical phenomena treated in the systems integration literature, i.e. large-scale, long-life, technology-intensive capital goods, but from the perspective of the firm buying them or, more likely, the performance they provide. A critical focus of this work is the design and management of contractual and non-contractual governance mechanisms between the buyer and the provider. PCP is a long way from the empirical settings of early service OM—running fast-food or hotel operations, say. Nevertheless (or maybe hence) it is a fruitful research area in its own right, because of the importance for the public sector alone of understanding things such as health facility provision and military procurement. But beyond that, it is also interesting as an extreme form of some of the phenomena more widely prevalent in contemporary business—networks of geographically dispersed operations involving the access and provision of complicated mixtures of products and services, under conditions of extreme uncertainty. As such, the issues we confront here are likely to be more central to service OM as time goes by.

Conclusion: Scalability and Innovation

This chapter has been a selective and partial review of some recent emerging issues in service OM, from both empirical and theoretical perspectives.

If services are different to manufacturing because they are necessarily entangled in a relationship between economic entities (Gadrey 2000; Araujo and Spring 2006) or because they involve a customer input (Sampson and Froehle 2006), then the service OM developments reviewed seem either to be ways to mitigate the effects of this (or, in some instances, make use of it) to achieve scalability, or to exploit and adapt it to achieve innovation.

Scalability and the elimination or reduction of the trade-off between variety and cost is at the heart of lean services, modular services, and some facets of the enrolment of the customer as employee. In their development and implementation, these approaches require innovation and change in the operations processes used, but they are not centrally concerned with generating new sources of revenue and new benefits for customers. New technologies such as the internet make it possible to involve the customer in self-service in new ways, and bring into play new considerations in the design of processes and the management of service quality, for example in virtual rather than face-to-face encounters (Sousa and Voss 2006). Lean and modular services clearly draw on once-innovative manufacturing approaches [although see White (1928) on some aspects of lean, and Starr (1965) on modular production] and reframe the quest for scale in services in the terms of those approaches. They certainly provide novel emphases and, particularly in the case of service modularity, have been enabled by advances in IT that allow rapid, low-cost customization of particular aspects of some information-intensive services, e.g. in banking. But they run into trouble, or at least different conditions that impede a full translation of the practices from manufacturing, due to some of the inherent characteristics of service operations. As we have seen, lean approaches seem to have been most successfully applied to back office 'quasi-manufacturing' aspects of operations in service settings, and modular services—which have been studied much less—seem to be limited by (or at least different because of) the permeability of interfaces between modules in service processes. Largely, then, these approaches seem to be new forms of old service OM principles, such as the customer contact model of Chase (1981). This is not to suggest that research on these is any the less valid: the challenge will be to understand and more clearly define limitations of these approaches, how they might be enabled by new circumstances provided by technological or cultural change, and under what circumstances they may be entirely inapplicable.

As we have seen, services have of late been defined in terms of the respective roles of the service provider and customer (e.g. Sampson and Froehle 2006), rather than by the IHIP criteria. Interesting new possibilities in the study of service innovation are beginning to emerge, partly because of this reframing. In B2C 'experience services' and in the (mainly) B2B domains of servitization, systems integration, and PCP, a major part of service innovation concerns changing roles of the supplier and customer, and of others in a wider network. Service innovations seem to be about finding new distributions of activities to owners of different combinations of capabilities and incentives, and about realizing new benefits from capabilities or combinations of capabilities: as Normann (2001: 108) puts it: 'this innovation comes about as a result of innovative linkages between hitherto unrelated resources which are revealed as under-utilized'. Not only are these innovations *in* the process of interaction, they are also innovations emerging *from* the process of interaction (in the general form and in particular instantiations). This contrasts with some OM treatments of NSD, which are somewhat constrained by the legacy of process models of NPD, and (particularly in B2C) leave the essential roles of customer and service provider largely unchanged. Such discussions also posit a fundamentally active and controlling role to the service provider, whereas service designs and specifications in B2B often arise from intense interaction between buyer and supplier (Selviaridis and Spring 2010), or within triads (Li and Choi 2009) and larger networks.

Notes

1. Total Quality Management, Just-in-Time, Statistical Process Control, Enterprise Resource Planning, Supply Chain Management, respectively.
2. This is not to suggest that all applications of OM and operational research (OR) take place in the private sector: for example, many more senior members of the UK OR community learned their trade in the now-defunct National Coal Board.
3. For example, the UK's National Health Service is the seventh largest employer in the world; over six million people work in the public sector in the UK.
4. It may surprise some OM researchers brought up on Slack *et al.* or similar OM texts to know that the centrality of the notion of 'process' only came along in the 1980s. Buffa (1963) and Wild (1977), for instance, frame the discussion of POM around the manufacturing or operating *system*, which did not have the clear input–transformation–output form of later approaches by, for example, Hill (1983) or Slack *et al.* (1995).
5. Business process re-engineering.
6. Computer-integrated manufacturing.
7. This is, of course, the case for manufacturers, too, as their products can be treated as 'value foundations'.

References

Abbott, A.D. (2001). *Chaos of Disciplines*. Chicago: University of Chicago Press.
Akkermans, H.A. and Vos, B. (2003). Amplification in service supply chains: an exploratory case study from the telecom industry. *Production and Operations Management*, **12**(2), 204–223.

Allway, M. and Corbett, S. (2002). Shifting to lean service: stealing a page from manufacturers' playbooks. *Journal of Organizational Excellence*, **21**(2), 45–54.

Araujo, L. and Spring, M. (2006). Products, services and the institutional structure of production. *Industrial Marketing Management*, **35**(7), 797–805.

Arruñada, B. and Vázquez, X.H. (2006). When your contract manufacturer becomes your competitor. *Harvard Business Review*, **84**(9), 135.

Axelsson, B., *et al.*, (Eds). (2005). *Developing Sourcing Capabilities: creating strategic change in purchasing and supply management*. Chichester: John Wiley.

Axelsson, B. and Wynstra, J.Y.F. (2002). *Buying Business Services*. Chichester: John Wiley.

Baines, T.S., *et al.* (2009). Servitized manufacture: practical challenges of delivering integrated products and services. *Proceedings of the Institution of Mechanical Engineers, Part B: Journal of Engineering Manufacture*, **223**(9), 1207–1215.

Basole, R.C. (2009). Visualization of interfirm relations in a converging mobile ecosystem. *Journal of Information Technology*, **24**(2), 144–159.

Basole, R.C. and Rouse, W.B. (2008). Complexity of service value networks: conceptualization and empirical investigation. *IBM Systems Journal*, **47**, 53–70.

Benedettini, O., *et al.* (2009). State-of-the-art in integrated vehicle health management. *Proceedings of the Institution of Mechanical Engineers, Part G: Journal of Aerospace Engineering*, **223**(2), 157–170.

Bourdieu, P. (1984). *Distinction: a social critique of the judgement of taste*. London: Routledge.

Bowen, D. (1986). Managing customers as human resources in service organizations. *Human Resource Management*, **25**(3), 371–383.

Bowen, D.E. and Youngdahl, W. E. (1998). 'Lean' service: in defense of a production-line approach. *International Journal of Service Industry Management*, **9**(3), 207–225.

Buellingen, F. and Woerter, M. (2004). Development perspectives, firm strategies and applications in mobile commerce. *Journal of Business Research*, **57**(12), 1402–1408.

Buffa, E. (1963). *Models for Production and Operations Management*. New York: Wiley.

Buzby, C.M., *et al.* (2002). Using lean principles to streamline the quotation process: a case study. *Industrial Management & Data Systems*, **102**(9), 513–520.

Caldwell, N. and Howard, M., (Eds). (2011). *Procuring Complex Performance: studies of innovation in product-service management*. New York: Routledge.

Chase, R.B. (1981). The customer contact approach to services: theoretical bases and practical extensions. *Operations Research*, **29**(4), 698–706.

Chase, R.B. (1996). The mall is my factory: reflections of a service junkie. *Production and Operations Management*, **5**(4), 298–308.

Clark, K.B. (1996). Competing through manufacturing and the new manufacturing paradigm: is manufacturing strategy passé? *Production and Operations Management*, **5**, 42–58.

Cooper, R.G. (1994). Third-generation new product processes. *Journal of Product Innovation Management*, **11**, 3–14.

Davies, A. (2003). Integrated solutions: the changing business of systems integration. In: *The Business of Systems Integration*, Davies, A., Hobday, M., and Prencipe, A. (Ed.), pp. 333–368. Oxford: Oxford University Press.

De Blok, C., *et al*. (2010). Modular care and service packages for independently living elderly. *International Journal of Operations & Production Management*, 30, 75–97.

Ellram, L.M., *et al*. (2007). Services Supply Management: the next frontier for improved organizational performance. *California Management Review*, 49(4), 44–66.

Ellram, L.M., *et al*. (2008). Offshore outsourcing of professional services: a transaction cost economics perspective. *Journal of Operations Management*, 26(2), 148–163.

Ettlie, J.E. and Rosenthal, S.R. (2011). Service versus manufacturing innovation. *Journal of Product Innovation Management*, 28(2), 285–299.

Fitzsimmons, J.A. and Fitzsimmons, M.J. (2008). *Service Management: operations, strategy, information technology*. New York: McGraw-Hill.

Forrester, J. (1961). *Industrial Dynamics*. Boston: MIT Press.

Froehle, C.M. and Roth, A.V. (2007). A resource-process framework of new service development. *Production and Operations Management*, 16(2), 169–188.

Fuchs, V.R. (1968). *The Service Economy. [By] Victor R. Fuchs...Assisted by Irving F. Leveson*. New York: National Bureau of Economic Research.

Furterer, S. and Elshennawy, A.K. (2005). Implementation of TQM and lean Six Sigma tools in local government: a framework and a case study. *Total Quality Management & Business Excellence*, 16(10), 1179–1191.

Gadrey, J. (2000). The characterisation of goods and services: an alternative approach. *Review of Income and Wealth*, 46(3), 369–387.

Gadrey, J. and Gallouj, F. (2002). *Productivity, Innovation, and Knowledge in Services: new economic and socio-economic approaches*. Cheltenham: Edward Elgar.

Gawer, A. (Ed.). (2009). Platform dynamics and strategies: from products to services In: *Platforms, Markets And Innovation*, pp. 45–77. Cheltenham: Edward Elgar.

Gershuny, J. and Miles, I. (1983). *The New Service Economy: the transformation of employment in industrial societies*. London: F. Pinter.

Giarini, O. and Services World Forum (Association) (1987). *The Emerging Service Economy*. Oxford: Pergamon Press.

Griffith, R., *et al*. (2003). The UK productivity gap and the importance of the service sectors. *AIM Briefing Note, December* 2003.

Grönroos, C. (2008). Service logic revisited: who creates value? And who co-creates? *European Business Review*, 20(4), 298–314.

Harvey, D. (1989). *The Condition of Postmodernity: an enquiry into the origins of cultural change*. London: Blackwell.

Hayes, R.H. (1992). Production and operations managements new 'requisite variety'. *Production and Operations Management*, 1(3), 249–253.

Hayes, R.H. (2008). Operations managements next source of galvanizing energy? *Production and Operations Management*, 17(6), 567–572.

Hayes, R.H. and Wheelwright, S.C. (1979). Link manufacturing process and product life-cycles. *Harvard Business Review*, **Jan-Feb**, 133–140.

Hayes, R.H. and Wheelwright, S.C. (1984). *Restoring our Competitive Edge: competing through manufacturing*. New York: John Wiley.

Hill, T. (1983). *Production/Operations Management*. London: Prentice-Hall International.

Hill, T.P. (1979). Do-it-yourself and GDP. *Review of Income and Wealth*, **25**, 31–39.

Holcomb, T.R. and Hitt, M.A. (2007). Toward a model of strategic outsourcing. *Journal of Operations Management*, **25**, 464–481.

Holweg, M. (2007). The genealogy of lean production. *Journal of Operations Management*, **25**(2), 420–437.

Imai, K., *et al.* (1985). Managing the new product development process: how Japanese companies learn and unlearn. In: *The Uneasy Alliance: managing the productivity-technology dilemma*. Clark, K.B., Hayes, R.H., and Lorenz, C. (Ed.), pp. 337–375. Boston MA: HBS Press.

Johnston, R. (1989). The customer as employee. *International Journal of Operations & Production Management*, **9**(5), 15–23.

Johnston, R. (1999). Service operations management: return to roots. *International Journal of Operations and Production Management*, **19**(2), 104–124.

Johnston, R. (2005). Service operations management: from the roots up. *International Journal of Operations & Production Management*, **25**(12), 1298–1308.

Judd, R.C. (1964). The case for redefining services. *Journal of Marketing*, **28**, 58–59.

Julien, D.M. and Tjahjono, B. (2009). Lean thinking implementation at a safari park. *Business Process Management Journal*, **15**(3), 321–335.

Kim, S., *et al.* (2007). Performance contracting in after-sales service supply chains. *Management Science*, **53**, 1843–1858.

Kotha, S. (1994). Mass customization: the new frontier in business competition. *Academy of Management Review*, **19**, 588–592.

Kotha, S. (1995). Mass customization: implementing the emerging paradigm for competitive advantage. *Strategic Management Journal*, **16**, 21–42.

Krafcik, J.F. (1988). Triumph of the lean production system. *Sloan Management Review*, **30**, 41–51.

Larsson, R. and Bowen, D.E. (1989). Organization and customer: managing design and coordination of services. *The Academy of Management Review*, **14**(2), 213–233.

Learner, E.E. and Storper, M. (2001). The economic geography of the internet age. *Journal of International Business Studies*, **32**(4), 641–665.

Lee, H. and Özer, Ö. (2007). Unlocking the value of RFID. *Production and Operations Management*, **16**, 40–64.

Lei, D. and Goldhar, J.D. (1991). Computer-integrated manufacturing (CIM): redefining the manufacturing firm into a global service business. *International Journal of Operations and Production Management*, **11**(10), 5–18.

Levitt, T. (1972). Production-line approach to service. *Harvard Business Review*, **Sept–Oct**, 41–52.

Levitt, T. (1976). The industrialization of service. *Harvard Business Review*, **54**, 63–74.

Li, M. and Choi, T.Y. (2009). Triads in services outsourcing: bridge, bridge decay and bridge transfer. *Journal of Supply Chain Management*, **45**, 27–39.

Lovelock, C. and Gummesson, E. (2004). Whither services marketing: in search of a new paradigm and fresh perspectives. *Journal of Service Research*, **7**, 20–41.

Manning, S., *et al.* (2008). A dynamic perspective on next-generation offshoring: the global sourcing of science and engineering talent. *Academy of Management Perspectives*, **22**(3), 35–54.

Mathiassen, L. and Sørensen, C. (2008). Towards a theory of organizational information services. *Journal of Information Technology*, **23**(4), 313–329.

McIvor, R. (2009). How the transaction cost and resource-based theories of the firm inform outsourcing evaluation. *Journal of Operations Management*, **27**, 45–63.

McLaughlin, C.P. (1996). Why variation reduction is not enough: a new paradigm for service operations. *International Journal of Service Industry Management*, **7**(3), 17–30.

Menor, L. and Roth, A. (2008). New service development competence and performance: an empirical investigation in retail banking. *Production and Operations Management*, **17**(3), 267–285.

Menor, L.J., Tatikonda, M.V., Sampson, S.E. (2002). New service development: areas for exploitation and exploration. *Journal of Operations Management*, **20**(2), 135–157.

Metters, R. and Verma, R. (2008). History of offshoring knowledge services. *Journal of Operations Management*, **26**(2), 141–147.

Monczka, R.M. and Trent, R.J. (1992). Worldwide sourcing: assessment and execution. *International Journal of Purchasing and Materials Management*, Fall, 9–19.

Neely, A. (2008). Exploring the financial consequences of the servitization of manufacturing *Operations Management Research*, **1**(2), 103–118.

Nie, W. and Kellogg, D. (1999). How professors of operations management view service operations. *Production and Operations Management*, **8**(3), 339–355.

Normann, R. (1991). *Service Management: strategy and leadership in service business.* Chichester: John Wiley.

Normann, R. (2001). *Reframing Business: when the map changes the landscape.* Chichester: John Wiley.

Normann, R. and Ramirez, R. (1993). From value chain to value constellation—designing interactive strategy. *Harvard Business Review*, **71**(4), 65–77.

Parker, G.G. and Anderson, E.G. (2002). From buyer to integrator: the transformation of the supply-chain manager in the vertically disintegrating firm. *Production and Operations Management*, **11**, 75–91.

Petit, P. (1985). *Slow Growth and the Service Economy.* London: Pinter.

Piercy, N. and Rich, N. (2009). Lean transformation in the pure service environment: the case of the call service centre. *International Journal of Operations & Production Management*, **29**, 54–76.

Pilkington, A. and Meredith, J.R. (2008). The evolution of the intellectual structure of operations management—1980–2006: A citation/co-citation analysis. *Journal of Operations Management*, **27**(3), 185–202.

Pine, B.J. (1993). *Mass Customization.* Boston, MA: HBS Press.

Ramirez, R. (1999). Value co-production: intellectual origins and implications for practice and research. *Strategic Management Journal*, **20**, 49–65.

Roth, A.V. and Menor, L. (2003). Insights into service operations management: a research agenda. *Production and Operations Management*, **12**(2), 145–164.

Sako, M. (2006). Outsourcing and offshoring: implications for productivity of business services. *Oxford Review of Economic Policy*, **22**(4), 499–512.

Sampson, S. (2000). Customer-supplier duality and bidirectional supply chains in service organisations. *International Journal of Service Industry Management*, **11**(4), 348–364.

Sampson, S. (2011). What are services?—an empirical investigation. In: *12th QUIS Annual Meeting*, v. d. Rhee, B. and Victorino, L. (Ed.), 897–906. Ithaca, NY: Cornell University, .

Sampson, S. and Froehle, C. (2006). Foundations and implications of a proposed unified services theory. *Production and Operations Management*, **15**(2), 329–343.

Sasser, W.E., *et al.* (1978). *Management of Service Operations: text, cases and readings*. Boston: Allyn and Bacon.

Schmenner, R.W. (1986). How can service businesses survive and prosper? *Sloan Management Review*, **27**(3), 21–32.

Schmenner, R.W. (2004). Service businesses and productivity. *Decision Sciences*, **35**(3), 333–347.

Schmenner, R.W. and Swink, M.L. (1998). On theory in operations management. *Journal of Operations Management*, **17**, 97–113.

Selviaridis, K. and Spring, M. (2010). The dynamics of business service exchanges: insights from logistics outsourcing. *Journal of Purchasing and Supply Management*, **16**(3), 171–184.

Sinha, K.K. and Van de Ven, A.H. (2005). Designing work within and between organizations. *Organization Science*, **16**(4), 389–408.

Skinner, W. (1969). Manufacturing—missing link in corporate strategy. *Harvard Business Review*, **May-Jun**, 136–145.

Skinner, W. (1974). The focussed factory. *Harvard Business Review*, **May-Jun**, 113–121.

Slack, N., *et al.* (1995). *Operations Management*. London: Pitman.

Slack, N. and Da Silveira, G. (2001). Exploring the trade-off concept. *International Journal of Operations and Production Management*, **21**(7), 949–964.

Slack, N., *et al.* (2004). The two worlds of operations management research and practice: can they meet, should they meet? *International Journal of Operations & Production Management*, **24**(4), 372–387.

Sousa, R. and Voss, C.A. (2006). Service quality in multichannel services employing virtual channels. *Journal of Service Research*, **8**(4), 356–371.

Sousa, R., *et al.* (2008). Customer heterogeneity in operational e-service design attributes: an empirical investigation of service quality. *International Journal of Operations & Production Management*, **28**(7), 592–614.

Spring, M. and Araujo, L. (2009). Products, service and services: re-thinking operations strategy. *International Journal of Operations & Production Management*, **29**(5), 444–467.

Staats, B.R., *et al.* (2011). Lean principles, learning, and knowledge work: evidence from a software services provider. *Journal of Operations Management*, **29**(5), 376–390.

Stalk, G. (1988). Time: the next source of competitive advantage. *Harvard Business Review*, **Jul-Aug**, 41–48.

Starr, M.K. (1965). Modular production: a new concept. *Harvard Business Review*, **Nov-Dec**, 131–142.

Swank, C.K. (2003). The lean service machine. *Harvard Business Review*, **81**, 123–129.

Thompson, J.D. (1967). *Organizations in Action: social science bases of administrative theory*. New York: McGraw-Hill.

Trent, R.J. and Monczka, R.M. (2003). International purchasing and global sourcing—what are the differences? *Journal of Supply Chain Management*, **39**(4), 26–36.

Vandermerwe, S. and Rada, J. (1988). Servitization of business: adding value by adding services. *European Management Journal*, **6**(4), 314–324.

Vargo, S.L. and Lusch, R.F. (2004). Evolving to a new dominant logic for marketing. *Journal of Marketing*, **68**, 1–17.

Vargo, S.L. and Lusch, R.F. (2008). Why 'service'? *Journal of the Academy of Marketing Science*, **36**, 25–38.

Voss, C.A. and Hsuan, J. (2009). Service architecture and modularity. *Decision Sciences*, **40**(3), 541–569.

Walsh, K. (1995). *Public Services and Market Mechanisms: competition, contracting and the new public management*. Basingstoke: Macmillan.

Wheelwright, S.C. and Clark, K.B. (1992). *Revolutionizing Product Development: Quantum leaps in speed, efficiency and quality*. New York: Free Press.

White, C.P. (1928). Hand-to-mouth buying. *Annals of the American Academy of Political and Social Science*, **139**, 136–145.

Wild, R. (1977). *Concepts for Operations Management*. Chichester: Wiley.

Wynstra, F., *et al.* (2006). An application-based classification to understand buyer-supplier interaction in business services. *International Journal of Service Industry Management*, **17**(5), 474–496.

Zomerdijk, L.G. and Voss, C.A. (2010). Service design for experience-centric services. *Journal of Service Research*, **13**, 67–82.

4

Employment in Service and the Service Sector

Irena Grugulis

Introduction

The service sector is an important location of work that accounts for the majority of employment in the developed world. There are more people working in McDonald's than US Steel (Macdonald and Sirianni 1996a) and it is retail work rather than the factory or assembly line that may be *the* new generic form of mass employment in the postindustrial socio-economic landscape (Bozkurt and Grugulis 2011: 2). In November 2012, 79% of all UK jobs were service sector jobs (ONS 2013). Understanding the service sector and service sector jobs is important. This chapter reviews the nature of work and skills in that sector. A great deal of current literature makes the case for difference, presenting service sector work as qualitatively distinct to that undertaken in manufacturing. This chapter acknowledges the importance of much of this research area but argues that the service sector itself is diverse and wide-ranging and proposes a new classification of service sector work.

The Nature of Service Sector Work

There is a question mark over the nature of work in the service sector. At one level, there is a reasonable amount of consensus, particularly between academics from human resources, employment, and industrial relations traditions that service sector work is qualitatively different to that undertaken in manufacturing. The physical presence of the customer and their involvement in 'managing' the labour process; the incorporation of the way workers look and feel as a legitimate area of work; and the corresponding dominance of 'soft' (ascribed or social) skills all serve to differentiate service work from that with more tangible outputs. There are also structural differences between service work and other sections of the economy as it is here that 83% of working women are located, together with the majority of part-time jobs (Self 2008). In addition, there are different implications for progression in service sector work as jobs tend to be polarized, demanding either high levels of skill (for doctors, accountants, consultants, and lawyers) or extremely low levels (for frontline service work, caring, cooking, and cleaning). In this hourglass economy (Nolan and Wood 2003) movement between low and high-skills work is limited and workers in the lower end of the labour market are often confined to horizontal moves within a narrow job range (Grimshaw *et al.* 2002).

So far, so distinctive. An impressive amount of research supports this differentiation providing analytical and theoretical insights into service work that are well supported by empirical evidence (see, for example Leidner 1993; Korczynski 2001; Bolton and Houlihan 2005). But researchers from other traditions, particularly operations management have been less inclined to support the case for 'difference'. Araujo and Spring (2006) have pointed out the similarities between the activities of firms located in services and those classified as manufacturing, blurring the boundaries between the two sectors. Accounts of service sector firms in this tradition, as well as in economics (see, for example Broadberry 2006) concentrate on parts of the service sector that seldom appear in research into employment including vehicle servicing and transportation.

A focus on these sectors has certain advantages, not least the fact that economic assessments of labour market productivity are possible. Indeed, in Broadberry's (2006) historic assessment of UK service sector performance, his data covers shipping, railways, road and air transport, telecommunications, wholesale and retail distribution, and banking and finance. In customer-facing work, performance and productivity are notoriously difficult to gauge, outputs may be subjective and standard economic assumptions questionable. A luxury hotel, for example, may improve customers' experience of their stay by hiring more low-skilled workers (to carry bags, run errands, advise on local theatres and restaurants, or replenish room supplies of fresh fruit). But such a move would mean a decline in labour productivity, as more workers were involved in, if not the same amount of work, then at least in processing the same number of guests (Keep *et al.* 2002).

Reference to the Office for National Statistics reveals the full diversity of the service sector (see http://www.statistics.gov.uk/iosmethodology). It includes not only the person-to-person industries so well covered by existing research on work such as hotels, restaurants, retailing, education, the public sector, and medicine, but also areas traditionally central to operations management work such as transportation, defence, postal services, and telecommunications where employment structures resemble those in traditional manufacturing, as well as beyond these to the public sector, hospitals, schools, universities, and the creative industries of theatres, museums, music, and IT.

Existing models only capture part of the diversity of this sector, a process facilitated by the reluctance of researchers to move beyond the established zones of interest traditional to their subject areas. This chapter will seek to go beyond that and offers a new analytical framework for service sector work. It proposes five different categories based on the role of the customer or client, nature of the work, tangibility of outputs, and skill levels demanded; these are: customer-facing, high touch service sector work; 'traditional' work; work in the creative industries; knowledge work and public sector service work. Each is analytically distinct. The chapter starts by setting out the case for difference, in areas of work McDowell (2009) describes as 'high touch' before going on to describe the new classification in detail. It goes on to consider the nature of service sector skills and the implications these have for work and workers.

Distinctive Service Sector Work

The distinctive nature of service sector work is premised on the presence of the customer and the simultaneous execution and consumption of work and work products. Because of this proximity the process of being served is as much a part of the transaction as any product being provided so the way workers feel and look, and the feelings they provoke in others become part of the wage effort bargain and a legitimate arena for management intervention (Noon and Blyton 2007).

This emotional engagement takes different forms, depending on the work undertaken. From charming glamorous and attentive flight attendants, bullying manipulative debt collectors (Hochschild 1983), and fun-loving Disneyland ride attendants (Van Maanen 1991) workers present different personas over which they enjoy varying levels of control; with the scripted sales encounters, jokes, and pauses of insurance sales people (Leidner 1993) and the regulations over how staff should modulate their voices in call centres (Callaghan and Thompson 2002) contrasting with the independent pugnacity of waitresses in a downmarket American diner seeking to maximize their tips (Paules 1991).

Appearance is also part of work and a legitimate area for management control both in glamorous 'style' labour markets (Nickson *et al.* 2001; Warhurst and Nickson 2001) and in more 'standard' jobs. Clothes stores recruit sales assistants with the right 'look' who can model the wares on and off the job (Gatta 2011). Candidates for jobs in fashionable bars, hotels, and boutiques are expected to be 'stylish', 'tasty', 'of smart appearance', 'trendier people', or 'very well presented' (Nickson *et al.* 2001:179–180) and staff are coached in aesthetic and emotional display; while flight attendants working for PSA had their bust, hips, and thighs measured on a regular basis (Hochschild 1983). Such a focus on aesthetics is not restricted to a glamorous elite, many standard restaurants and shops set dress codes and presentation rules (Paules 1991; Leidner 1993). And appearance can feature in assessments of applicants for even the most mundane tasks. One female candidate to the National Westminster Bank with an IQ of 172 was even told by an interviewer that her weight of 16 stone made it unlikely that she would be offered work (Cook 1997).

At their worst, judgements of aesthetics can be both gendered and racialized with workers sorted into different occupations by skin colour. In the USA, employers' tendency to allocate white staff to customer-facing roles and black and minority ethnic people (BMEs) to the back office is widely mocked as 'if she's white put her in the light, if she's black, put her in the back'. As Noon (2007) points out, there is a long history of such behaviour and Patterson's (1965) study of 1950s immigrants to London reveals both small numbers of BMEs actively employed by retail chains to stimulate business with the BME community as well as a more widespread reluctance to hire BMEs because (p. 123) 'the public might not like it'.

Customers are also the often attributed source of gendered stereotypes (Erickson *et al.* 2000) with workers penalized for not conforming or performing to prescribed gender roles. So in Pierce's (1995) study of American paralegals women were expected to flirt or nurture in marked contrast to the simple professional courtesy demanded of men; research in a call centre reveals men rewarded for hitting sales targets while women were expected to display specific behavioural norms as well (Taylor and Tyler 2000); and the skill lists against which managers are judged may be heavily politicized and gendered (Rees and Garnsey 2003). There is little indication that dividing the workforce into gender-specific roles is in decline; indeed, recent research reveals work actively being redesigned on a gendered basis with women located in less well paid, career limiting customer-facing work (Hebson and Grugulis 2004; Skuratowicz and Hunter 2004). Essentially this is about work as *being* as well as work as *doing*. People are hired for jobs because they are, or appear to be, members of certain categorical groups (white, male, female, middle class, good looking) or rejected for membership of other groups (black, Asian, male, female, working class, non-working class).

For this type of work, the customer is key analytically as well as practically. Essentially the employment relationship is a triangular one incorporating customer, employee, and employer (Leidner 1993). This way of organizing work has implications for both the traditional control pattern and the established model of resistance. So employees of McDonald's are accountable for their appearance and expressions to every customer who enters the restaurant (Leidner 1996), Disneyland staff are expected to stay in character (Van Maanen 1991), flight attendants may be taken to task by passengers for not smiling, or not smiling *enough* (Hochschild 1983), and call centre workers may be blamed for mistakes that they had little to do with (Carroll *et al.* 2001; Korczynski 2001).

This triangle of relations is dynamic with alliances and allegiances neither straightforward nor fixed. Employers and employees may find common interests 'against' their customers to increase sales or because working together encourages mutual solidarity against the strangers. Work scripts and practices present the customer as the outsider who is there to be sold to or dealt with, not admitted into organizational secrets (Leidner 1993). Alternatively, managers may elicit customers' help in setting or monitoring service standards and customers may volunteer this assistance (Bolton and Houlihan 2005). Questionnaires on the quality of service are now a standard feature of most customer-facing workplaces (Fuller and Smith 1996; Noon and Blyton 2007). And finally, employees may take pride in the service they offer, allying themselves with customers against management. So the waitress who wants higher tips may deliberately serve a more generous portion of chips, or give additional condiments free in defiance of management orders (Paules 1991). To make this shifting pattern of alliances more confusing, the demands of each of these parties may not be clearly articulated and customers can exist in both a notional and a real form. This means that all three parties can lay claim to the right to speak for customers and set out whatever it is that customers really want. As serving the customer is, rhetorically at least, the principal aim of this type of service work, this appeal is a powerful legitimation device.

A New Typology of Service Work

The proximity of the customer, the incorporation of emotions and aesthetics into the employment contract, and the focus on soft skills contribute to the qualitative differences between service sector work and that performed in the wider economy. Understandably much existing research into work has focused on areas such as call centres (which combine sophisticated technological innovation with restrictive employment practices and deskilling), restaurants or frontline services; an effective counter to the previous dominance of studies of male manufacturing workers in industrial sociology.

However, while these 'customer-facing' or 'high touch' (McDowell 2009) occupations are distinctive and are certainly worthy of study, they do not represent the service sector as a whole. Rather, as Korczynski and Macdonald (2008) point out, there is a distinctive subset of workers who are customer facing, below the rank of professional. They estimate that such a category accounts for 29% of those in work.

Given this, and given the need to satisfactorily account for all service sector workers, rather than a subset of them, it is worthwhile to attempt to construct a typology for service sector work as a whole. Here, five categories are proposed. The categories have been drawn up analytically and are based on the role of the customer or client, the nature of the work, tangibility of outputs, and skill levels demanded. The categories are:

1. Customer-facing, High Touch Service Work

   Following Korczynski and Macdonald this type of work is considered in some detail above. Customers are central to work processes and outputs are often intangible. This category covers retail work, hotels, restaurants, and many personal care occupations (Macdonald and Sirianni 1996b; Grugulis and Bozkurt 2011).

2. 'Traditional' Work

   'Traditional' occupations can be observed in transportation, defence, postal services, and telecommunications. The customer plays a less significant role here and these resemble traditional manufacturing jobs both in the means of control, as the relationship between the employee and employer is mediated by institutions, law and custom, and practice, without a triangular relationship developing between employees, employers, and customers. While few physical products are made, this work does have tangible outcomes in the form of repaired vehicles, packages delivered, and trains running on time, which make performance easier to gauge. Workers in this part of the service sector are also more likely to be male, employed full-time, and members of unions than those working elsewhere.

3. Work in the Creative Industries

   The third category is that of work in the creative industries. According to the UK Department for Culture, Media and Sport this includes advertising, architecture, art and antiques, computer games, crafts, design, designer fashion, film and video, music, the performing arts, publishing, software, and TV and radio. As with 'traditional' service sector occupations, these too may result in tangible outputs: a theatrical production, a musical recording, or a computer game. But they are worth considering separately for a number of reasons. Their relationship with customers is more direct, although it differs from that in high touch work as the customers here are audiences, readers, and players. Work is self-consciously creative (although this subsector includes many mundane and support functions) and many jobs are dominated by hobbyists. They can present statistical problems (see, for example Skillset 2007; Skillset/UKFilmCouncil 2008) as freelance and project-based work inevitably does; although here that may be compounded by worker's self-identification with a particular profession whether or not they spend most of their working time in it or earn their living from it.

4. Knowledge Work

Knowledge workers, or in Reich's (1991) terms, symbolic analysts are the expert and educated manipulators of symbols. Professionals, consultants, and analysts, all possess expertise in their specialist areas, with corresponding status (though see Brown *et al.* 2011). Customers are central to knowledge workers' work and the employment relationship is triangular. Aesthetics and emotions are still important as Haynes details in her chapter in this book and accountancy firms, the Law Society and investment banks provide grooming and fashion advice to staff (Anderson-Gough, Grey and Robson 2000; McDowell 1997). However the emotional expectations of knowledge workers are different; Mann (1999) summarizes the expected professional detachment as 'have a cool day', and they have status and substantive knowledge to bring to client relationships, shifting the balance of power in their favour (Sturdy *et al.* 2009).

5. Public Sector Service Work

Finally come public sector services, those provided by the state. In the UK, occupations that are primarily publicly funded include education, health, government, and public services. In these, customers and clients are present but the relationship that doctors have with patients and teachers with pupils differs from those of waitress and diner, or management consultant and CEO. Teachers may discipline and assess as well as support, just as doctors may deny treatment as well as provide it, and the qualifications that pupils gain or the health patients enjoy are as much, if not more, the results of their own actions, as they are those of the teachers and doctors who support them. The nature of public sector goods shapes the employment relationship (Foster and Hoggett 1999; Boyne 2003). Public sector service may have objectives such as social justice, equity, and democracy, which are not readily achieved and for which the 'customer' cannot choose to go to another provider if they are dissatisfied. Understandably, demand for such services tends to exceed supply (Fountain 2001) and, while excellent service in the private sector may stimulate both demand and resources, in the public sector, good service may mean securing reasonable delivery when faced with declining or limited real resources (Martinez Lucio and MacKenzie 1999; Rainbird *et al.* 2004).

It should be stressed that, as it stands, this classification is a working document. There are overlaps between categories and a considerable diversity within them. Art, antiques, and crafts are, following the Department for Culture, Media and Sport's definition of the creative industries, located in the section on creative work, yet the actual occupation may more closely resemble retail work, which figures under high touch customer-facing work. 'Traditional' workers may also have customers, who post and take delivery of parcels, travel on trains, and get their cars fixed, and this will impact on their work processes. 'Traditional' work, the creative industries and public sector work all encompass a considerable diversity of jobs and occupations with very different skill levels, status, and pay rates.

None the less, these are still categories worth preserving and developing. Providing a typology of service sector work is helpful in two ways. First, it overcomes the myopic characteristic of particular subject areas: the assumption by operations management writers that all work is the same and that service sector occupations can be read off from manufacturing ones and the assumption by organization studies and human resource management researchers that the service sector is fundamentally different to all other forms of labour.

Second, it allows some of the diversity of the sector to emerge. There is academic work on all of these areas but that on traditional work, creative industries, and public sector occupations is rarely classified under services so in part this acknowledgement of diversity takes the form of bringing together (often disparate) research and analysis. But it also enables researchers to challenge the way very different occupations are conflated. So, for example, Stewart's (1997) figure that knowledge workers constitute 59% of the workforce (cited in Storey and Quintas 2001) is achieved by an uneasy amalgamation of high touch customer-facing work, knowledge work, and (probably) the creative industries and public sector as well, assuming that because knowledge work is located in the service sector then all service sector work must be knowledge work (see Thompson 2004 for a critique of this). A more nuanced classification should help to prevent such combinations of categories.

Having established just how varied service sector work is (as well as the form that variety takes) this chapter will go on to review the increasing emphasis on soft and social skills that has characterized the labour force over the last few decades (Payne 2000; Keep 2001).

Service Sector Skills

Traditionally skills have been associated both with manipulating physical objects and with work that is male, full-time, and unionized, so skilled workers were able to demonstrate tangible results and their unions would take action to protect, develop, and reward those skills (Turner 1962). In recent years that has changed and the skills now most in demand by employers are soft and social skills, with 84% of US employers looking for soft skills at recruitment and 75% mentioning soft skills before any other factor (Moss and Tilly 2001: 59). Lists of desired qualities vary, from communication and customer service skills to positive attitudes towards change, team-working, self-awareness, self-promotion, networking, action planning, political focus, coping with uncertainty, and self-confidence (Confederation of British Industry 1989; Whiteways Research 1995; National Skills Task Force 2000).

A focus on soft skills is apparent in manufacturing (Thompson *et al.* 1995) but it is the rise of the service sector and focus on customers and clients that have materially contributed to much of their prominence. In part of course, this is simply relabelling employers' longstanding interest in character and personality. Most jobs involve a mixture of technical and social skills: teaching a class will require knowledge of a particular subject but also the ability to present it in an engaging, accurate, and informative way, to design a lesson and to speak coherently and audibly; putting a new roof on a house demands knowledge and skills about construction materials and an appreciation of the ways these fit together most securely, but it may also require team-working, communication, and problem solving to co-operate with colleagues and work round obstacles. Unsurprisingly, Green *et al.*'s (2007) analysis of pay for highly skilled IT workers reveals that it is not technical skills alone that secure the highest wage premia, but technical skills in combination with social skills. In the workplace, it is not enough to know how to do a task, an individual must also possess the social skills needed to put the task into operation. Such skills are appreciated by both colleagues and employers, indeed, in a slightly worrying finding Casciaro and Lobo (2005) revealed that, in the absence of socially pleasant experts ('stars') most workers would rather ask sociable colleagues who knew little about a subject ('lovable fools') for advice than more knowledgeable but less amenable peers ('competent jerks').

So, soft skills are important, they are a key feature of work, and particularly customer-facing service sector work and they feature most significantly at key points in employees' careers such as recruitment, appraisal, and promotion. Yet these advantages notwithstanding, soft skills also present both analytical and practical problems. First, they are not skills. They are personal qualities, competences, aspects of relationships, and virtues but they are not individual skills. This does matter, as labelling them as skills effectively strips them of their reciprocal and relational aspects, making the individual worker, rather than the nature of their work, the management systems or the terms and conditions they operate under, responsible for exercising them. Yet as Lafer (2004: 117–118) comments:

> traits such as discipline, loyalty and punctuality are not 'skills' that one either possesses or lacks; they are measures of commitment that one chooses to give or withhold based on the conditions of work offered.

Second, soft and social skills are exceptionally hard to measure with any degree of confidence. Like beauty, they exist largely in the eye of the beholder and are attributed rather than convincingly demonstrated. Such judgements as are made tend to rely on proxies such as gender, race, or class and there is certainly evidence that male and female, white and BME, working- and middle-class workers are all judged very differently. So, for example, enthusiasm for the job, which would be considered assertive in a man becomes aggressive when a woman displays it (Collinson *et al.* 1990), black workers are considered less loyal than their white colleagues (Maume 1999) and Asian women who dress traditionally less career minded (PeopleManagement 2003). In the workplace women are expected to flirt or nurture male bosses, and are marked down in performance reviews if they do not, while male assistants are required only to be professional and courteous (Pierce 1995).

Often the rationales behind these judgements go beyond casual sexism and racism. Moss and Tilly (1996, 2001) in a detailed study of US employers' recruitment practices found a marked variation between views of different racial groups and between women and men in the same racial group with many employers happy to hire black women for customer-facing work for which they would not consider black men (who were deemed too aggressive or too difficult to manage). The reciprocal aspects of soft skills are key here too. If women, BMEs, and other minority groups are treated differently during recruitment or at work, they are likely to respond differently, as Lafer points out above. Such unequal treatment can result in a 'dialectic of defiance' (Vallas 2003) with members of disadvantaged groups responding in negative ways to discrimination, so demonstrating fewer positive soft skills at work than their more privileged colleagues. In other words, disadvantage and discrimination can itself create disadvantage and discrimination. It seems that a great deal of soft skills depends on the extent to which the workplace is either welcoming or hostile (Vallas 1990).

Third, while soft skills may actively disadvantage those workers who are already underprivileged in the labour market, it is not clear whether they facilitate progression in any way. Traditional technical skills and formal educational achievements aid progression in the labour market by certifying achievements and enabling potential employees and employers to find one another. Soft skills are far less successful at this. In part this is a reflection of service sector work where jobs are polarized and it can be difficult to establish progression routes between low- and high-skilled jobs. But this can also be attributed to the intangibility of soft skills that are far harder to substantiate and evidence than more technical skills. And there is certainly a dissonance between employers' insistence on their importance for low-level work and their reluctance to translate this into any kind of pay premia (Bolton 2004).

It seems there is tension between the discretion that soft skills seem to require and the way work is designed and controlled. Human interaction is, by its very nature, complex and difficult to script (Hochschild 1983; Bolton and Boyd 2003; Bolton and Houlihan 2005; though see also Payne 2009). However, despite some claims (Tsoukas and Vladimirou 2001) it is difficult to label most frontline service jobs as knowledge work as they are tightly controlled. Korczynski (2001, 2002) terms this paradox the customer-oriented bureaucracy in which both the controlled aspects of bureaucracy and the 'personalized' customer service are expected to operate (though see Brook 2007).

Worryingly, much of the training designed to equip the unemployed for work in Canada and the USA is now focused on soft skills (Butterwick 2003; Lafer 2004). These may give access to minimum wage jobs but this is the sector of the labour force where there is a great deal of churn (McDowell 2009) and soft skills seem to equip workers only for rapid and regular transitions between employment and unemployment.

While soft skills actively disadvantage workers at the bottom end of the labour market, they have a very different effect on those at the top. Grugulis and Vincent's (2009) study of IT consultants and housing benefit caseworkers reveals that, while a focus on soft skills was used to discount and marginalize the caseworkers' skills, materially disadvantaging female workers who were disproportionately allocated to unskilled customer service roles, they were considered an addition to the highly skilled IT professionals' expertise. Ironically, here, graduates hired for the personal qualities of entrepreneurship, flexibility, and ambition used them to select 'sexy, hot projects', master the latest software, and leave for better paid work elsewhere.

It seems that soft skills are transitive (Grugulis and Lloyd 2010), in the sense that they depend on technical skills, particularly for highly-skilled workers. This makes sense, after all, to communicate or problem solve, workers require situational knowledge and experience as well as communication or problem-solving skills, and it is the interaction between these hard and soft elements of work, which earns pay premia (Dickerson and Green 2002). It also seems, that despite early hopes, soft skills have not provided a language by which occupational disadvantage can be overcome. Indeed, it seems that labelling skills makes employers more likely to allocate women to tasks considered 'feminine' than to increase the rewards available (Grugulis and Vincent 2004, 2009). This is not a ladder, it is, as Keep (2001) perceptively notes, an escalator. Everyone is going up, as the lists of skills that people possess are getting longer, but the people who started on the bottom rung are still on the bottom rung.

Discussion and Conclusions

A number of significant conclusions emerge from this. Work in the service sector is incredibly diverse. The five categories developed here encompass a wide range of occupations with very different levels of contact with and responsibilities towards, frontline service. Such diversity is neglected in the existing literature, which tends to either omit customer-facing roles entirely or focus exclusively on them. A classification that covers all service sector occupations and distinguishes between them is long overdue.

This diversity notwithstanding, we should not lose sight of the distinctive elements in some service sector jobs. There is a subsection of service sector work where the presence and role of customer and client are key and these jobs are highly distinctive. The existing organizational studies and employment literature has done excellent research into exploring the nature and details of the way such jobs are carried out, the importance of appearance and emotions and the integration of the employee into the exchange. In these jobs the process of being served may be as much a part of any purchase as physical products affecting the nature of work, the way it is controlled and the skills demanded of individual workers. An appreciation of the distinctive nature of such occupations is key to any form of workplace analysis.

Related to this is the role of the customer in this literature. The customer plays a key role in most accounts of the service sector but the way that role is presented varies greatly. In marketing literature, customers tend to be depicted in relatively simplistic terms, as both all-powerful and homogeneous. Firms simply have to provide what the customer wants, create that 'moment of delight' (Carlzon 1987) and their markets are established. Yet as Keep *et al.* (2002) point out, this obscures the complicated and varied reasons behind most purchases. Swissair, which won awards for its customer service went bankrupt while Easyjet, which is famed for its neglect, continues to thrive. Moreover customers may value neglect, and, through it, speed of service, over customer care. In this chapter, customers have a rather more varied and complex role as they are involved in the employment practices and may be included in both management and service worker alliances. These alliances are shifting and transitory but the customer is present in all. This is not customer as a universal panacea to ensure the smooth running of the market that we see elsewhere but a rather more nuanced triangular relationship between employees, employers, and customers. Their importance is not denied, rather an analytical framework is used to engage with detailed empirical research to illuminate workplace relations (see, for example Leidner 1993, 1996).

Finally, this chapter has engaged with the changing nature of skills and the shift to soft and social skills. Soft skills are an important and integral part of every job. Without them, it is difficult to imagine how work groups might function effectively. But they also raise both conceptual and practical problems in the workplace, problems that are exacerbated by the fact that such 'skills' are ascribed. At best soft skills facilitate organization, at worst they provide a legitimation for stereotypes and prejudice, damaging groups already disadvantaged in the workplace.

Where then, does this chapter take us? Any attempt to describe work in a sector that accounts for more than 80% of jobs necessarily simplifies the occupations it presents. Here, by offering a new typology of service work, an attempt is made to do this without distorting. The work undertaken in the service sector is important, as is understanding the form, content, and drivers of that work. This chapter is an attempt to illuminate that work.

References

Anderson-Gough, F., Grey, C., and Robson, K. (2000). In the name of the client: the service ethic in two professional service firms. *Human Relations*, **53**(9), 1151–1174.

Araujo, L. and Spring, M. (2006). Services, products and the institutional structure of production. *Industrial Marketing Management*, **35**(7), 797–805.

Bolton, S.C. (2004). Conceptual confusions: emotion work as skilled work. In: *The Skills that Matter*, Warhurst, C., Grugulis, I., and Keep, E. (Ed.), pp. 19–37. Basingstoke: Palgrave Macmillan.

Bolton, S.C. and Boyd, C. (2003). Trolley dolly or skilled emotional manager? Moving on from Hochschilds *Managed Heart*. *Work, Employment and Society*, **17**(2),289–308.

Bolton, S.C. and Houlihan, M. (2005). The (mis)representation of customer service. *Work, Employment and Society*, **19**(4), 605–703.

Boyne, G.A. (2003). What is public service improvement? *Public Administration*, **81**(2), 211–227.

Bozkurt, O. and Grugulis, I. (2011). Why retail work demands a closer look. In: *Retail Work*, Grugulis, I. and Bozkurt, O. (Ed.), pp. 1–21. Houndsmills: Palgrave Macmillan.

Broadberry, S. (2006). *Market Services and the Productivity Race 1850-2000: British performance in international perspective*. Cambridge: Cambridge University Press.

Brook, P. (2007). Customer oriented militants? A critique of the Customer Oriented Bureaucracy theory on front-line service worker collectivism. *Work, Employment and Society*, **21**(2), 363–374.

Brown, P., Lauder, H., and Ashton, D. (2011). *The Global Auction*. Oxford: Oxford University Press.

Butterwick, S. (2003). Life skills training: 'open for discussion'. In: *Training the Excluded for Work*, Cohen, M.G. (Ed.), pp. 161–177. Vancouver: UBC Press.

Callaghan, G. and Thompson, P. (2002). We recruit attitude: the selection and shaping of routine call centre labour. *Journal of Management Studies*, **39**(2), 233–254.

Carlzon, J. (1987). *The Moment of Truth*. Cambridge, MA: Ballinger.

Carroll, M., Cooke, F.L., Grugulis, I., Rubery, J., and Earnshaw, J. (2001). Analysing diversity in the management of human resources in call centres. Presented at the Human Resource Management Journal conference Call Centres and Beyond: the HRM implications, 6 November, Kings College London.

Casciaro, T. and Lobo, M.S. (2005). Competent jerks, lovable fools and the formation of social networks. *Harvard Business Review*, **83**(6), 92–99.

CBI (Confederation of British Industry). 1989. *Towards a skills revolution—a youth charter*. London: CBI.

Collinson, D., Knights, D., and Collinson, M. (1990). *Managing to Discriminate*. London: Routledge.

Cook, E. (1997). Fattism: a hard act to swallow. *The Independent on Sunday*, 9 July.

Dickerson, A. and Green, F. (2002). *The Growth and Valuation of Generic Skills*. SKOPE Research Paper. Oxford and Warwick: Universities of Oxford and Warwick.

Erickson, B.H., Albanese, P., and Drakulic, S. (2000). Gender on a jagged edge: the security industry, its clients and the reproduction and revision of gender. *Work and Occupations*, **27**(3), 294–318.

Foster, D. and Hoggett, P. (1999). Change in the benefits agency: empowering the exhausted worker? *Work, Employment and Society*, **13**, 19–39.

Fountain, J.E. (2001). Paradoxes of public sector customer service. *Governance*, **14**, 55–73.

Fuller, L. and Smith, V. (1996). Consumers' reports: management by customers in a changing economy. In: *Working in the Service Society*, Macdonald, C.L. and Sirianni, C. (Ed.), pp. 24–49. Philadelphia: Temple University Press.

Gatta, M. (2011). In the blink of an eye—American high-end small retail businesses and the public workforce system. In: *Retail Work*, Grugulis, I. and Bozkurt, O. (Ed.), pp. 49–67. Basingstoke: Palgrave Macmillan.

Green, F., Felstead, A., Gaillie, D., and Zhou, Y. (2007). Computers and pay. *National Institute Economic Review*, **201**, 63–75.

Grimshaw, D., Beynon, H., Rubery, J., and Ward, K. (2002). The restructuring of career paths in large service sector organisations: 'delayering', up-skilling and polarisation. *Sociological Review*, **50**, 89–116.

Grugulis, I. and Bozkurt, O. (Ed.). (2011). *Retail Work: critical perspectives on work and employment*. Basingstoke: Palgrave Macmillan.

Grugulis, I. and Lloyd, C. (2010). Skill and the labour process: conditions and consequences of change. In: *Working Life: renewing Labour Process Analysis*, Thompson, P. and Smith, C. (Ed.), pp. 99–192. Houndsmills: Palgrave.

Grugulis, I. and Vincent, S. (2004). Changing boundaries, shaping skills: the fragmented organisational form and employee skills. In: *Fragmenting Work: blurring organisational boundaries and disordering hierarchies*, Marchington, M., Grimshaw, D., Rubery, J., and Willmott, H. (Ed.), Oxford: Oxford University Press.

Grugulis, I. and Vincent, S. (2009). Whose skill is it anyway? Soft skills and polarisation. *Work, Employment and Society*, 23(4), 597–615.

Hebson, G. and Grugulis, I. (2004). Gender and new organisational forms. In: *Fragmenting Work: blurring organisational boundaries and disordering hierarchies*, Marchington, M., Grimshaw, D., Rubery, J., and Willmott, H. (Ed.), Oxford: Oxford University Press.

Hochschild, A.R. (1983). *The Managed Heart: commercialization of human feeling*. Berkley, CA: University of California Press.

Keep, E. (2001). If it moves, its a skill. Presented at ESRC seminar on The Changing Nature of Skills and Knowledge, 3–4 September, Manchester.

Keep, E., Mayhew, K., and Corney, M. (2002). Review of the Evidence on the rate of return to employers of investment in training and employer training measures. In: *SKOPE Research Paper*: Universities of Oxford and Warwick, SKOPE.

Korczynski, M. (2001). The contradictions of service work: call centre as customer-oriented bureaucracy. In: *Customer Service: empowerment and entrapment*, Sturdy, A., Grugulis, I., and Willmott, H. (Ed.), pp. 79–101. Basingstoke: Palgrave.

Korczynski, M. (2002). *Human Resource Management in Service Work*. Basingstoke: Palgrave.

Korczynski, M. and Macdonald, C.L. (2008). Service work and critical perspectives: an introduction. In: *Service Work and Critical Perspectives*, Korczynski, M. and Macdonald, C.L. (Ed.), pp. 1–10. New York: Routledge.

Lafer, G. (2004). What is skill? In: *The Skills that Matter*, Warhurst, C., Grugulis, I., and Keep, E. (Ed.), pp. 109–127. Basingstoke: Palgrave Macmillan.

Leidner, R. (1993). *Fast Food, Fast Talk: service work and the routinizations of everyday life*. Berkeley, CA: University of California Press.

Leidner, R. (1996). Rethinking questions of control: lessons from McDonalds. In: *Working in the Service Society*, Macdonald, C.L. and Sirianni, C. (Ed.), pp. 29–49. Philadelphia, PA: Temple University Press.

Macdonald, C.L. and Sirianni, C. (1996a). The service society and the changing experience of work. In: *Working in the Service Society*, Macdonald, C.L. and Sirianni, C. (Ed.), pp. 1–28. Philadelphia: Temple University Press.

Macdonald, C.L. and Sirianni, C. (Ed.). (1996b). *Working in the Service Society*. Philadelphia: Temple University Press.

McDowell, L. (1997). *Capital Culture: gender at work in the City*. Oxford: Blackwell.

McDowell, L. (2009). *Working Bodies: interactive service employment and workplace identities*. Chichester: Wiley-Blackwell.

Mann, S. 1999. *Hiding What we Feel, Faking What we Dont: understanding the role of your emotions at work*. Shaftesbury: Element.

Martinez Lucio, M. and MacKenzie, R. (1999). Quality management. A new form of control? In: *Employee Relations in the Public Sector: themes and issues*, Corby, S. and White, G. (Ed.), pp. 156–178. London: Routledge and Cardiff University.

Maume, D.J.J. (1999). Glass ceilings and glass escalators: occupational segregation and race and sex differences in managerial promotions. *Work and Occupations*, **26**(4), 483–509.

Moss, P. and Tilly, C. (1996). Soft skills and race: an investigation into black mens employment problems. *Work and Occupations*, **23**(3), 252–276.

Moss, P. and Tilly, C. (2001). *Stories Employers Tell: race, skill and hiring in America*. New York: Russell Sage Foundation.

National Skills Task Force. (2000). Skills for all: research report of the National Skills Task Force. Sudbury: DfEE.

Nickson, D., Warhurst, C., Witz, A., and Cullen, A.-M. (2001). The importance of being aesthetic: work, employment and service organisation. In: *Customer Service: empowerment and entrapment*, Sturdy, A., Grugulis, I., and Willmott, H. (Ed.), pp. 170–190. Basingstoke: Palgrave.

Nolan, P. and Wood, S. (2003). Mapping the future of work. *British Journal of Industrial Relations*, **41**(2), 165–174.

Noon, M. (2007). The fatal flaws of diversity and the business case for ethnic minorities. *Work, Employment and Society*, **21**(4), 773–784.

Noon, M. and Blyton, P. (2007). *The Realities of Work*. Houndsmills: Palgrave.

ONS. (2013). Employment by Industry. Office for National Statistics.

Patterson, S. (1965). *Dark Strangers: a study of West Indians in London*. Harmondsworth: Penguin.

Paules, G.F. (1991). *Dishing it Out: power and resistance among waitresses in a New Jersey restaurant*. Philadelphia, PA: Temple University Press.

Payne, J. (2000). The unbearable lightness of skill: the changing meaning of skill in UK policy discourses and some implications for education and training. *Journal of Education Policy*, **15**(3), 353–369.

Payne, J. (2009). Emotional labour and skill: a reappraisal. *Gender, Work and Organization*, **16**(3), 348–367.

People Management (2003) News, 6 September.

Pierce, J.L. (1995). *Gender Trials: emotional lives in contemporary law firms*. Berkley, CA: University of California Press.

Rainbird, H., Munro, A., and Holly, L. (2004). Employer demand for skills and qualifications. In: *The Skills that Matter*, Warhurst, C., Grugulis, I., and Keep, E. (Ed.), pp. 91–108. Basingstoke: Palgrave Macmillan.

Rees, B. and Garnsey, E. (2003). Analysing competence: gender and identity at work. *Gender, Work and Organization*, **10**(5), 551–578.

Reich, R. (1991). *The Work of Nations: preparing ourselves for 21st century capitalism*. New York: Vintage Books.

Self, A. (2008). *Social Trends*. Basingstoke: Palgrave Macmillan and Office for National Statistics.

Skillset. (2007). *Employment Census 2006: the results of the sixth census of the audio visual industries*. London: Skillset.

Skillset/UKFilmCouncil. (2008). *Feature Film Production Workforce Survey 2008*. London: Skillset/UKFC.

Skuratowicz, E. and Hunter, L.W. (2004). Where do womens jobs come from? Job resegregation in an American Bank. *Work and Occupations*, **31**, 73–110.

Stewart, T. (1997). *Intellectual Capital: the new wealth of organisations.* London: Nicholas Brealy.

Storey, J. and Quintas, P. (2001). Knowledge management and HRM. In: *Human Resource Management: a critical text*, Storey, J. (Ed.), London: Thomson Learning.

Sturdy, A., Handley, K., Clark, T., and Fincham, R. (2009). *Management Consultancy: boundaries and knowledge in action.* Oxford: Oxford University Press.

Taylor, S. and Tyler, M. (2000). Emotional labour and sexual difference in the airline industry. *Work, Employment and Society*, **14**, 77–96.

Thompson, P. (2004). Skating on thin ice: the knowledge economy myth. Glasgow: University of Strathclyde/Big Thinking.

Thompson, P., Wallace, T., Flecker, J., and Ahlstrand, R. (1995). It aint what you do, its the way that you do it: production organisation and skill utilisation in commercial vehicles. *Work, Employment and Society*, **9**(4), 719–742.

Tsoukas, H. and Vladimirou, E. (2001). What is organisational knowledge? *Journal of Management Studies*, **38**(7), 973–993.

Turner, H.A. (1962). *Trade Union Growth, Structure and Policy.* London: George Allen and Unwin Ltd.

Vallas, S.P. (1990). The concept of skill: a critical review. *Work and Occupations*, **17**(4), 379–398.

Vallas, S.P. (2003). Rediscovering the colour line within work organisations: the knitting of racial groups revisited. *Work and Occupations*, **30**(4), 379–400.

Van Maanen, J. (1991). The smile factory: work at Disneyland. In: *Reframing Organisational Culture*, Frost, P., Moore, L., Luis, M., Lundberg, C., and Martin, J. (Ed.), pp. 11–24. Thousand Oaks, CA: Sage.

Warhurst, C. and Nickson, D. (2001). *Looking Good, Sounding Right.* London: Industrial Society.

Whiteways Research. (1995). *Skills for Graduates in the 21st Century.* London: Association of Graduate Recruiters.

5

Gender and Diversity Challenges in Professional Services Firms

Kathryn Haynes

Introduction

The term 'professional services firm' (PSF) refers to firms that apply specialist technical knowledge to the creation of customized solutions to client's problems (Empson 2001). Traditionally the term has been used to apply to firms working within formally regulated professions, particularly accounting and law, although it may also be extended to those within advertising, consulting, or investment banking (von Nordenfycht 2010). The sector represented one of the fastest growing economic segments of most Western economies in the 1990s, expanding at an annual rate of 20% per annum (Boojihawon and Young 2002). Although it was affected by the recent global economic downturn, the sector rallied and remains important and dominant within many economies.

The professional services sector draws from the historical characteristics of the various professions from which it originates, while it has expanded rapidly into new areas. Because of its historical relationship with the professions, which were a bastion of male control since their inception in the nineteenth century (Walker 2011), the sector was traditionally dominated by predominantly middle-class, white, men. Yet in recent decades, it has been subject to major demographic changes with the opening up of higher education to a much larger number of students from a wider range of social backgrounds (Panel of Fair Access to the Professions 2009), and has seen much larger numbers of women entering PSFs.

This chapter explores the progress, outcomes, and implications of this social and demographic shift in the workforce in PSFs. While the chapter is predominately located in the UK professional services sector, it draws from research that explores issues more widely around the globe. It examines the role of the professions in providing professional services, the role and influence of PSFs, the nature of professional service work, and relationships with clients, in conjunction with concepts of gender and diversity. Specifically it examines whether, and how, long-existing closure regimes have shifted in professional services, bringing about new challenges for the firms themselves and for professional workers.

The chapter is structured as follows: First, it considers the scope and significance of PSFs by drawing from debates about the nature of PSFs, and then examining their impact within the economy and as employers. Second, it begins to look at the way professional services limit their membership through closure regimes based on the traditional nature of professionals and professionalism. The main focus of the discussion is on gender challenges in the professional services context as a form of social closure through the need to have appropriate social and physical capital. However, the chapter also considers other forms of social closure, based on class and race among other factors, which also may interact with each other. Finally, the chapter draws out some implications for equality within PSFs and potential for further research. While I mostly refer to literature and studies in the context of PSFs in accounting and law, the issues have relevance to other areas of professional services, as I will go on to discuss.

The Scope and Significance of Professional Services Firms

Before going into gender challenges in the professional services sector, we need to understand the scope and significance of professional services. Yet, there remains debate about what constitutes a professional service firm. The comprehensive taxonomy of PSFs provided by von Nordenfycht (2010) allows for some clarity by considering three identifying characteristics. He points out that although the characteristic of knowledge intensity is often assumed to be a key defining characteristic of firms derived from the basis of a profession, the extent to which this makes all PSFs distinctive is problematic. Knowledge intensity might be a fundamental distinctive characteristic of PSFs, but how it is enacted is different within different types of firms and depends on whether it is seen as informing knowledge embodied in individuals, or in equipment, products, and organizational routines. In which case, von Nordenfycht (2010) suggests, if a firm relies on an intellectually skilled workforce across its front-line workers, 'human capital intensity' might be a better term for this first characteristic. The second characteristic is low capital intensity, which 'indicates that a firm's production does not involve significant amounts of nonhuman assets, such as inventory, factories and equipment, and even intangible nonhuman assets like patents and copyrights' (von Nordenfycht 2010: 162). The third characteristic is a professionalized workforce, which means that individuals have to study for rigorous professional qualifications, in conjunction with experiential elements, to achieve professional status. Hence, the *classic* PSF would comprise accounting, law, and architecture, as these firms incorporate high knowledge intensity, low capital intensity, and a highly professionalized workforce. These characteristics allow for more weakly professionalized workforces such as within management consulting or advertising to be characterized as *neo-PSFs*. They also preclude organizations such as hospitals being defined as PSFs, due to their high capital intensity investment in equipment and buildings, despite their knowledge intensity and partly professionalized workforce. Von Nordenfycht's (2010) characterization captures the shifting ground from profession to knowledge-based service firm.

The significance and contribution of professional services to the economy and working environment is also subject to wide debate, as it relies heavily on these former definitions of what constitutes a PSF. A recent UK Treasury report, for example, acknowledges that official data do not capture the complete picture. However, the most relevant category in the Annual Business Inquiry, which sources data from the Office of National Statistics, demonstrates the significance of the sector's contribution to the economy, revealing that the turnover of the sector was £75.2 billion in 2006 and £84.3 billion in 2007 (HM Treasury 2009). It is worth noting, however, that these official UK government figures include within the PSF context, shipping and elements of construction, not areas that would enter von Nordenfycht's (2010) taxonomy, as well as more traditional forms of professional services such as the legal profession, accountancy, and management consultancy. None the less, the UK legal profession employed 330,000 people in 2007; provided services for which clients paid over £10.82 billion; and generated a surplus of £2.46 billion in exports, while the UK accountancy profession employed 245,000 people in 2007; provided services for which clients paid over £9.36 billion; and generated a surplus of £1.01 billion in exports (HM Treasury 2009).

At the global level, PSFs arose from a collective body of professionals and practitioners in a particular professional discipline into sites of specific operation and delivery of service through increasingly large partnerships of professionals. Many of these firms within the sector have expanded into extensive global organizations through growth and international acquisition and merger activity. Over twenty of the largest global law firms, for example, have revenues of over $1bn,[1] while the largest global accounting firm,

PricewaterhouseCoopers, with global revenue of over \$29.2 bn,[2] currently employs over 168,000 people in 158 countries. Such firms play an increasingly significant role not only in the economy but also in society. Many accounting or consulting firms may be as large as the clients they seek to serve, often deeply embedded in client firms through long-term and broadly defined relationships, including outsourced activities of their clients (Empson 2007). Hence, the professional services sector is a significant player in the servitization of Western capitalist economies, and a major employer of skilled professionals.

The opening up of the professions and the condensing of the delivery of professional services into increasingly large PSFs has brought about some considerable and continuing challenges in recent decades in respect of gender and diversity, arising from social and demographic changes in the workforce.

Recent decades have seen significant increases each year in the numbers of women attracted to professions, and to the PSFs within them. In the case of law, the percentage of female students enrolling with the Law Society in the UK consistently reached about 62% in the years from 2001 to 2009 (Law Society 2010), whereas within accounting, worldwide female student members of the six major UK accounting bodies between 2002 and 2009 was consistent at 48% (Professional Oversight Board for Accountancy 2010; Professional Oversight Board for Accountancy 2008).

Yet, despite the increasing numbers of women entering PSFs, many newly qualified accountants exit the profession at an early stage (*Accountancy* 2008) and the possibility of widening the demographics of those pursuing long-term careers in law remains problematic (Sommerlad 2004). The proportion of women progressing to the higher levels of PSFs remains low despite the surge of programmes and policies in many of the large ones designed to support women's progression. I argue in this chapter that these difficulties relate to the historical nature of the professions, and their historical closure regimes, but with some important shifts in the nature of closure in a modern context.

Closure Regimes

Professional closure is the sociological term derived given to the way that professions limit their membership to those who meet stringent entry requirements (Larson 1977; Weber 1978). It refers to the way that groups with interest in common circumscribe their membership to pursue their collective interest or to defend it from outsiders (MacDonald 1995). Closure regimes include both explicit criteria, such as educational qualifications, and more implicit criteria, relating to class, race, and gender, or other credentials (Bolton and

Muzio 2007; O'Regan 2008). In the case of law, for example, the feminization of the profession, with increasing numbers of women entering it, have caused what Ackroyd and Muzio (2007) argue is a shift from external closure mechanisms, which sanction access to the profession, to internal ones, which regulate progression through the ranks and control access to the most prestigious and rewarding positions.

Hence, to understand how closure is enacted within professions, we need first to address the nature of professionalism, and the requirements to become professional, which forms the basis of social closure.

The Nature of Professionalism

The early twentieth century role of the profession was as a body offering a public service. Under modern capitalism, professions were deemed a major force capable of opposing the rampant individualism of the acquisitive society, through their promise to advance the community interest (Tawney 1921). Professional organizations acted as a form of moral community based on occupational membership (Durkheim 1957), while simultaneously serving the twin themes of altruism towards the public good and the service ethic (Carr-Saunders and Wilson 1933). According to Greenwood (1957), members of professions are generally deemed to have attributes of professional competence, which brings about public recognition and community sanction, through a recognized code of ethics, embedded in the culture of the profession.

However, professions are also seen as a form of occupational labour market with specialist qualifications, acting as distinct modes of occupational organization and segregation (Sommerlad and Sanderson 1998). Their supposedly distinguishing characteristics and technical expertise are used by professions to justify their, often monopolistic, provision of specific services offered (Abbott 1988; Johnson 1972). It is this ability of professions to exclude outsiders from the technical and legal basis of their practice, which enables skills to be both materially and symbolically rewarded, that maintains the power to the profession (Larson 1977).

Classic PSFs are members of professional bodies, which regulate practitioners and the firms themselves. For example, solicitors are regulated by The Law Society in the UK and the Bar Association in the USA. Accountants are regulated by their membership of one of six professional accounting institutes in the UK,[3] and in the USA by the Certified Public Accountants (CPA). Accounting institutes and law societies regard themselves as professional and are controlled and organized in similar ways to other groups deemed as professional in society, largely through self-regulation and professional standards of ethics and conduct. As a result, almost all conceptualizations of professionalism tend to concern issues of knowledge or expertise, and, more particularly, control and licensing of specialist knowledge or expertise in the public interest (Johnson 1972; Abbott 1988; Sikka *et al.* 1989) or, arguably, in defence of members' interests (Willmott 1986). Accountants and lawyers are not simply regarded as professional for undertaking accounting and law work, or for using accounting and law techniques or specialist knowledge; rather, only those who are professionally qualified with one of the professional institutes are regarded as professionals. The stringent qualification and experience requirements act as a barrier to entry and maintain the technical basis of membership—a form of explicit social closure. The professional, as an individual, is defined through membership of a profession and adherence to its rules and standards, so in the case of accounting:

> being a professional accountant would refer to accredited competence in the specific skills and knowledge associated with particular professional bodies. In short, on this view, a professional is someone who has passed the exams. (Grey 1998: 572)

However, Grey (1998) also suggests that, while qualifications and knowledge are factors taken for granted, legitimating the accountant as a professional, the predominant way in which professional accountants *themselves* use the term 'professional' in discursive practice is more concerned with appropriate forms of behaviour, or ways of conducting oneself, rather than with issues of accreditation to practise or the possession of technical skills. In the accounting context, the locus of this behavioural aspect of professional identity, and the key source of its influence, is the socialization process undertaken within the PSF itself, in which the individual is moulded into the archetypal, desirable accountant, such that he or she possesses both the technical *and* behavioural attributes required (Anderson-Gough *et al.* 1998b, 2000, 2001, 2005). In law, there is evidence that processes of professional socialization occur earlier, within higher education institutions and law schools (Thornton 1998; Sommerlad 2008), and during recruitment (Collier 2005), although the large law firm remains an important locus of professionalization whereby professional priorities and objectives are increasingly supported by organizational systems and initiatives (Faulconbridge and Muzio 2008).

Hence, if the professional has to achieve both tangible professional qualifications and less tangible behavioural requirements, this raises the potential different forms of social closure. Despite professions appearing to have accepted as 'ideological necessity' the close tying of educational credentials to meritocratic access, their role in supporting access to status requires restricted entry (Larson 1977: 51). Hence, professional practices may contribute to historical and continued professional closure for those seen as 'other' (Hammond 2002; Sommerlad 2007; Francis and Sommerlad 2009). These concepts and closure regimes will now be examined in more detail.

Gender Challenges

Professions, such as accounting and law, have previously been considered masculine territories from which women have been excluded through barriers to entry. Historically, the opportunity for women to become accountants was problematic, as gender conflicts restricting women's access to the profession persisted since the early 1900s and women were seen by some as both physically and intellectually unfit for such a role (Lehman 1992). Their oppression within accountancy interacted with the development of power and influence in the profession itself and the constitution of its knowledge base in terms of gender (Kirkham 1992). Until the latter half of the twentieth century, the professional echelons of accounting were a male preserve in the UK, as the masculine qualities required of accounting professionals 'contrasted markedly with the image of the weak, dependent, emotional "married" woman of mid-Victorian Britain' (Kirkham and Loft, 1993: 516). Similarly, in the law profession women were historically subjected to significant barriers to entry. In many Western countries, women's admission to law occurred at the turn of the nineteenth to the twentieth century or during the first decades of the twentieth century as the progress of professionalization grew apace, but entry to the judiciary occurred much more slowly (Schultz 2003). For example, in England and Wales, women struggled to achieve equality with men and were often subordinated into the least prestigious sections of the profession (Sommerlad and Sanderson 1998), and in Canada, monopolies on legal services gave law societies significant power to exclude women from the profession (Brockman 2001).

Despite the inclusion of more women into professional services, discussed above, and the breakdown of barriers to entry, new forms of gendered closure regimes appear to be occurring in recent decades. Women attempting to progress to the higher echelons of PSFs, particularly in the critical promotion to partnership, may find their progress inhibited due to the persistence of a glass ceiling (Stumpf 2002). A number of issues contribute to the existence and maintenance of these barriers to women's progression, including sexual discrimination (Nicolson 2005); the combination of professional and family commitments (Johnson *et al.* 2008); stereotypical assumptions about parenting, inferring that women eventually abandon their careers to take care of home and children (Hagan and Kay 1995); the need to fit a prevailing masculine model of performance or success (Kumra and Vinnicombe 2008;

Jonnergård *et al.* 2010); and 'marked segmentation between largely feminine, community orientated and relatively underpaid specialisms on the one side and male-dominated, corporate oriented and remunerative practice areas on the other' (Bolton and Muzio 2007: 58). The stratification of law into different types of firms, legal specialisms, and organizations fractures women's experiences of law, and accentuates hegemonic masculinity in mainstream law by the feminization of the profession occurring in niches of legal practice, which are 'naturalized' as female and where women play a 'maternal' caring role (Sommerlad 2003). As a result, large numbers of women leave PSFs dissatisfied or distressed or seek part-time solutions, and those women who do stay in practice often find there is a ceiling on their status and monetary compensation (Hagan and Kay 1995).

Professional identities may also be gendered due to stereotypes associated with masculine and feminine social and cultural norms within professions and PSFs. Organizational decision-makers in hiring decisions perceive candidates through the lens of gender stereotypes (Gorman 2005) and as women attempt to pass through organizational hierarchies in corporate law firms, traditional male domination of upper level positions intensifies these decision-maker biases (Gorman and Kmec 2009). Moreover, women are subjected to stricter performance standards than men when undertaking the same job (Gorman and Kmec 2007) and are likely to be rewarded less than their male counterparts (Kay and Gorman 2008). In the context of PSFs, the professional and organizational discourses forming the socialization processes within accounting and law exercise a significant degree of institutional power in the shaping of the individual (Anderson-Gough *et al.* 1998a; Sommerlad 1998), which may have significant gendered effects.

Some of these gendered effects are seen in the representation of social and physical capital in PSFs.

Social Capital

Social capital theory relates to an individual's position in a social network of relationships and focuses on the resources contained in, accessed through, or stemming from these networks (Kumra and Vinnicombe 2010). Essentially, it derives from Bourdieu's concepts of practice and his concern with how various forms of capital support symbolic power and dominance (Bourdieu 1977, 1984, 1986). He outlines a form of *cultural capital*, which is accumulated in part from educational credentials and institutionalized within social systems and practices, supported by *social capital* arising from powerful social networks (Bourdieu, 1986). Hence, it relates to the explicit forms of social closure in terms of education qualifications, but importantly to the implicit forms of social closure derived from fitting into the cultural norms of an organization and being supported through linkages and networks.

Both men and women are aware of the need to acquire social capital to progress their career (Broadbridge 2010). In the context of professional services, the accumulation of social capital is essential to promotion opportunities in terms of being invited into partnership. Kumra and Vinnicombe's (2010) study of social capital accumulation strategies within a consulting PSF, concurs with the view that women are aware of the need to amass social capital to advance their career, particularly in the form of influential sponsors within the firm. However, they suggest that women are often excluded from both formal and informal networks, which negatively impacts on their ability to accumulate social capital, because they often occupy less influential positions, find it more difficult to network, have fewer women to network within same sex networks than men do, and are unable to access such resources so readily as their male counterparts due to underlying organizational processes. Such barriers have also been found elsewhere in professional services (Tonge 2008), and are exacerbated for female managers when moving into part-time employment (Durbin and Tomlinson 2010). Unlike technical ability, which can be evaluated using qualifications and objective appraisal systems (though it is debatable whether these are always wholly objective), the influence of internal connections in PSFs is highly subjective and difficult to measure (Malos and Campion 1995). As a result, Kumra and Vinnicombe (2010) go on to suggest that women professionals use impression management strategies, based on being seen to be ambitious, likeable, and available, to dispel negative gender stereotypes that may otherwise accrue to them and impede their ability to access key social networks and thereby accumulate social capital. Women have to be seen to be committed, available for long working hours, and not overburdened with explicitly obvious caring responsibilities (Anderson-Gough *et al.* 2005; Gammie *et al.* 2007; Kornberger *et al.* 2010).

Hence, while it is clear that barriers to entry have improved for women within professional services, other forms of social closure are faced by women in their attempts to progress their careers in PSFs. Promotion to the higher levels of professional services remains problematic for women (Kumra and Vinnicombe 2008). They face the double burden of being technically excellent and hardworking, while also dispelling negative gendered stereotypes to acquire social capital to succeed.

Physical Capital

Physical capital is a second form of capital that is relevant to professional identity and potential aspects of social closure. Again, this notion derives from Bourdieu (1986), and, like social capital, is inter-related with forms of cultural capital. For Bourdieu, the physical body and the form of capital associated with it, physical capital, is a bearer of symbolic value and a possessor of power, status, and distinctive symbolic forms, which is integral to the accumulation of various resources linked to the acquisition of status and distinction (Shilling 1993). So, although professional expertise and qualifications are essential criteria for meritocratic access to professions, other forms of social closure may be at play here.

In the context of the law profession, Thornton (2007) has argued that women's promotion to the judiciary is based on highly gendered notions of merit whereby a woman must position herself close to the masculine norm to ensure a semblance of authority. She also suggests that the physical form of the professional is embodied as inherently masculine (Thornton 2007), so that merit, far from being an objective criterion operates as a rhetorical device shaped by power. In professional services, the norm of bodily presence is an integral dimension of the culture of service work, where there is often a sense of performativity in engaging with the work, especially in legal practice (Thornton and Bagust 2007).

Haynes' (2008) study of women accounting professionals demonstrated the significance of the physical body in the formation of the personal and professional self, where the body becomes a vehicle for displaying conformity, or indeed non-conformity, to gendered social norms, which affects embodied practices, emotions, and identities both within and without the workplace. The focus of this study was on women transitioning between a professional form of physical capital as accounting professionals and other forms of gendered embodied self, such as that experienced during pregnancy and in early motherhood. In some ways, it might be expected that new mothers addressing practical pressures might find returning to work a negotiable and potentially difficult process, even when supported by the firm in doing so. However, in this study the two forms of physical capital clashed, leading to disillusion and disengagement (Haynes 2008).

A further extended study of lawyers and accountants in PSFs found that professional identity was inherently related to physical capital (Haynes 2012). The physical body is an important facet of defining professionalism, such that professionals are expected to dress, act, and behave in ways that conform to cultural norms within that context. Professionalism is related to embodied conduct, or 'carrying oneself', as if the degree of expertise and professionalism is encapsulated in the physical body. However, the exact nature of professional embodiment and professionalism is elusive and ephemeral, relating to self-presentation and demeanour. This, the article argues, is more difficult in masculine contexts for women to negotiate because of the need to be assertive but is not perceived as overly aggressive even though the nature of the job requires a degree of physical presence, performativity, and authority, such as when advocating in court. Women who are deemed as acting contrary to femininity, embodying more masculine attributes required by the law profession for example, are subject to negative characterizations for being too assertive or too shrill. Control of the body and its outward display, through being physically fit, healthy, and an appropriate weight, can be said to be indicative of being in control of one's rationality and corporeal presence, central to the embodiment of the professional in accounting and law. Moreover, in professional services, the relationship with the client is likely to be of a longer-term nature and more relational than in low-skilled service work, allowing the client to act as a regulating force in defining service provision (Anderson-Gough *et al.* 2000; Kornberger *et al.* 2010). The role of the client in PSFs is therefore central to defining the nature of professionalism and how this is embodied. The expectations of the client impact on the need for a professional image and those that do not conform to this norm struggle to attain the professional demeanour and professional embodiment so prized in PSFs (Haynes 2012).

Other Forms of Social Closure

Gender has been the primary focus of this chapter so far, especially in terms of the shifting landscape of professional services; as the sector becomes feminized, barriers to entry are largely broken down, but new barriers to progression might be said to be forming. However, there are other forms of social closure, which need to be addressed, and which also intersect with gender and each other. Social and physical capital is also affected, among others, by class, race, and ethnicity.

Class has been the subject of a number of studies in the professional services context. Nicolson (2005) argues that the main reason why class matters so much in law, for example, is because of the way it interacts with the selection criteria used by educational and professional gatekeepers to discriminate indirectly against those from less privileged backgrounds who do not have the financial capital to attend fee-paying schools or the social capital derived from expectation and parental support of middle-class homes, which increases the chance of entering a prestigious law school. Class encompasses another form of cultural capital on which social closure is predicated. The largest, most prestigious law firms have been criticized for recruiting from a limited number of elite universities resulting in candidates being more likely to be of middle-class and white origin (Rolfe and Anderson 2003). However, while increasing numbers of women entering into the law profession in recent years tend to be from middle-class backgrounds, thus further eroding the social equality of the profession, gender remains a significant discriminatory factor in law (Nicolson 2005). In addition, male lawyers seem to have responded protectively by intensifying the masculine culture (Sommerlad and Sanderson 1998), despite the adoption of diversity strategies, which do little to change underlying organizational cultures (Ashley 2010).

Race is also an area of concern in terms of equality of opportunity in professional services. In the accounting context, race acted as a historical barrier to entry for black accountants in the USA (Hammond and Streeter 1994) due to discriminatory experience requirements for professional membership, while other ethnic groups such as Maori and Chinese in New Zealand suffered more recent discrimination (Kim 2004; McNicholas *et al.* 2004). Race remains a contentious area for equality of progress in UK professional services (*Accountancy* 2009). Nicolson (2005) suggests that the increasing numbers of ethnic minorities in UK legal practice now substantially exceeds their general social presence not just in terms of admissions but also total numbers, with ethnic minority lawyers now breaking into the more lucrative specializations and prestigious law firms, being awarded silk and obtaining partnerships. However, it is important to recognize that the hegemonic form of cultural capital in legal practice remains Eurocentric as well as masculine, with an over-representation of ethnic minorities in those who come from lower socio-economic backgrounds. So there is potential 'intersectionality' occurring here, referring to the interaction between categories of difference in individual lives, social practices, institutional arrangements, cultural ideologies, and the outcomes of the interactions in terms of power (Davis 2008). In other words, there is a complex set of potential discrimination for some professionals within the professional services sector, arising from the interaction of race, gender, and class.

Moreover, while the 'big three' in terms of gender, race, and class, have been most visible, wide-ranging, problematic in critiques of professions, other forms of social, cultural, and physical closure may also apply to other demographic factors such as age, religion, sexuality, and disability (Nicolson 2005). There is generally a lack of research on these issues within professional services, although in terms of physical capital being needed to fit a prevailing professional norm, the issue of disability has begun to be addressed in the accounting context. Despite disability rights legislation, PSFs have been found to have a minimal understanding of disability, lagging behind other organizations in their attitudes, and in which disability is not a significant component of their diversity and equality policies (Duff and Ferguson 2007). Moreover, institutionalized practices within PSFs, such as an emphasis on the image and appearance of staff, discourse of the client, and importance of temporal commitment serve to exclude or marginalize disabled professionals (Duff and Ferguson 2011). These facets might be said to echo similar forms of exclusionary practice in the context of gender.

Implications for Equality in Professional Services

While the professional services sector continues to grow apace, with increasing numbers of new recruits entering firms each year, there continues to be a concern over equality of opportunity within the sector. The very nature of a profession is that it operates as a specialist labour market based on technical and meritocratic expertise, which excludes those who do not meet its stringent entry requirements, thus maintaining its professional power (Larson 1977; Abbott 1988). Formal closure regimes in terms of qualifications remain but the opening up of higher education to a wider demographic means that classic barriers to entry may have been largely overturned, as more women and ethnic minorities achieve the entry requirements.

However, entry barriers give way to more implicit and subtle forms of social closure operating in terms of gender, race, class, and other forms of exclusion, especially in the pursuit of promotion to higher levels and prestigious areas of work. Progression through the hierarchy remains problematic and women, for example, are not being retained in PSFs in the numbers that might be expected (Law Society 2010; Professional Oversight Board for Accountancy 2010).

This is an issue, which even the UK government is concerned about, suggesting in a recent report that:

> The glass ceiling has been raised but not yet broken. Despite the narrowing of the gender pay gap, the top professional jobs still tend to go to men not women. Despite increasing numbers of people from black and ethnic minority backgrounds in professional jobs, many professions are still unrepresentative of the modern society they serve. And most alarmingly of all there is strong evidence, given to the Panel, that the UK's professions have become more, not less, socially exclusive over time. (Panel of Fair Access to the Professions 2009: 6)

The report suggests that PSFs in the UK are recruiting from a narrow set of elite universities, in which lower socio-economic groups are under-represented, and that the default position in too many professions, particularly at the higher echelons, is still to recruit from too narrow a part of the social spectrum (Panel of Fair Access to the Professions 2009). Skilled knowledge workers are crucial to PSFs, who are large employers of graduates, as their service relies on higher skills and knowledge. However, there are some issues to tackle within recruitment and retention. Perceptions of macho cultures of long hours, informal social networks, masculine identities, and lack of support for diverse social groups, within PSFs raises the need for improved policies and practices within firms to support equality. While many firms are implementing such policies, further research might usefully address their effectiveness in bringing about change. Moreover, while there is research on issues concerning gender and to some degree class and race in professional services, little research has been undertaken that addresses their intersectionality, or other areas of difference, such as age, disability, or sexuality. These are areas for potential further research.

Notes

1. www.law.com The American Lawyer. *Global Law* **100**, May 2011.
2. PricewaterhouseCoopers, 2011, Global Annual Review (2009 £26.2bn, 150,000 people).
3. In accounting, the six professional institutes in the UK are the Institute of Chartered Accountants in England and Wales (ICAEW); Institute of Chartered Accountants in Scotland (ICAS); Chartered Accountants Ireland (CAI); Chartered Institute of Management Accountants (CIMA); Association of Chartered Certified Accountants (ACCA); and the Chartered Institute of Public Finance Accountants (CIPFA).

References

Abbott, A. (1988). *The System of Professions: An essay on the division of expert labour,* Chicago, IL: Chicago University Press.

Accountancy (2008). Accountants fear graduate exodus. *Accountancy Magazine,* **59**.

Accountancy (2009). It does matter if you are black or white. *Accountancy Magazine,* February, 22–23.

Ackroyd, S. and Muzio, D. (2007). The reconstructed professional firm: explaining change in English legal practices. *Organization Studies,* **48**, 1–19.

Anderson-Gough, F., Grey, C., and Robson, K. (1998a). *Making Up Accountants: The organisational and professional socialisation of trainee chartered accountants.* Aldershot: Ashgate.

Anderson-Gough, F., Grey, C., and Robson, K. (1998b). 'Work hard, play hard': an analysis of cliché in two accountancy practices. *Organization,* **5**, 565–592.

Anderson-Gough, F., Grey, C., and Robson, K. (2000). In the name of the client: the service ethic in two professional service firms. *Human Relations,* **53**, 1151–1174.

Anderson-Gough, F., Grey, C., and Robson, K. (2001). 'Tests of time': organisational time reckoning and the making of accountants in two multi-national accounting firms. *Accounting, Organizations and Society,* **26**, 99–122.

Anderson-Gough, F., Grey, C., and Robson, K. (2005). 'Helping them to forget…': the organizational embedding of gender relations in public audit firms. *Accounting, Organizations and Society,* **30**, 469–490.

Ashley, L. (2010). Making a difference? The use (and abuse) of diversity management at the UK's elite law firms. *Work, Employment and Society,* **24**, 711–727.

Bolton, S. and Muzio, D. (2007). Can't live with 'em; can't live without 'em: gendered segmentation in the legal profession. *Sociology,* **41**, 47–64.

Boojihawon, D. and Young, S. (2002). Understanding international strategy in professional services industries. In: *International Business: Adjusting to new challenges and opportunities,* McDonald, F., Tuselmann, H., and Wheeler, C. (Ed.), pp. 166–180. Basingstoke: Palgrave.

Bourdieu, P. (1977). *Outline of a Theory of Practice.* Cambridge: Cambridge University Press.

Bourdieu, P. (1984). *Distinction: A social critique of the judgement of taste.* London: Routledge.

Bourdieu, P. (1986). The forms of capital. In: *Handbook of Theory and Research for the Sociology of Education,* Richardson, J.G. (Ed.), pp. 241–258. New York: Greenwood Press.

Broadbridge, A. (2010). Social capital, gender and careers: evidence from retail senior managers. *Equality, Diversity and Inclusion,* **29**, 815–834.

Brockman, J. (2001). *Gender in the Legal Profession: fitting or breaking the mould.* Vancouver: UBC Press.

Carr-Saunders, A.M. and Wilson, P.A. (1933). *The Professions.* Oxford: Clarendon Press.

Collier, R. (2005). 'Be Smart, be successful, be yourself'?: representations of the training contract and trainee solicitors in advertising by large law firms. *International Journal of the Legal Profession,* **12**, 51–92.

Davis, K. (2008). Intersectionality as buzzword. *Feminist Theory,* **9**, 67–85.

Duff, A. and Ferguson, J. (2007). Disability and accounting firms: evidence from the UK. *Critical Perspectives on Accounting,* **18**, 139–157.

Duff, A. and Ferguson, J. (2011). Disability and the socialization of accounting professionals. *Critical Perspectives on Accounting,* **22**, 351–364.

Durbin, S. and Tomlinson, J. (2010). Female part-time managers: networks and career mobility. *Work, Employment and Society,* **24**, 621–640.

Durkheim, E. (1957). *Professional Ethics and Civic Morals.* London: Routledge.

Empson, L. (2001). Fear of exploitation and fear of contamination: impediments to knowledge transfer in mergers between professional service firms. *Human Relations,* **54**, 839–862.

Empson, L. (2007). Professional service firms and the professions. In: *International Encyclopaedia of Organization Studies,* Clegg, S. and Bailey, J. (Ed.), London: Sage.

Faulconbridge, J. and Muzio, D. (2008). Organisational professionalism in globalizing law firms. *Work, Employment and Society,* **22**, 7–25.

Francis, A. and Sommerlad, H. (2009). Access to legal work experience and its role in the (re)production of legal professional identity. *International Journal of the Legal Profession,* **16**, 63–86.

Gammie, E., Gammie, B., Matson, M., and Duncan, F. (2007). *Women of ICAS Reaching the Top: The demise of the glass ceiling*. Edinburgh: Institute of Chartered Accountants of Scotland.

Gorman, E.H. (2005). Gender stereotypes, same-gender preferences, and organizational variation in the hiring of women: evidence from law firms. *American Sociological Review*, **70**, 702–728.

Gorman, E.H. and Kmec, J.A. (2007). We (have to) try harder: gender and required work effort in Britain and the United States. *Gender & Society*, **21**, 828–856.

Gorman, E.H. and Kmec, J.A. (2009). Hierarchical rank and women's organizational mobility: Glass ceilings in corporate law firms. *American Journal of Sociology*, **114**, 1428–1474.

Greenwood, E. (1957). Attributes of a profession. *Social Work*, **2**, 44–55.

Grey, C. (1998). On being a professional in a Big 6 firm. *Accounting, Organizations and Society*, **23**, 569–587.

Hagan, J. and Kay, F. (1995). *Gender in Practice: a study of lawyers' lives*. Oxford: Oxford University Press.

Hammond, T. (2002). *A White-collar Profession: African American certified public accountants since 1921*. Chapel Hill, NC: University of North Carolina Press.

Hammond, T. and Streeter, D. (1994). Overcoming barriers: early African-American certified public accountants. *Accounting, Organizations and Society*, **19**, 271–288.

Haynes, K. (2008). (Re)figuring accounting and maternal bodies: the gendered embodiment of accounting professionals. *Accounting, Organizations and Society*, **33**, 328–348.

Haynes, K. (2012). Body beautiful?: gender, identity and the body in professional services firms. *Gender, Work & Organization*, **19**, 489–507.

HM Treasury (2009). *Professional Services Global Competitiveness Group Report*. London: HM Treasury.

Johnson, E.N., Lowe, D.J., and Reckers, P. (2008). Alternative work arrangements and perceived career success: current evidence from the Big 4 firms in the US. *Accounting, Organizations and Society*, **33**, 48–72.

Johnson, T. (1972). *Professions and Power*. London: Macmillan.

Jonnergård, K., Stafsudd, A., and Elg, U. (2010). Performance evaluations as gender barriers in professional organizations: a study of auditing firms. *Gender, Work & Organization*, **17**, 721–747.

Kay, F. and Gorman, E.H. (2008). Women in the legal profession. *Annual Review of Law and Social Science*, **4**, 299–332.

Kim, S.N. (2004). Racialized gendering of the accountancy profession: toward an understanding of Chinese women's experiences in accountancy in New Zealand. *Critical Perspectives on Accounting*, **15**, 400–427.

Kirkham, L. (1992). Integrating herstory and history in accountancy. *Accounting, Organizations and Society*, **17**, 287–297.

Kirkham, L. and Loft, A. (1993). Gender and the construction of the professional accountant. *Accounting, Organizations and Society*, **18**, 507–558.

Kornberger, M., Carter, C., and Ross-Smith, A. (2010). Changing gender domination in a Big Four accounting firm: flexibility, performance and client service in practice. *Accounting, Organizations and Society*, **35**, 775–791.

Kumra, S. and Vinnicombe, S. (2008). A study of the promotion to partner process in a professional services firm: how women are disadvantaged. *British Journal of Management,* **S1**, S65–S74.

Kumra, S. and Vinnicombe, S. (2010). Impressing for success: a gendered analysis of a key social capital accumulation strategy. *Gender, Work & Organization,* **17**, 521–546.

Larson, M. (1977). *The Rise of Professionalism: A sociological analysis.* Berkeley, CA: University of California Press.

Law Society (2010). *Trends in the solicitors' profession: Annual statistical report 2009.* London: The Law Society of England and Wales.

Lehman, C. (1992). Herstory in accounting: the first eighty years. *Accounting, Organizations and Society,* **17**, 261–285.

MacDonald, K. (1995). *The Sociology of the Professions.* London: Sage.

McNicholas, P., Humphries, M., and Gallhofer, S. (2004). Maintaining the Empire: Maori women's experiences in the accounting profession. *Critical Perspectives on Accounting,* **15**, 57–93.

Malos, S.B. and Campion, M.A. (1995). An options based model of career mobility in professional services firms. *Academy of Management Review,* **20**, 611–644.

Nicolson, D. (2005). Demography, discrimination and diversity: a new dawn for the British Legal Profession? *International Journal of the Legal Profession,* **12**, 201–228.

von Nordenfycht, A. (2010). What is a professional service firm? Toward a theory and taxonomy of knowledge-intensive firms. *Academy of Management Review,* **35**, 155–174.

O'Regan, P. (2008). 'Elevating the profession': the Institute of Chartered Accountants in Ireland and the implementation of social closure strategies 1888–1909. *Accounting, Business & Financial History,* **18**, 35–59.

Panel of Fair Access to the Professions. (2009). *Unleashing Aspiration: summary and recommendations of the full report.* London: Cabinet Office.

Professional Oversight Board for Accountancy. (2008). *Key Facts and Trends in the Accounting Profession.* 6th edn. London: Financial Reporting Council.

Professional Oversight Board for Accountancy. (2010). *Key Facts and Trends in the Accounting Profession.* London: Financial Reporting Council.

Rolfe, H. and Anderson, T. (2003). A firm choice: law firm's preferences in the recruitment of trainee solicitors. *International Journal of the Legal Profession,* **10**, 315–334.

Schultz, U. (2003). Introduction: Women in the world's legal professions: overview and synthesis. In: *Women in the World's Legal Professions,* Schultz, U. and Shaw, G. (Ed.), pp. xxv–lxi. Oxford: Hart Publishing.

Shilling, C. (1993). *The Body and Social Theory.* London: Sage.

Sikka, P., Willmott, H., and Lowe, E. (1989). Guardians of knowledge and the public interest: evidence and issues of accountability in the UK accountancy profession. *Accounting, Auditing and Accountability Journal,* **2**(2), 47–71.

Sommerlad, H. (1998). The gendering of the professional subject. In: *Legal Feminisms,* McGlynn, C. (Ed.), pp. 3–20. Aldershot: Ashgate.

Sommerlad, H. (2003). Can women lawyer differently? A perspective from the UK. In: *Women in the World's Legal Professions,* Schultz, U. and Shaw, G. (Ed.), pp. 191–224. Oxford: Hart Publishing.

Sommerlad, H. (2004). Shaping the size and composition of the Profession. *International Journal of the Legal Profession, 11*, 67–79.

Sommerlad, H. (2007). Researching and theorising the processes of professional identity formation. *Journal of Law and Society, 34*, 190–217.

Sommerlad, H. (2008). 'What are you doing here? You should be working in a hair salon or something': outsider status and professional socialization in the solictors' profession. *Web Journal of Current Legal Issues*, 2 [http://webjcli.ncl.ac.uk/2008/issue2/sommerlad2.html].

Sommerlad, H. and Sanderson, P. (1998). *Gender, Choice and Commitment: Women solicitors in England and Wales and the struggle for equal status*. Aldershot: Ashgate.

Stumpf, S.A. (2002). Becoming a partner in a professional services firm. *Career Development International, 7*, 115–121.

Tawney, R.H. (1921). *The Acquisitive Society*. London: G. Bell.

Thornton, M. (1998). Technocentrism in the law school: why the gender and colour of law remain the same. *Osgoode Law Journal, 36*, 369–398.

Thornton, M. (2007). 'Otherness' on the bench: how merit is gendered. *Sydney Law Review, 29*, 391–413.

Thornton, M. and Bagust, J. (2007). The gender trap: flexible work in corporate legal practice. *Osgoode Hall Law Journal, 45*, 773–811.

Tonge, J.L. (2008). Barriers to networking for women in a UK professional service. *Gender in Management, 23*, 484–505.

Walker, S.P. (2011). Professions and patriarchy revisited: accountancy in England and Wales, 1887–1914. *Accounting History Review, 21*, 185–225.

Weber, M. (1978). *Economy and Society*. Berkely, CA: University of California Press.

Willmott, H. (1986). Organising the profession: a theoretical and historical examination of the development of the major accountancy bodies in the UK. *Accounting, Organizations and Society, 11*, 555–580.

6

Management Innovation in the UK Consulting Industry

Joe O'Mahoney

Introduction

Management innovation concerns the creation and development of new management techniques, tools, and products (Hamel 2006; Lei-Yu 2010). Mol and Birkinshaw argue that management innovation is one of the most important and sustainable sources of competitive advantage for firms because of its context-specific nature among other reasons (Mol and Birkinshaw 2009). Despite the importance of management innovations for organizations, very little is known about the forces that enable and constrain the *production* rather than diffusion of management innovation. Much of what we do know about the former tends to be focused on micro-level issues such as strategic decision-making (Hansen *et al.* 1999), managerial agency (Birkinshaw *et al.* 2008; Hamel 2008), entrepreneurs, and change-agents (Clark 2004), or the internal dynamics by which innovations are developed (Greenwood and Suddaby 2001; Heusinkveld and Benders 2005).

While this micro-level lens sheds light upon important activites associated with the development of management innovations, the approach often ignores or downplays the role of the socio-economic context in changing how innovation happens, thus ignoring a dynamic perspective on innovation that might explain how changes occur. This leaves a gap in our understanding concerning questions regarding the firm, industry, and market contexts in which management innovation is likely to happen. For this reason, this chapter seeks to depict how the shifting meso- and macro-level processes generate changes in innovative activity within the UK consulting industry. Specifically, drawing on a four-year qualitative and quantitative study, the chapter seeks to understand *how and why management innovation is changing in the UK consulting industry.* The study focuses on the consulting industry because of its prominent position as a generator of management innovation (O'Mahoney 2010; Heusinkveld *et al.* 2009). The analysis develops a dynamic model of innovation, proposing a series of inter-related and emergent generative processes that constrain and enable innovative activity, and a specification of the underlying assumptions of the model, which might be developed and tested in future research. In doing so, the chapter sheds light on the important socio-economic and structural processes that constrain and enable management innovation in consulting firms. At a theoretical level, the contribution involves developing a model of how macro-level forces change innovative activity within organizations.

To achieve this, the chapter first distinguishes management innovation as a verb from innovation as a noun, arguing that most research has focused on the latter. When considering the former, the chapter argues that many studies focus on the micro-level of analysis and often ignore the socio-economic and institutional trends that underpin shifts in innovative activity. Next, the chapter outlines the methodology, detailing how a critical, realist ontology can support a dynamic perspective that links micro-level agency with structures at a meso- and macro-level of analysis. The research methods illustrate how qualitative and quantitative research of primary and secondary sources was deployed over a four-year period. The subsequent findings suggest that innovation in the consulting industry is changing due to a number of underlying dynamics, and these are then developed into a model in the analysis, which highlights the contingent and complex nature of management innovation over time, stressing how macro- and meso-level processes influence the changing nature of innovation in the consulting industry.

Innovation: Verb and Noun

In the field of management innovations, including those of management fashions, studies use macro, meso, and micro lenses to understand how management tools and practices are selected and diffused. Macro-level analyses emphasize the way in which factors such as economic trends (Barley and Kunda 1992), institutional logics (Abrahamson 1996), social networks (Coleman *et al.* 1966), or national politics (Cole 1985) influence the diffusion and adoption of management innovations. Meso-level studies investigate the influence of organizational culture (McCabe 2002), structure (Gosselin 1997) or ownership (Lapsley and Wright 2004). Micro-level studies examine differing aspects of agential influence on the selection of, resistance to, or translation of management practices by examining the rational choices of managers (Rogers 1983), their identities (Knights and McCabe 2000), or the agency of 'champions' (Stjernberg and Philips 1993). These studies generally represent 'innovation' as a noun—an entity that is selected, diffused, and translated *after* its invention.

If we wish to consider 'innovation' as a verb, we must study the creation of new management practices or tools, what Birkinshaw *et al.* (2008: 7) call the 'invention' stage: 'an initial act of experimentation out of which a new hypothetical management practice emerges'. The consideration of management innovation as a verb has received considerably less attention than the noun variety. Perhaps for this reason, the analyses deployed have been considerably more limited, with attention focused more on the micro/agential levels of analysis than those considering the post-invention stage. In Hammel's (2007) *The Future of Management*, for example, his exhortations are primarily aimed at individuals ('. . . OK, you're inspired! You have some great ideas for management innovation. . . .'), and do not consider the socio-economic contexts that might encourage or inhibit the generation of innovative management activity. Similarly, Birkinshaw *et al.* (2008) follow a similar trajectory, detailing the different types of agency (internal and external) that influence both the motivation to search for new managerial solutions and the actual invention phase itself. In another well-known article, Hansen *et al.* (1999) argue that aspects of knowledge in consulting firms can be managed strategically with virtually no reference to environmental factors. Those that *do* consider the external context generally do so in terms of the innovating firm's exposure to new knowledge (for example, Mol and Birkinshaw 2009) rather than its socio-economic environment.

Others, coming from alternative perspectives, also prioritize the individual or firm level of analysis over macro considerations. The sociology of knowledge perspective, for example, championed by Huesinkveld and Benders (2002, 2005), demonstrates how new management concepts are developed within a firm and contested by different individuals and groups in an attempt to colonize and legitimize distinctive knowledge claims. Other academics examine the role of management gurus (Huczynski 1993; ten Bos and Heusinkveld 2007) and other 'knowledge entrepreneurs' (Clark 2004) in developing and disseminating new management ideas. Others still, take a rhetorical view of management fashions, emphasizing the role of insecurity, talk, and performance in encouraging both the creation and adoption of new management ideas (Jackson 1986; Gill and Whittle 1993; Fincham 1995; Keiser 1997). Yet, all of these perspectives tend to emphasize individual agency within the organization or, at best, the agency by which external ideas are bought inside the organization (Birkinshaw *et al* 2008; Heusinkveld *et al* 2009). The theoretical concepts such papers use, such as 'knowledge entrepreneurs', 'idea linking', 'rational decision-making', and 'performances' emphasize the agency of managers and consultants rather than the socio-economic contexts in which they act.

The gap in the literature identified in this chapter is, therefore, that studies of management innovation (as a verb) prioritize micro-levels of analysis rather than the macro- and meso-levels. Such a position fails to grasp the embeddedness of agency within a changing structural environment, treating individuals or organizations, as free-floating entities devoid of a historical trajectory or socio-economic dynamics. This gap is important because without such embeddedness, changing levels of innovation can only be effected by different strategies deployed by decision-makers within consultancies or clients rather than traced to the changing political, economic, and legal contexts within which these activities occur.

The Context: Management Consultancy

Despite its relative youth compared to other professional services such as law or accountancy, consultancy has been one of the most successful of the knowledge industries, with revenues expanding over 10,000% in the last thirty years alone (O'Mahoney 2010). Yet, its interest for innovation studies is not due simply to its success but also because, at its most basic, management consultancy sustains itself through the generation, development, and dissemination of management innovations for client organizations (Engwall and Kipping 2002; Clegg *et al.* 2004).

Innovation in consultancies is a relatively cheap exercise. Unlike technological innovation, there are no raw materials, long development processes, or complex testing procedures. For this reason, while consulting services have one of the lowest R&D spends as a percentage of turnover at 0.7% (NESTA 2009a) they generate one of the highest reported levels of innovation among UK sectors (NESTA 2009b). That consultancies will witness management issues many times, which an individual client will experience perhaps only once, enables them to develop and hone solutions and expertise in the same way that other companies create and test services or technologies. These efforts have meant that many of the most prolific management innovations such as total quality management or business process re-engineering have been created through partnerships with consultancies (Wood 2001).

Yet, despite the growing importance and influence of the consulting industry as a site of service innovation, we still know relatively little about the dynamics, constraints, and enablers of the phenomena. As a result, debates regarding innovation are, for example, frequently stymied by polarized assumptions regarding consulting innovation. On the one hand, some academics simply assume that consultancies are, at their most basic, 'innovation factories' (Hargadon and Sutton 2000: 161) developing effective new solutions that have a positive impact upon clients and the wider global economy (Anand *et al.* 2007; Birkinshaw and Mol 2008). On the other hand, some writers represent consulting innovations and interventions as 'old wine in new bottles' (Sahlin-Andersson and Engwall 2002: 278), depicting the consultants that sell them as witch-doctors or charlatans (Clark 1998; Argyris 2000; Whittle 2005). As a consequence, consulting innovation often tends to be represented rather simplistically on a bipolar scale, with consultancies either being 'innovative' or 'not innovative', a characterization which belies the myriad of ways in which knowledge and service companies can generate innovations (Nabil *et al.* 2009).

In recent years, several commentators have implied that consultancies are moving from the more creative end of this scale to the other. In academia, several studies have suggested that consultants now perform relatively standardized roles (Sturdy *et al.* 2008), maintaining stability rather than pushing for change (Furusten 2009). From an industry perspective, surveys have noted client's dissatisfaction with the creativity consultants bring to projects (Czerniawska 2006) while *The Economist* (2008) blamed the narrowing margins of the industry on their lack of a 'big idea'. Certainly, as we see later, there are reasons to think that innovation might be under pressure. However, many of the studies that indicate this were either based on single case studies or were not in-depth studies of innovation *per se.* Indeed, there have been virtually no studies that have sought a detailed, qualitative, and quantitative understanding of management innovation in consultancies, especially in relation to socio-economic trends.

Method

A Critical Realist Research Perspective

The research seeks to answer the question *how, and why, is management innovation changing in the UK consulting industry?* The research assumes a critical realist ontology (Bhaskar 1975; Archer *et al.* 1998; Ackroyd and Fleetwood 2004) that commits to:

> emergence: that 'higher' strata, such as society or a brain, emerge from and are dependent upon 'lower' strata, such as people or atoms. This commitment enables

> structure and agency distinction: while related, structure and agency should not be conflated as they are in many post-modernist or structuration theories

stratified ontology: which distinguishes what is 'real' (the underlying processes and structures in the world) from the 'actual' (the events that occur in space and time, which are generated by those processes), which are distinct from the 'empirical' (what we perceive reality to be)

generative processes: the social as well as the physical world is changed through causal tendencies, which operate at different levels of reality.

Contrary to studies that accept only a discursive or an empirical realm of reality, this layered ontology accepts the mutual dependence but separation of agency and structure. Critical realism is well suited, therefore, to explaining the embeddedness of strategic action within social and other structures, as well as the identification of causal processes in generating empirical events. This chapter therefore stresses that the agency of any consultant, or strategy of any organization, forms part of a complex interplay of causal processes that underpin, enable, and constrain social and organizational life. In the analysis, some of these underlying processes and their influences are outlined with respect to the structural embeddedness of innovative activity.

Research Design

The research design sought first to understand how management innovation was changing over time and then to develop a tentative explanation of the reasons for these changes (Figure 6.1). It achieved this through an inductive theory-building process in which the focus of the research became more refined over time first using qualitative data and then using quantitative. The quantitative data were not meant to test hypotheses to generate levels of significance, but in line with inductive mixed-methods research (Teddlie and Tashakkori 2009), to provide greater clarity on the themes and concepts that had been used to explore the research question.[1]

Preliminary interviews were undertaken with fifty-five industry leaders from a wide range of consultancies, professional organizations, and industry analysts, as part of a project to understand the strategic challenges

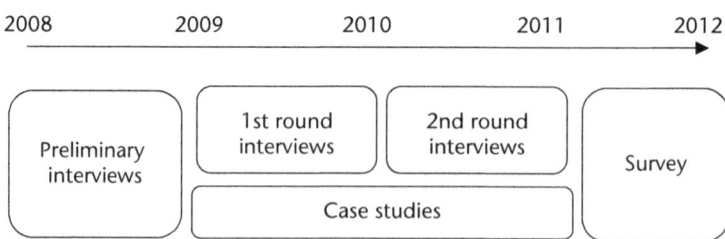

Figure 6.1 Research design (2008–2012)

of the consulting industry in the UK. These sixty-minute, transcribed, semi-structured interviews, focused on eliciting the difficulties UK firms were facing in 2008. One of the challenges that emerged, which many participants thought was worthy of further consideration, was the challenge of managing innovation (O'Mahoney *et al.* 2008). This prompted a second project in 2009, which focused more specifically on this challenge. Initially, thirty-five semi-structured, transcribed interviews were undertaken with a range of management consultants, clients, and procurers (see Table 6.1), which focused on what enabled and constrained innovation within consultancy practice, examples of innovative activity and any trends or patterns they could discern over the last five years. Procurers and client managers were chosen because earlier interviews suggested these roles potentially had a significant impact on consultancy practice. The procurers and client managers were from the same companies. No small-sized users of consultants were approached as these can rarely afford teams of consultants.

Almost a year later, after initial themes had begun to emerge, a second round of interviews was conducted with the same interviewees to provide more detail on specific topics that had emerged from previous interviews. These themes included the role of procurement, manifestation of competition in the sector, and life cycle of innovations. These more structured interviews lasted an average of forty-one minutes, which were also transcribed.

In addition, the author undertook two participant–observation case studies of management innovation, which involved working with two consultancies to develop new consulting services, marketing them, and deploying them with clients (Table 6.2). The first company (Alpha) was a consultancy with fifteen full-time consultants and about thirty associates that could be called on for large projects. The service was a survey-based tool that allowed companies to benchmark their innovative practice. The author worked with this company

Table 6.1 Interviews by company size and interviewee seniority

	Company size (FTE)	Consultants	Procurers	Client managers
1st stage	1000+	3 Partners 5 Consultants	1 Manager 2 Procurers	1 Manager 2 Employees
	20–1000	3 Partners 5 Consultants	1 Manager 2 Procurers	1 Managers 1 Employees
	0–20	3 Partners 5 Consultants	None	None
2nd stage	1000+	3 Partners 5 Consultants	1 Manager 2 Procurers	1 Manager 2 Employees
	20–1000	3 Partners 5 Consultants	1 Manager 2 Procurers	1 Managers 1 Employees
	0–20	3 Partners 5 Consultants	None	None

to develop the benchmarking tool and test it with some 'guinea-pig' clients. The second company (Beta), employing two people, developed a workshop based around psychometric testing to develop the creativity of senior managers. The author worked with the consultancy to develop, use, and improve the product in eight client engagements. In total, the participant observation amounted to thirty days of 'face time', spread over about twelve months, generating seventy-five pages of single-spaced transcribed notes.

The qualitative research generated a number of statements about what was happening to innovation and a number of statements about why this might be the case (see Table 6.2). It was felt that greater clarity could be developed about the importance and definition of these statements by distributing a survey to a range of management consultants. To this end, a survey that asked both open and closed questions was developed, which asked questions about:

the definition of management innovation

types of management innovation

the reasons for and causes of innovation

the life cycle of management innovations

the enablers and constraints of innovation

the role of procurement in influencing innovation

The questionnaire was distributed to consultancies listed in two databases, the Institute of Consulting (3315 consultancies) and the Advanced Institute of Management (312 consultancies). The response rate was 11% ($n = 399$). The author was also provided with access to the findings from the Community Innovation Surveys (CIS). These surveys, conducted by the UK Government every two years, examine innovation in all industries. The data from this survey had not previously been analysed at the level of consultancy and doing so provides a useful longitudinal analysis to supplement the static survey introduced above. The results for this survey were analysed at the level of 'Business and Management Consultancies' ($n = 133$) over three collection phases: 2005, 2007, and 2009.

The analysis of the data adopted a grounded theory approach in which theory development emerges from constant comparison between data and emerging concepts (Turner 1981; Strauss and Corbin 1994; Suddaby 2006). During a constant process of analysis, the emergence of themes fed into subsequent interviews and participant observation. Open coding was undertaken in which the transcripts and notes were examined with a focus on how innovation was changing and why this was the case. In critical realist terms, the former was elicited using the coding based primarily around interviews (for example, whether innovation was increasing or not) and the latter was generated by both seeking causal processes in the cases (for example, how procurement might affect innovation) and what interviewees thought might be the case. This process helped identify and conceptually separate the epi-phenomena of empirical events and the causes of these events. These are described in the analysis.

Results

Given the amount of data generated by participant observation, surveys, and interviews, it is necessary to focus this section specifically on the question *'what is happening to management innovation in the UK consulting industry and why?'* The results are organized into a set of inter-related themes, which together suggest that management innovation in the UK consulting industry is increasing but also changing. The data suggest that although a number of socio-economic trends such as the rise of procurement, decrease in consultancy profit margins, and increase in utilization levels tend towards lower levels of innovation, the increased competition in the sector has generated greater levels of innovation. The results also indicate that, to minimize costs and create customer 'stickiness' innovation is increasingly being done in conjunction with clients, which leads to more 'local' innovations with shared intellectual property rights rather than big name services such as total quality management or business process re-engineering.

Tendencies that Constrain Innovation

Most interviewees reported that profit margins in consultancies had declined significantly over the last ten years. This was linked to a number of factors, perhaps best summarized by a partner at a medium-sized consultancy:

> pressure on prices has come from a number of sources. Clients are more sophis-ticated...they shop around using procurement who then batter us down on prices... there are more consultancies in the market meaning we drive our own prices down in order to compete....

Furthermore, the recession, and perhaps the increasing size of projects has led to a reassessment of risk on behalf of clients. As a partner at a large IT consultancy firm suggested:

> it's not just spending it's also risk. [*In the current environment*] clients want tried and tested solutions... [*Also*] as IT and Outsourcing projects have grown into the tens of billions, it focuses [*Clients'*] minds on something that will work rather than something that is experimental.

These views were reiterated by other consultants, clients, and procurers who suggested that it was not simply the recession that had affected client spending patterns, but a longer-term trend towards the minimization of risk through the introduction of procurement:

> procurement are primarily rewarded by...getting costs down. To achieve this you cut out the bells and whistles...what you call innovation [*consultant, small firm*] [*procurement*] bureaucracy is the biggest barrier to our working with consultants in new ways. They sit in-between the business owner and the consultancy and you're not allowed to talk to each-other until they arrive on site. Crazy. (Client Manager, University)

In the case studies, the author was struck by the difference that the procurement process made to the dynamic between client and consultant as this note shows:

> we were told that 60% of the success criteria for the proposal would be cost which meant that we needed to remove all the internet applications and go for a paper form...moreover, the tendering process was so tightly specified that there was no space for a discussion about ideas with the client. (Alpha, 10.03.10)

In the survey, this message was repeated, with 83% of consultants believing that procurement 'hampers the sale of innovative services' and only 35% reporting that it was a 'cost effective way of tendering for projects'.

This story of increasingly cost-aware clients using procurement to negotiate down prices from an ever-expanding pool of consultants was a common one in all sizes and specialisms of consultancy and had several reported consequences. First, consultancies responded to diminishing margins by pushing up consultant utilization rates. As one consultant suggested:

> it is simply unsustainable...ten years ago, my utilisation was 65%. It's now 95...I don't have time for training, thinking or anything apart from billable hours.

This was especially true of large PLCs, where the need to generate immediate returns put pressure on senior management to maximize revenues without increasing the headcount. In the survey, the top three constraints listed by PLCs and companies with more than 1000 employees were; (1) lack of time; (2) utilization rates; and (3) cost of innovation. The impact of cost constraints was equally reflected in the CIS data (Table 6.2) where the biggest increases and the biggest absolute factors in constraining innovation were all financial. However, within small and private partnerships, financial constraints were less of an issue. A partner at a private strategy firm suggested:

> our rates are high so our utilisation doesn't have to be, We work at about 65% and spend the rest of the time innovation, going to conferences and learning.

Table 6.2 The percentage increase in responses to 'what constrained your innovation?' 2005–2009

	2005	2007	2009	% Increase
Cost of finance	35	32	47	33
Availability of finance	35	31	45	28
Need to meet UK Government regulations	22	23	27	24
Lack of qualified personnel	35	38	43	21
Lack of info on technology	28	28	34	20
Excessive perceived economic risks	44	35	52	18

Source: CIS Data 2005, 2007, 2009

For smaller companies, especially private ones, it was the client, rather than internal finances that were constraining innovation, with the top three constraints listed as: (1) clients not taking risks; (2) client finances; and (3) lack of time. Here, it is evident that the state of the economy in the period 2008–2011 has played an important part in cutting client spending on consultancy services, especially in the public sector.

Second, reductions in profits reportedly led to a difficulty in paying, and therefore recruiting, highly-skilled individuals, especially in middle and senior positions, which two interviewees argued damaged the firms' ability to innovate. The inability to pay high salaries was frequently made in comparison to investment banks that were rightly perceived as having increased salaries significantly for similar recruits over the last twenty years.

Finally, four interviewees suggested that leverage ratios (the number of consultants for every partner) had increased in many firms, especially PLCs, which led to a more commodified 'cookie-cutter' approach to services, rather than a personal approach tailored to each client. This trend was said to have been exacerbated by a shift in the market away from strategy consulting, characterized by low leverage ratios and utilization rates towards the middle market (programme and management), which tends to be more standardized. The assumption being that the latter form of work mitigates against innovation.

Tendencies that Enable Innovation

Despite the constraints on consultancy innovation, it became clear in interviews and surveys that consultants perceived innovation to be increasing in the industry and suggested the main reason for this was increased competition in the field. One owner of a medium-sized consultancy stated:

> there are just simply more consultancies than there were ten, or even five years ago ... [*which means*] we need to innovate to stand out from the crowd.

Table 6.3 The percentage of different sized companies answering 'Over the last five years do you believe innovation in your consultancy has....'

FTE	Increased	Stayed the same	Decreased
1–20	68	9	21
21–1000	72	18	10
1000+	62	27	5

In the primary survey (Table 6.3) respondents across the board suggested that innovation had increased over the last five years. In addition, 65% of respondents believed that innovation would continue to increase in the future, compared to only 5% who thought it would decrease. When asked to give a reason for this, most respondents suggested that they expected the consulting space to continue to get more competitive.

In the CIS survey (Figure 6.2) the number of consultancies reporting the introduction of new or improved services jumped from 33% in 2005 to 45% in 2009. When asked why there had been this increase, 64% of respondents put 'Differentiation from the competition' as very important, ahead of 'Demonstrating knowledge/excellence' (59%) and gaining new clients (48%).

Squaring the Circle

The results above highlight two contradictory trends. On the one hand, consultancies report, in both surveys and interviews, that management innovation in their organizations is on the increase. On the other hand, they report

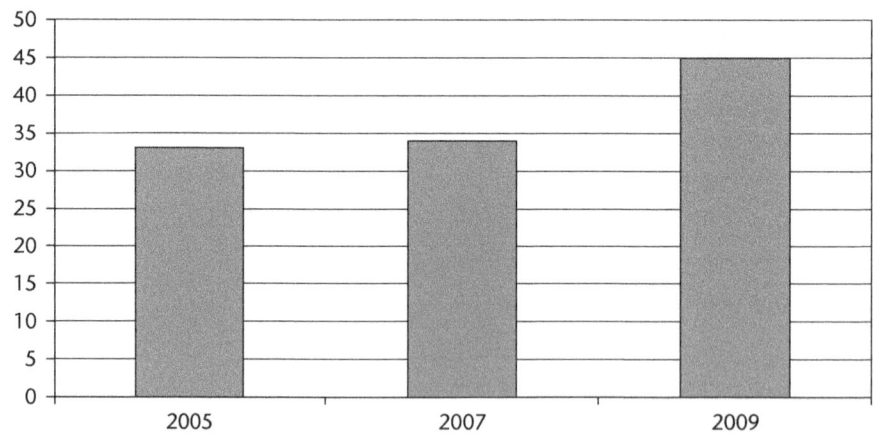

Figure 6.2 The percentage of respondents answering 'yes' to 'did you introduce new or significantly improved services?'

Source: CIS Data 2005, 2007, 2009.

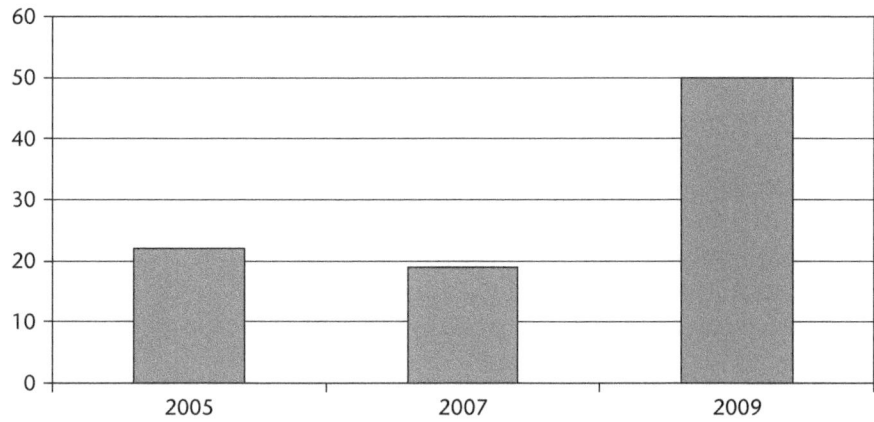

Figure 6.3 The percentage of consultancies reporting co-operation with external organizations in the development of innovation

Source: CIS Data 2005, 2007, 2009.

that there is less time, money, and resources available for such innovation. The solution to this paradox can be found in the increasing tendency of consultancies to work with partners in developing innovative services. In Figure 6.3, we can see a significant increase in the number of co-innovation projects after the 2008 recession had begun.

In Table 6.4, we can see that the most common form of these partnerships, and that which has experienced the greatest increase, is working with clients. Furthermore, when asked about what things make them more innovative, two of the top three enablers of innovation were client focused: 'brainstorming with clients' and 'service testing with clients'.

Again, the interview data here provides depth to the figures. Several interviewees explained not only that external partnerships were a useful way of sourcing new ideas, but also a way of sharing the costs of innovation and building loyalty with clients. Examples of this 'shared innovation' were incredibly

Table 6.4 The percentage of respondents reporting different partners in the innovation process

Stakeholder	2005	2007	2009	% Increase
Clients	16	14	40	154
Suppliers	16	12	26	64
Competitors	12	7	18	50
Consultants	10	9	15	42
Universities	9	6	10	13
Government	13	5	12	−13

Source: CIS Data 2005, 2007, 2009

varied, ranging from large co-funded 'innovation centres' co-staffed with clients and consultants sharing expertise and intellectual property rights to micro-level interactions where sole-owner consultants would develop proprietary programmes specifically for one client. While these types of interactions are not new to consultancy, most interviewees suggested that they were an increasingly prominent feature of the innovation landscape.

From interviews, there were two noticeable consequences of greater levels of co-innovation reported. First, both clients and consultants suggested that co-innovation produced more tailored and less generic projects. This outcome was also mentioned in reference to clients simply refusing to accept the 'big name' innovations of previous years:

> when you're working together you get something specific to your needs [*Client manager*]
>
> [*clients are*] too experienced these days to just buy something because of it's name.... [*they*] want something practical that they are involved with. [*Co-innovation*] allows them to get their hands dirty...develop transferable skills.... Know what we're up to [*Managing Consultant*].

Thus, co-innovation does offer both consultants and clients advantages. However, several consultants also mentioned that this method of working also raised difficulties for exploiting intellectual property:

> these tailored, shared projects do occasionally raise issues about intellectual property...we can't then take the solution and sell it to their competitor...[*also*] something that specific takes considerable effort to turn into a generic service.

The findings then, indicate that, while there are strong forces that mitigate against innovation, the increasing competition in the sector has forced firms to innovate to differentiate themselves from each other and attract new clients. However, the consequences of declining profit margins have meant that consultancies now look to share innovation costs with their clients, something that clients are keen to reciprocate with.

Analysis

In the analysis, this chapter seeks to identify and clarify the generative processes changing management innovation in the UK consulting industry. In critical realist terms, these processes illustrate a trend, such as declining profit margins, and link it to a consequence related to the production of management innovation, such as the lack of available time for R&D. Each mechanism has an enabler associated with it, the activity or condition that links the underlying trend with the consequence. It will be noticed from Table 6.5 that

Table 6.5 Underlying processes and epiphenomena of management innovation

Causal process	Consequence	Enabler	Impact on innovation	Corroborating literature
Increased supply of consultancies combined with client spending cuts.	Competition drives prices down, thus reducing profit margins.	Market mechanism.	Less money available for innovation.	Kennedy Information (2011); Office of National Statistics (2011)
	Greater competition prompts differentiation strategies.	Strategic decision-making to attract clients.	Greater effort to innovate.	NA
Shift away from strategy consultancy to operations consultancy.	More competition generated in operations market driving down daily rates.	Market mechanism.	Less money available for innovation.	MCA (2011) FEACO (2011)
	Lower daily rates.	Lower rates are paid for operations consultancy than strategy work.	Less money available for innovation.	MCA (2011)
Increased use of procurement by clients.	Innovation is left out of project proposals to minimize costs.	Procurement rewarded for cost-cutting.	Less demand for innovation by clients.	O'Mahoney (2011)
	Tendering process decreases consultancy day rates.	Market mechanism.	Less money available for innovation.	Czerniawska and Smith (2010)
	Lack of communication between business owner and consultant.	Legal requirement in the public sector.	Consultant has less understanding of business problem.	Furusten and Werr (2005).
Accumulation of client experience with consultancies.	Client requires tailored, bespoke solutions rather than one-size-fits-all services.	Growth in client expertise.	More local, less generic innovative solutions.	NA
Increasing leverage ratios.	High leverage ratios create a more commodified and standardized form of work.	Strategic decision-making to maximize profits, especially in PLCs.	Perceived to lead to lower levels of innovation.	Adams and Zanzi (2005)
Declining profit margins.	Difficulty in funding salaries that attract talent.	Executive decision to prevent wage inflation to protect profit margins.	Lack of talent to resource innovation projects.	Kennedy Information (2011), Wetfeet (2011), Vault (2011), BLT (2009), Office of National Statistics (2009)
	Increase in utilization levels leaving less time for R&D and training.	Executive decision to maximize billable hours to protect profit margins.	Less time for innovative activity.	Brett Howell (2009); AMCF (2009); Sako (2006).
	Seeking co-innovation partnerships.	The need to increase innovation combined with lower margins.	Greater innovative activity, but sharing of intellectual property.	NA

many of the central forces affecting innovation are inter-related and thus difficult to separate out. Within this complexity, it is possible to tease out some tentative processes that underpin changes in innovation in firms. An effort has been made, where possible, to seek corroborating literature:

- The increased number of consultancies in the market, which has the effect of increasing competition, which in turn both drives down prices and prompts consultancies to seek greater differentiation from the competition through innovation. The growth in both the absolute numbers of consultancies, the number of consultants and the revenue of the industry is attested to by a number of publications both globally (Kennedy Information 2011) and in the UK (MCA 2011; Office of National Statistics 2011).

- The shift in the market away from strategy and towards operational work is a trend mentioned by interviewees, and evidenced by the MCA reports over the last five years. According to both sources, the shift is due to clients doing much strategy work themselves and has had the consequence of increasing competition in the operations consulting market.

- The increased use of procurement by clients in recruiting consultants was mentioned by many interviewees and has been noted by a number of industry commentators and reports (NAO 2006; Czerniawska and Smith 2010). The impact of procurement on consulting innovation was argued by interviewees to have a dampening effect on day rates by performing a reverse auction for projects, which in turn prompts consultancies to aim at cost reduction over innovation. Others also argued that the position of procurement between consultants and client managers hampers communication, which in turn hits innovation. These findings are corroborated by the little academic work that has been undertaken on this topic (Furusten and Werr 2005; O'Mahoney 2011).

- The accumulation of management experience and learning is a well-established theme in academia (Zollo and Winter 2002); however, analysts have not turned their attention to the effects of the exponential increase in use of consultants by managers. Interviews suggest that this has had the effect of educating managers to tailor projects to their needs, negotiate fee rates down, and do many less complicated projects themselves.

- The growth in leverage ratios, especially in PLCs tends towards the more commodified form of work characterized by say Accenture, rather than McKinsey, and so, some interviewees suggested, lower levels of innovation. The relationship between commodified work and high leveraged PLCs has had some attention in the literature (Suddaby and Greenwood 2001; Maister 2003), as has the growing number of firms that have moved from private partnerships to PLCs. However, few if any studies have looked at the impact of this on innovation. Further work is needed here.

Many of these underlying processes have had the consequence of reducing profit margins in the industry. This is a well documented trend (AMCF 2009; Brett Howell 2009; MCA 2011) and it is evident from the interview that this squeeze has hit consultancies hard, affecting their ability to recruit talent and invest in innovation. It is this pressure on innovation that has caused consultancies to seek partnerships in innovation, primarily with their clients.

Together these underlying forces produced the contradiction that strategic decision-makers in consultancies have faced: the need to differentiate themselves in an increasingly crowded market combined with reduced finances available for innovation. The solution, as we have seen, has been to partner with companies, especially clients, in sharing the costs of developing new management solutions. It is this that forms the centrepiece to the changing dynamic in management innovation within the 2008–2011 recession, and the contribution of this chapter has been to show how this strategic shift is embedded in, though not determined by, the meso- and macro-level processes that we have examined above.

Conclusions

This analysis of the shifting forms of innovation within the UK consulting industry is important because it clearly embeds management innovation (as a verb) within its socio-economic context. In Figure 6.4, these dynamic processes are shown in relation to the supply and demand of innovation. Square boxes represent client dynamics and lozenge boxes represent consultancy dynamics. It is clear from this figure and Table 6.5 that innovation within a consultancy firm cannot simply be represented in terms of micro-level factors such as agency (Clark 2004), strategy (Hansen *et al.* 1999), external agency (Birkinshaw *et al.* 2008), or identity and insecurity (Gill and Whittle 1993; Fincham 1995). Yet, all of these perspectives tend to emphasize the individual or, at best, the group.

Instead, these micro-level issues are shown to be embedded within an analysis that links management innovation with the micro- (strategic decisions regarding investment in training, levels of pay, and utilization rates),

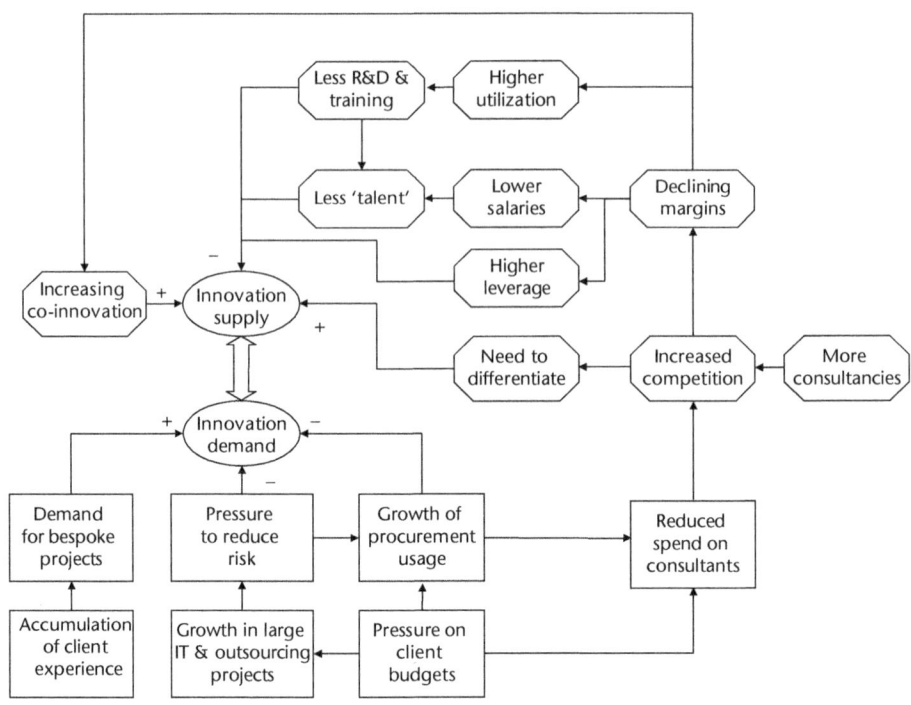

Figure 6.4 A dynamic model of management innovation

meso- (firm leverage structure, client learning cycles, and role of procurement), and macro-levels (market supply and demand, recessionary budget cuts, and firm ownership). This model has been promoted through a critical realist analysis, which actively encourages an understanding of organizations at different ontological levels, which embed agency within a socio-economic structure.

The chapter has several limitations, and in identifying these points to potential new directions in research for management innovation. First, this chapter cannot comprehensively pronounce on all the processes that it has identified. Table 6.5, for example, provides a useful guide to where more research is needed. The 'NA', which is written beside the suggestions that co-innovation partnerships and accumulation of client experience are argued to be important, indicates that academic research in these areas is lacking, something this chapter hardly makes up for. Second, statistical figures here have been used primarily to support the qualitative analysis and have not been used to test formal hypotheses. Future studies might want to test more thoroughly some of the propositions that are made here. Finally, it is clear that this study has been made in the context of a recession. This provides a useful test-bed to examine how the changes in the economy influence the dynamics of innovation. It would be interesting to examine how these dynamics change during a boom rather than a bust.

Acknowledgments

This study was supported by the Economic and Social Research Council grant number RES-RES-331-27-0071. The funder had no role in directing the study. The author would like to thank Prof. Rick Delbridge for his advice during this project, and Tim Edwards and Daniel Muzio for their comments on the chapter.

Notes

1. The mix of qualitative and quantitative data in inducing theory was embedded in its original exposition of grounded theory (Glaser and Strauss 1967). However, this approach fell out of fashion as deductive research claimed quantitative methods as its own. Fortunately, in recent years, mixed methods have undergone resurgence in theory building, first under the guise of triangulation and more recently as an explicit research strategy (Shah and Corley 2006).

References

Adams, S. and Zanzi, A. (2005). The consulting career in transition: from partnership to corporate. *Career Development International*, **10**(4), 325–338.

AMCF (2009). Operating ratios for management consultancy firms. www.amcf.org

Anand, N., Gardner, H., and Morris, T. (2007). Knowledge-based innovation: emergence and embedding of new practice areas in management consulting firms. *Academy of Management Journal*, **50**(02), 406–428.

Argyris, C. (2000). *Flawed Advice and the Management Trap*. New York: Oxford Press.

Barley, S.R. and Kunda, G. (1992). Design and devotion: the ebb and flow of rational and normative ideologies of control in managerial discourse. *Administrative Science Quarterly*, **37**, 1–30.

Bhaskar, R. (1975). *A Realist Theory of Science*. London: Version.

Birkinshaw, J., Hamel, G., and Mol, M. (2008). Management innovation. *Academy of Management Review*, **33**(4): 825–845.

Birkinshaw, J. and Mol, M. (2006). How management innovation happens. *MIT Sloan Management Review*, **47**(4), 81–88.

Birkinshaw, J. and Mol, M. (2009). The sources of management innovation: when firms introduce new management practices. *Journal of Business Research*, **62**(12), 1269–1280.

BLT (2009). Management Consultancy Salary Survey. www.blt.co.uk

Brett Howell Associates (2009). *Financial Benchmarks: management Consultants Survey.* Portsmouth, Hants: BHA.

CIS (2005, 2007, 2009). *The UK Community Innovation Survey.* London: Department for Business Innovation and Skills.

Clark, T. (1998). Telling tales: management guru's narratives and the construction of managerial identity. *Journal of Management Studies,* **35**(2), 137–161.

Clark, T. (2004). Strategy viewed from a management fashion perspective. *European Management Review,* **1**, 105–111.

Clegg, S., Kornberger, M., and Rhodes, C. (2004). Noise, parasites and translation: theory and practice in management consulting. *Management Learning,* **35**, 31–44.

Cole, R. (1985). The macropolitics of organizational change: a comparative analysis of the spread of small group activities. *Administrative Science Quarterly,* **30**, 560–585.

Coleman, J., Katz, E., and Menzel, H. (1966). *Medical Innovations.* New York: Bobbs-Merril.

Consulting Magazine (2011). Best Firms to Work For, 23 August.

Czerniawska, F. (2006). *Ensuring Sustainable Value from Consultants.* MCA/PWC Report. London: MCA.

Czerniawska, F. and Smith, P. (2010). *Buying Professional Services: how to get value for money from consultants and other professional service providers.* London: John Wiley & Sons.

Engwall, L. and Kipping, M. (2002). Introduction: management consulting as a knowledge industry. In: *Management Consulting: emergence and dynamics of a knowledge industry,* Kipping, M. and Engwall, L. (Ed.), pp. 1–16. Oxford: Oxford University Press.

Fincham, R. (1995). Business process reengineering and the commodification of management knowledge. *Journal of Marketing Management,* **11**(7), 707–719.

Furusten, S. (2009). Management consultants as improvising agents of stability. *Scandinavian Journal of Management,* **25**, 264–274.

Furusten, S. and Werr, A. (2005). *Dealing with Confidence.* Copenhagen: Copenhagen Business School Press.

Gill, J. and Whittle, S. (1993). Management by panacea. *Journal of Management Studies,* **30**, 281–295.

Glaser, B.G. and Strauss, A. (1967). *Discovery of Grounded Theory. strategies for qualitative research.* Mill Valley, CA: Sociology Press.

Gosselin, M. (1997). The effect of strategy and organizational structure on the adoption and implementation of activity based costing. *Accounting, Organizations and Society,* **22**(2), 105–122.

Hamel, G. (2007). *The Future of Management.* Boston, MA: Harvard Business School Press.

Hargadon, A. and Sutton, R. (1997). Technology brokering and innovation in a product development firm. *Administrative Science Quarterly,* **42**, 716–750.

Heusinkveld, S. and Benders, J. (2002). Between professional dedication and corporate design: exploring forms of new concept development in consultancies. *International Studies of Management and Organization,* **32**(4), 104–122.

Heusinkveld, S. and Benders, J. (2005). Contested commodification: consultancies and their struggle with new concept development. *Human Relations,* **58**(3), 283–310.

Heusinkveld, S., Benders, J., and Van Den Berg, R. (2009). From market sensing to new concept developments in consultancies: the role of information processing and organizational capabilities. *Technovation,* **29**, 509–516.

Huczynski, A. (1993). *Management Gurus: what makes them and how to become one.* London: Routledge.

Jackson, B. (1996). Re-engineering the sense of self: the manager and the management guru. *Journal of Management Studies,* **33**, 571–90.

Kennedy Information. (2009). *The Global Consulting Marketplace: key data.* Fitzwilliam, NH: Forecasts and Trends Kennedy Information Inc.

Kennedy Information. (2011). *The Global Consulting Marketplace: key data.* Fitzwilliam, NH: Forecasts and Trends Kennedy Information Inc.

Kieser, A. (1997). Rhetoric and myth in management fashion. *Organization,* **4**, 49–74.

Knights, D. and McCabe, D. (2000). 'Aint Misbehavin?' Opportunities for resistance under new forms of 'quality management'. *Sociology,* **34**(3), 421–436

Lapsley, I. and Wright, E. (2004). The diffusion of management accounting innovations in the public sector: a research agenda. *Management Accounting Research,* **15**(3), 355–374.

Lei-Yu, W. (2010). Which companies should implement management innovation? A commentary essay. *Journal of Business Research,* **63**(3), 321–323.

Maister, D. (2003). *Managing the Professional Service Firm.* London: Simon & Schuster.

National Audit Office (2006). Central governments use of consultants. *Volume 128 of HC, Session 2006–2007, House of Commons papers.* London: The Stationary Office.

NESTA (2009a). The Innovation Index: measuring the UKs investment in innovation and its effects. November.

NESTA (2009b). *Measuring Sectoral Innovation Capability in Nine Areas of the UK Economy.* November.

NESTA (2010). *Sourcing Knowledge for Innovation.* May.

OMahoney (2010). *Management Consulting.* Oxford: Oxford University Press.

OMahoney, J. (2011). *Innovation in the UK Consulting Industry. Report for the Chartered Management Institute.* October. London: CMI.

OMahoney, J., Adams, R., Antonocopolou, E., and Neeley, A. (2008). *Challenges of the UK Management Consulting Industry: report for the ESRC.* Swindon: ESRC.

Office of National Statistics (2009). *Annual Survey of Hours and Earnings.* Newport: Office of National Statistics, UK Government.

Office of National Statistics (2011). *Business Population Estimates for the UK and Regions.* October. Newport: Office of National Statistics.

Rogers, E. (1983). *Diffusion of Innovations.* New York: Free Press.

Sahlin-Andersson, K. and Engwall, L. (2002). Carriers, flows, and sources of management knowledge. In: *The Expansion of Management Knowledge,* Sahlin-Andersson, K. and Engwall, L. (Ed.), pp. 3–32. Stanford, CA: Stanford University Press.

Shah, S.K. and Corley, K.G. (2006). Building better theory by bridging the quantitative–qualitative divide. *Journal of Management Studies,* **43**(8), 1821–1835.

Stjernberg, T. and Philips, A. (1993). Organizational innovations in a long-term perspective: legitimacy and souls-of-fire as critical factors of change and viability. *Human Relations,* **46**(10), 1193–1221.

Strauss, A. and Corbin, J. (1994). Grounded theory methodology. An overview handbook of qualitative research. In: *Handbook of Qualitative Research,* Denzin, N.K. and Lincoln, Y.S. (Ed.), pp. 273–285. Thousand Oaks, CA: Sage.

Sturdy, A., Handley, K., Clark, T., and Fincham, R. (2008). Rethinking the role of management consultants as disseminators of business knowledge. In: *The Evolution of Business Knowledge,* Scarborough, H. (Ed.). Oxford University Press.

Suddaby, R. (2006). What grounded theory is not. *Academy of Management Journal,* **49**(4), 633–642.

Suddaby, R., and Greenwood, R. (2001). Colonizing knowledge: commodification as a dynamic of jurisdictional expansion in professional service firms. *Human Relations,* **54**(7), 933–953.

Teddlie, C. and Tashakkori, A. (2009). *Foundations of Mixed Methods Research: integrating quantitative and qualitative approaches in the social and behavioral sciences.* London: Sage.

ten Bos, R. and Heusinkveld, S. (2007). The Gurus Gusto: management fashion, performance and taste. *Journal of Organizational Change Management,* **20**(3), 304–325.

The Economist. (2008). *Giving Advice in Adversity.* 25 September.

Top-Consultant. (2010). Salary Benchmarking Report. www.top-consultant.com

Turner, B.A. (1981). Some practical aspects of qualitative data analysis: one way of organising the cognitive processes associated with the generation of grounded theory. *Quality & Quantity,* **15**, 225–247.

Wetfeet. (2008). Wetfeet Consultancy Career Guide.

Whittle, A. (2005). Preaching and practising flexibility: implications for theories of subjectivity at work. *Human Relations,* **58**(10), 1301–1322.

Wood, P. (2001). *Consultancy and Innovation: the business service revolution in Europe.* London: Routledge.

Zollo, M. and Winter, S.G. (2002). Deliberate learning and the evolution of dynamic capabilities. *Organization Science,* **13**(3), 339–351.

7

Society's Grand Challenges: What Role for Services?

Andy Neely

The Servitization of Manufacturing

Manufacturing's shift to services is not a new phenomenon. For at least twenty years, academics have argued that firms should seek to supplement their product revenues with service revenues. In a manufacturing context, the term 'servitization' is usually traced back to the work of Vandermerwe and Rada (1988). Their paper is upbeat about the potential for services, arguing that services are sweeping the industrial landscape:

> Servitization is happening in almost all industries on a global scale. Swept up by the forces of deregulation, technology, globalization and fierce competitive pressure, both service companies and manufacturers are moving more dramatically into services (Vandermerwe and Rada 1988: 315).

Other authors, however, point out that many manufacturers have been service providers ever since the day they provided their first product—certainly, ever since the day they had their first product breakdown! Manufacturers have long sold spares and offered repairs. They have offered maintenance and overhaul services, in many cases for as long as they have been selling products. In other sectors of the economy, we can see an evolution—through periods of service provision to periods of product sales and then back to service provision. In the music industry, for example, before records and tapes were available, music was embodied in the service delivered by live bands. Then we had a period where products—tapes, records, and

CDs—were widely available. Now we are re-entering a phase where the physical product is becoming obsolete, as it is replaced by a digital asset accessed through a complex service system that involves the internet, electronic banking payments, music access rights, and the exchange of digital information. This evolution from service to product and back again is apparent not just in high-tech industries. In a historical review, Roger Schmenner explains how at one time pineapples were such a rarity that they were rented for dinner parties. The hosts would proudly display their rented pineapple on the dinner table, only to return it to the store the next day for someone else to rent and use that evening (Schmenner 2009). This has to be one of the earliest and most unusual versions of Lovelock and Gummesson's rental access paradigm (Lovelock and Gummesson 2004).

So if the servitization of manufacturing is not a new phenomenon, why then is it an important topic to explore now? This chapter argues that there are three broad reasons why we should take notice of the servitization of manufacturing today. First, the changing structure of the global economy—now, more than ever, services may offer opportunities for manufacturers in developed economies to create value. Second, the technological dimension—it seems we are at a technological tipping point, where new sensors and data capture systems open up new opportunities for service business model innovation. Third, the future—at this time there are some significant stresses and strains on society and these are set to grow. An ageing population, coupled with changing societal expectations means that we need new service innovations that will help people live the lives they wish to as they age. Environmental pressures and the demand on the earth's resources mean that we have to look for ways of changing notions of ownership and production, especially as we look forward to an economically active world with a global population of over seven billion inhabitants. Significant economic shifts, with power moving to the East, mean that Western economies are searching for new ways of ensuring they create and capture economic value.

The structure of the chapter is as follows. It starts by reviewing the traditional reasons why manufacturing is servitizing and exploring the technological tipping point. The chapter then offers a framework for thinking about servitization, identifying five options that firms appear to be pursuing. Next the chapter then turns to the future, looking at the illustrative challenges that society faces—most notably demographic, economic, and environmental—and explores the implications of these challenges for the phenomenon of servitization. Finally, the chapter combines five servitization options with the previously discussed societal challenges, offering some thoughts on what the future might hold.

The Rationale for Servitization

Before exploring the reasons why firms are servitizing it is worth stepping back and asking what is servitization. The academic literature appears to use the term somewhat loosely. Some authors describe servitization as 'the shift to services' (Vandermerwe and Rada 1988), suggesting that servitization involves a shift in positioning. Others describe servitization as a strategy. Slack (2005) states that servitization is 'any strategy that seeks to change the way in which product functionality is delivered to its markets'. Some define servitization relatively narrowly, thinking about it solely in terms of repair and overhaul (Cheng *et al.* 2010). While others think about it broadly, suggesting that servitization is a phrase that describes 'the bundling or integration of services with products' (Schmenner 2009). Further complexity is introduced when one considers related terms in the literature. There is a wide stream of work on Product–Service Systems (PSS), much of it exploring issues of sustainability (Mont 2004; Tukker and Tischner 2006). Other authors talk about firms 'going downstream' (Wise and Baumgartner 1999), 'transitioning from products to services' (Oliva and Kallenberg 2003), and offering 'integrated solutions' (Davies 2004).

For the purposes of this chapter, we will distinguish between three related concepts: servitization, a PSS, and a servitized organization. We define servitization in terms of the transformation journey—hence servitization is a transformation process, which involves a manufacturing firm 'innovating its capabilities and processes so that it can better create mutual value through the shift from selling products to selling Product-Service Systems'. We draw on the PSS literature to define PSS as 'integrated product and service offerings that deliver value-in-use'. And we assume that these PSS are delivered by servitized organizations that 'design, build and deliver one or more integrated product and service offerings that deliver value-in-use' (Neely 2009).[1]

Why are manufacturing firms choosing to servitize? It appears there are three broad categories of reason: (i) economic; (ii) strategic; and (iii) environmental (see Figure 7.1). In terms of the economic—the first reason for servitization is that manufacturers in developed economies recognize they cannot compete based on cost. Hence, they have to innovate and look for new ways of adding value, one of which is by offering services. This theme—service as a means of manufacturing competing in developed economies—features heavily in many government and policy publications (Porter and Ketels 2003; Sainsbury 2007). The second economic reason is that of the installed base. This is particularly prevalent in sectors that offer complex, expensive, and long-lasting equipment. Estimates suggest that the ratio of installed-base-to-new-sales is 13 to 1 for automobiles, 15 to 1 for civil aircraft, and 22 to 1 for

Economic rationale	1. Manufacturing firms in developed economies cannot compete on the basis of cost (technological developments are enabling them to add innovative services).
	2. The installed base argument (e.g. for every new car sold there are already 13 in operation, 15 to 1 for civil aircraft and 22 to 1 for trains).
	3. Stability of revenues—services vs. products.
Strategic rationale	1. Lock in customers (sell the original equipment at cost, make money on spares & suppliers—e.g. razors and printers).
	2. Lock out competitors.
	3. Increase the level of differentiation (e.g. equipment provider offers to take customer' s risk and give predictable maintenance costs).
	4. Customers demand it (e.g. contracting for capability).
Environmental rationale	1. Environmental rationale (change notions of ownership and resource use—e.g. Mobility cars).

Figure 7.1 The reasons why manufacturing firms are servitizing

locomotives (Wise and Baumgartner 1999). With products that have a thirty-to forty-year operating life, it makes economic sense for the manufacturer of the original equipment to seek to offer through life support and servicing. The third economic reason for servitization is stability of revenues. This has been particularly important in recent years, with the economic downturn. Manufacturers have recognized that product revenues are often 'lumpy'. When you sell a large product, you receive significant revenues, but you do not make sales all of the time. With service contracts, the revenues may be smaller, but they are regular. Hence, many firms are searching for a balance between product and service revenues to smooth the peaks and troughs in income.

The second set of reasons why manufacturing firms are servitizing can broadly be categorized as strategic. In some cases, firms deliberately adopt business models that seek to lock in customers. They sell the original equipment at or close to cost and seek to make their profits through the ongoing sale of associated spares and services. Classic examples include printers and ink cartridges, mobile phones and calling contracts, and razors and replacement blades. Interestingly others also recognize the value in these spares and services, so a second reason why some original equipment manufacturers enter into services is to lock out potential competitors, who might otherwise attack the spares market. This strategy is not always successful. Witness the ink cartridge replacement market, where there is now a booming business in recycling and refilling used cartridges. Clearly, these new competitors reduce the margins that the original equipment manufacturers are able to demand. Perhaps the most significant strategic rationales for servitizing, however, centre on risk, predictability, and customer demand. In terms of risks, many customers—especially those in the public sector—are seeking to shift the balance of risk. Governments across the world are now declaring that they will contract for capability rather than buy specific products (Ministry of Defence 2005). The UK defence industrial strategy makes it clear that the Ministry of Defence is interested in procuring the capability to carry out operations, rather than the physical equipment itself. Hence the growth in outsourced support services offered by firms such as BAE Systems and Rolls-Royce. As Slack (2005) points out, this trend has advantages for both suppliers and customers. From a supplier perspective, servitization is a way of increasing sales revenues, while from a customer perspective servitization offers a route of reducing risk and decreasing or at least stabilizing and making predictable maintenance and support costs. Interestingly in the public sector customers are often powerful, not least because of their purchasing spend. Hence, the final strategic reason for shifting to services—sometimes the customers of manufacturers demand that they make this shift.

The third broad category of reasons why manufacturers are servitizing is environmental. This is less prevalent today, but one might expect this to change in the future. Indeed, there is extensive literature in the environmental arena that highlights potential for servitization to have a positive impact on environmental performance (Goedkoop *et al.* 1999). The core thesis is that it is possible to reduce the adverse environmental impact of products if firms change their business models and customers revise their conceptions of ownership. An illustration that is often quoted is the rented washing machine. Customers no longer buy washing machines, but instead they rent them and pay a fixed fee per washing cycle. The revised business model means that it is in the customers' interest to minimize the number of washes they undertake—they pay less as a consequence. It is also in the provider's interest to maximize the product life cycle. Once the machine is installed, the provider does not want to have to undertake any maintenance. This revised business model changes the incentives for both the customer and provider—encouraging both parties to pursue courses of action that minimize the environmental impact of the product (Mont and Plepys 2003; Mont 2004).

While these three broad categories are important, the related issue is that recent technological developments appear to be speeding up the servitization of manufacturing. This is particularly the case when one considers asset heavy industries, where there is increasing use of intelligent vehicle health monitoring technologies. In the construction industry, for example, firms such as Caterpillar use remote asset management technologies to monitor equipment health. By tracking variables such as engine temperature and oil pressure, Caterpillar is able to identify potential engine failures at an early stage, intervening before a critical equipment failure. The net result is that customers end up replacing $100 bearings, rather than facing bills for complete engine overhauls. They are also able to achieve higher uptimes for their equipment, a key driver of competitiveness in the construction equipment industry.

Other technological advances open up new opportunities for service. In the agricultural sector, John Deere offers precision farming solutions through its GreenStar solutions. These employ GPS technology to monitor the position of farming equipment in a field. The iGuide system tracks the position of farming equipment—ploughs and harvesting implements—ensuring that the overlap between runs through the field is minimized and hence wasted effort reduced. Other solutions include automatic steering systems, which allow operators to drive hands-free, by linking steering mechanisms to GPS trackers. The same technology is used to control the application of fertilizer and the process of spreading seeds. Using GPS technology to monitor the position of farming equipment allows systems to be turned on automatically at the right time. Through the innovative integration of GPS technology and farming equipment, John Deere has been able to develop creative and valuable services and solutions for its customers.

Beyond the asset-heavy industries, advances in information communications technologies and new methods of data collection are creating new opportunities. For example, mobile phones can now double as people tracking devices. The movement of mobile phones can be used to monitor traffic flows. If, on a major motorway all of the mobile phones are only moving along that route at five miles an hour it is safe to assume that there is a traffic jam and the phones are sitting in cars that are stuck in the traffic jam. Google maps uses positioning data from mobile phones to provide real-time updated maps through smart phones. Smart metering systems in the home mean that energy companies can help householders understand, manage, and reduce their fuel consumption. The list of innovative services, being provided by traditional manufacturers appears endless and is limited primarily by our imagination. Technology plays a crucial enabling role in these developments. Whether it is GPS systems, handheld devices, or smart meters a unifying theme in many services is the creation and integration of data via the internet. Without these enabling technological platforms, many of the services we see today would simply not be feasible (Gawer 2009).

Five Options for Servitization

Traditionally the literature discusses three different forms of PSS—product-oriented PSS, use-oriented PSS, and result-oriented PSS (Hockerts and Weaver 2002). In a product-oriented PSS, ownership of the tangible product is transferred to the customer, but the manufacturer provides additional services that are directly related to the product. For a use-oriented PSS, ownership of the tangible product is retained by the service provider, who sells the functions of the product, via modified distribution and payment systems, such as sharing, pooling, and leasing, while in a result-oriented PSS, the PSS replaces services for products—e.g. voicemail service replacing answering machines. While useful this categorization is not comprehensive (Neely 2009), for it misses two addition options for servitization—integration-oriented PSS and service-oriented PSS. Integration-oriented PSSs result when firms seek to add services by going downstream and vertically integrating. Service-oriented PSSs result when firms add services to products, by integrating those services into the product, e.g. intelligent vehicle health monitoring services.

In essence, these five options for servitization form a spectrum, ranging from integration-oriented PSSs to result-oriented PSSs. Major oil companies, for example, have servitized through the integration-oriented PSS route. They have established retail infrastructures, initially to sell their own products—oil and gasoline—and then increasingly to sell the products of others. Indeed many service stations now operate as mini-supermarkets, offering a wide range of consumables.

A classic example of the product-oriented PSS would be automobile servicing and financing services. The consumer still takes physical ownership of the product, but buys additional product related services from the provider. In the case of financing, the finance is tied directly to the purchase of the product, a model used to great effect in many sectors—just look at the size and scale of GE's financial services business.

The third option—service-oriented PSS—is a subtly different development. Here the service becomes embedded in the product. John Deere's use of GPS technology, along with Rolls-Royce's power by the hour are classic examples of service-oriented PSSs. Both involve the use of advanced technologies embedded in the product to enable the service. Often these services involve remote monitoring and predictive maintenance. Data are gathered during the product's operation and are used by the original equipment provider to advise when maintenance services are required.

In the use-oriented PSS the change lies in ownership. Here legal ownership of the product does not transfer to the user of the product. Instead the user buys the right to use the product as needed. Some of Rolls-Royce's customers operate this way, paying just for the thrust aero-engines deliver rather than for the engine itself. The use-oriented model, however, is becoming increasingly widespread. ZipCar has adopted a use-oriented PSS, providing customer access to cars only when they need them. Indeed any rental- or access-based model is effectively a use-oriented PSS.

The most extreme form of service involves the service completely replacing the product. Sometimes products are made obsolete through these innovations. Take, for example, answer machines. We used to all have answer machines by our phones, but now the technology has developed to such an extent that the answering service is embedded in another product—the telephone itself—or provided as an additional service (e.g. by phone operating companies). Whenever the product (or the functionality it provides) can be digitized then there is scope for result-oriented PSS. This is a particularly important phenomenon in the entertainment and telecommunications industries, where traditional videos and DVDs have been replaced by e-enabled services, such as video on demand.

These five forms of PSS offer interesting opportunities for manufacturing firms seeking to servitize. The remainder of this chapter explores how these five forms may offer solutions to some of the grand challenges facing society in the twenty-first century.

Society's Grand Challenges

In 2011, the earth's population surpassed 7 billion. Although the overall rate of population growth is decreasing, the population in developing economies continues to grow at about 2%. In many developed economies, the picture is slightly different, in that declining birth rates, coupled with increased life expectancy means that populations are ageing. The United Nations forecasts that by 2050 the median age of people in developed countries will be 45.5 years, up from 29.0 years in 1950. Increased longevity has particular implications for services, especially public services. In the UK, the prediction is that by 2050 one in four people will be over 65. Today the figure is one in six (Cracknell 2010). Government data suggest that spending by the National Health Service on retired households is nearly double that on non-retired households. And, spending on people aged 85 and over is almost three times greater than spending on people aged 65–74. In 2009/10, state benefits and the National Health Service accounted for just under half of all government spending. The financial demands that an ageing population will impose mean that we have to look for new and innovative ways of much more efficiently delivering healthcare services in the future (Cracknell 2010).

Let us turn to a different grand challenge facing society—namely economic growth. Even before the current turmoil in financial markets, significant questions were being asked of manufacturing's future in developed economies. The UK and the USA have lost swaths of industry to emerging and other developed economies. Consider automotive manufacturing, consumer electronics, computer and IT systems, or machine tools—in the UK, with the exception of aerospace and pharmaceuticals—much of the country's manufacturing capacity is foreign owned. Indeed the country's economic strength is founded on financial services—a fact that has increasingly worried commentators, who are now calling for a rebalancing of the economy. How do you rebalance an economy, however, when your labour costs are significantly higher than the competition and in some cases, you have lost the production capabilities needed to support economic activity? Pisano and Shih (2009) neatly summarize this issue in their provocatively entitled article 'Restoring American Competitiveness'. They argue that the USA has lost much of its industrial commons—'the collective R&D, engineering, and manufacturing capabilities that sustain innovation'. Through decades of outsourcing, the US has decimated its local capabilities, making it almost impossible to re-establish certain industrial activities. If we cannot recreate old industries then to stimulate growth, developed economies have to innovate new industries—hence the significant interest in novel technologies and exotic materials ranging from electronics to biomedicine. The question is what role will services play in enabling and supporting these developments and the return to growth of many industrialized economies?

A third grand challenge that is often discussed is that of the environment. The Stern Report, published in 2006, outlined some significant challenges that will arise from climate change. Significantly, the report claimed that average temperatures could rise by 5 degrees centigrade from pre-industrial levels if climate change goes unchecked. With rises of 3–4 degrees centigrade, 200 million people may be permanently displaced because of rising sea levels, heavier floods, and drought. Even with a 2 degree centigrade warming, between 15 and 40% of species face extinction (Stern 2006). There are critics of Stern's analysis and ongoing debates about the size of the impact of climate change, but it is clear that it poses some significant challenges for society, especially if we continue to consume resources at an increasing rate.

These three grand challenges make an interesting framework to pose the question—what can PSSs offer in terms of addressing the grand challenges facing society?

The Demographic Challenge: What role for services?

As previously discussed, the demographic challenge relates to population growth. There are different causes of population growth, although three important factors are birth rates in developing economies, migration (often from developing economies)—a phenomenon that may become more pronounced given the impact of the environmental challenge—and population ageing, a consequence of increased life expectancy, because of improvements in medical and healthcare provision. Taken together these factors mean that our healthcare systems will come under increasing strain. We do not have enough hospital capacity and cannot afford to create enough capacity as the cost of healthcare is increasing rapidly. As the low hanging fruit of drug discovery is picked, it becomes increasingly expensive to create ever more sophisticated pharmaceuticals. Indeed the pharmaceutical industry also faces a crisis, as many of the traditional 'blockbuster' drugs are coming to the end of their patent and so pharmaceutical firms are questioning what role they should play in the future.

What do these challenges mean? First, we know that members of the ageing population value their independence and freedom. Many express a preference for living in their own homes. Technology—especially assisted living technology—makes this more feasible. Remote patient monitoring and diagnostics are becoming more common. These developments offer a new opportunity for pharmaceutical firms, as they seek to overcome the business challenges they face with their drugs coming off patent. Hence, we see more and more pharmaceutical firms redefining themselves as healthcare firms, interested not just in the sale of product, but in the provision of a wider range of healthcare services.

In terms of integration-oriented PSSs, the implication is that pharmaceutical firms will increasingly seek to integrate vertically. They will seek to position themselves as healthcare providers offering assisted living technologies, as well as healthcare support. How far this vertical integration will spread is an interesting question? In other manufacturing sectors, we have seen firms diversify into providing financial services to support their products. Will the same happen in the pharmaceutical sector? Is there scope for pharmaceutical firms to offer health insurance services or private healthcare, as we shift towards personalized healthcare provision? Even more outlandish, how far could pharmaceutical firms expand in terms of product-oriented PSSs? Could they start to offer customized and personalized drugs? Or even replacement organs?

In terms of service-oriented PSSs, the obvious developments lie in remote diagnostics and monitoring technologies. Patient adherence—the requirement for patients to complete courses of prescribed drugs—is a significant issue in healthcare today. With remote monitoring technologies, it may be possible to monitor whether patients are following their proscribed treatment plans. Indeed, with remote monitoring technologies it is also possible to track remotely blood sugar levels in diabetics, irregular heartbeats in patients at risk from heart attacks, and breathing patterns in asthmatics. A particularly interesting recent development is IBM's Watson, a supercomputer that recently won the American quiz show *Jeopardy*. Watson uses complex analytics to answer questions and has the potential to support patient diagnosis. Indeed IBM is now exploring how Watson could be used to support, if not replace, doctors in the patient diagnosis process.

Use-oriented PSS tend to focus on use of assets without exchange of ownership. Already we have examples of use-oriented PSS when it comes to population ageing—retirement homes, for example, provide access to assets (accommodation, entertainment, and sustenance) on an as-needed basis. At a broader level one can consider what other resources might an ageing population need access to on a sporadic basis—transportation services (cars with wheelchair access), healthcare services (shared nursing and medical advice), and leisure services are all obvious candidates.

The final category of PSSs—result-oriented PSSs—poses particular challenges for the demographic challenge. What would outcome-based healthcare constitute? Is there scope for a lifetime health contract—where individuals pay for support and advice that would increase their life expectancy? Coupling a 'pay per year' model, with remote monitoring and diagnostic technologies opens up interesting opportunities to offer dietary and exercise advice designed to maximize an individual's healthy life.

The Economic Challenge: What role for services?

The economic challenge is clearly topical. Even before the financial crisis and the current turmoil in Europe, there was widespread recognition that the economic landscape was changing. The emergence of the BRIC (Brazil, Russia, India, and China) countries as economic powerhouses, coupled with the relative economic lethargy in many developed economies, meant that many commentators were asking how firms in developed economies will complete in the future. Numerous policy reports called for 'Western' firms to compete through innovation and creativity—a call that was especially loud in the manufacturing sector.

There are, of course, numerous ways in which firms can innovate. Some commentators appear to equate innovation with technology, confusing high value with high tech. It is clear, however, that high tech is just one opportunity. There are low-tech opportunities to create value for firms that think creatively. Take, for example, recent thinking about two concepts—the last mile and the long tail. The last mile refers to the act of getting products to consumers. The long tail refers to the fact that there is a long tail of products with low individual demand, but which collectively are valuable. Amazon has exploited these two—the last mile and the long tail—to particularly good effect. They have captured significant value simply by retailing products—initially books, but now a much wider range of goods. The long tail is important to Amazon because changes in printing technologies mean that they can economically offer a wide range of products, even if some have very low demand. In a traditional bookstore shelf space is a limiting factor.

You can only display the books you can physically hold in store. In a virtual store, you have no such constraints; hence, you can offer a far wider product range, with effectively no stock holding costs. The implication is clear—in terms of integration-oriented PSS we will see increasing numbers of firms seeking to capture the value created in the last mile, by selling directly to their own (and others') consumers. To do so they will rely on online stores—either self-owned, or created in partnership with others.

When it comes to product-oriented PSS and service-oriented PSS two major trends we will see are increased systems and solutions offerings, coupled with innovations in business outsourcing services. The former—systems and solutions offerings—can already be seen in some sectors. In the automotive and aerospace manufacturing sectors, for example, there has been a significant shift to corner or modular engineering, where first tier suppliers take responsibility for the design and delivery of entire systems or modules that the original equipment manufacturers integrated into the final product. In service-oriented PSS, many manufacturers are offering through-life services for their product and equipment. This is especially the case in asset-heavy industries with a large installed base. As previously discussed, if you operate in a mature sector with a large installed base of capital equipment that has a long operating life then offering through-life services is a natural extension. A key element of this extension is the alignment of incentives between provider and customer. In the past, it was often in the original equipment manufacturer's interest for their equipment to be unreliable. In some sectors—notably aerospace—original equipment was often sold at or close to cost and the margin was made on the provision of spares and repairs or time and materials. With the advent of remote product monitoring equipment, manufacturers and customer can now minimize maintenance, often only intervening when maintenance is needed rather than working to a fixed schedule. This approach can significantly reduce the costs of maintenance, or make them far more predictable, reducing the risk and exposure of the customer.

Use-oriented PSS often involves the shared use of assets. Some firms are seeking to innovate their business model in this way, although interestingly these are often new entrants to the market—consider ZipCar, for example, which offers customers the opportunity to join a car sharing club and Better Place, the Israeli company that offers batteries for electric vehicles. One of the challenges in the electric vehicle market is the range that cars can travel before they need a battery recharge. The Better Place business model involves sharing batteries. Drivers buy their vehicles, but they borrow Better Place batteries, use them until they run out of charge, drive to a Better Place station, swap their battery, and drive off. Better Place recharges the battery to make it ready for another customer to use.

In the most extreme form of PSS—result-oriented PSS—the product is replaced by a service. Again, when responding to the economic challenge, result-oriented PSS often involves significant business model innovation. Frequently this is associated with a shift to outcome-based contracting, where the customer pays for the desired outcome, not the product. The classic example is Rolls-Royce, with its power-by-the-hour contracting model. But other firms have also adopted result-oriented systems—ranging from the provision of men and women's underwear (see www.manpacks.com and www.panty-bypost.com) through to a wide variety of drive-through services, including drive through libraries in Milwaukee and Ottawa.

The Environmental Challenge: What role for services?

The environmental challenge has multiple dimensions, but at its heart is the pressure on the earth's limited resources—a pressure that is clearly set to grow as the economies of the BRIC countries, among others, develop rapidly. A significant challenge that society faces is that of the consumer economy—we define ourselves as consumers—and yet consumption is at the heart of the environment challenge we face. Hence, one can argue that business models that rely on shared use of and access to resources, rather than consumption may provide a more sustainable future.

In integration-oriented PSSs this shift away from consumption implies a shift towards life cycle management. Considerations of recycling and reuse of resources will become more central, especially as the price of resources increases. There are already some interesting developments in the reuse of resources, especially when a systems perspective is taken. Some industrial estates now, for example, take the by-products from one factory and use them as inputs in another. In furniture manufacturing, wood and offcuts are produced as by-products, but these can be inputs to woodchip mills and used for fuel. Other manufacturing processes, which require significant cooling, produce heat as a by-product that can be captured, stored, and reused as thermal energy. In the oil industry, the use of extended well-life technologies has allowed firms such as Cairn Energy to start to extract additional oil and gas efficiently from wells that were uneconomical to the oil majors.

As firms seek to address the environmental challenge from a product-oriented PSS perspective, they will increasingly focus on life cycle operating costs, not initial manufacturing costs. Design for service and through-life operation will be much more deliberate, with growing attention paid to end of life disposal and reuse. Similar trends will be observed in the service-oriented PSS. Here manufacturers will use technology to offer timely services, rather than scheduled services. We have already mentioned the use of remote product sensors

Table 7.1 How the different forms of servitization might address grand challenges

	Demographic	Economic	Environmental
Nature of the challenge	• Significant growth in population. • Migration resulting in changing population profiles within countries. • Improved healthcare increasing life expectancy. • Ageing population, especially in developed economies.	• Emergence of new low-cost competitors. • Rapid industrialization of BRIC countries. • Concerns about financial stability and economic growth, particularly in developed economies.	• Growing pressure on earth's resources. • Concerns over the sustainability of the carbon economy. • Food shortages and wastage. • Global water shortages with uneven impacts.
Implications of the challenge	• As the population ages we will see more opportunities for assisted living and remote healthcare, with older members of society wishing to remain independent.	• Firms in developed economies will look for new ways to differentiate and add value, possibly through service provision.	• Society today is a 'consumer' society. One can question whether consumption is sustainable in the longer term. Business models that encourage shared use of resources may become more popular.
Opportunities for integration-oriented PSS	• Greater vertical integration from pharmaceutical providers. As drugs come off patent, firms may redefine themselves as healthcare providers, seeking to offer through life healthcare services. • Other equipment manufacturers will innovate healthcare provision, questioning whether we need the same hospital-based healthcare structure that we have today.	• It is clear that significant value lies in the last mile: the retail and distribution end of the value chain. • Product manufacturers will increasingly seek to capture more of this value by creating their own distribution channels, partiucarly online.	• Considerations of reuse and re-cycling will become more dominant. • Exploring the scope for reuse through systems thinking will become prevalent. • We are already seeing examples of industrial parks, where the by-products from one firm become the input to another. • Reuse waste heat, produced as part of a production process, to provide heat input to central heating systems.

Opportunities for product-oriented PSS	• Pharma companies become healthcare companies. • Customized and personalized drugs and organs.	• Digital printing—product innovation. • Systems integration. • Design and development.	• Efficient design that takes account of through-life operational costs, not short term.
Opportunities for service-oriented PSS	• Remote patient monitoring. • Patient adherence.	• Remote equipment monitoring. • Outsourced to reduce cost of operation.	• Managed maintenance—as needed, not when scheduled. • Advice on equipment utilization based on remote monitoring.
Opportunities for use-oriented PSS	• Hotel hospitals, for example, will become more prevalent.	• Shared factories. • Shared production. • Shared design.	• Shared resources and assets.
Opportunities for result-oriented PSS	• Outcome based healthcare. • Pay per year of life. • Offer remote monitoring and diagnosis (with supplementary dietary and exercise advice).	• Outcome-based contracting—provide outcome.	• Digitization—replace the product with the service.

to minimize maintenance. As well as having a cost-benefit, remote sensing equipment and predictive maintenance can be used to avoid unnecessary maintenance and repair, hence reducing the use of materials and components. Additionally, remote sensing equipment on vehicles, for example, can be used to give feedback and advice to the asset operators on how to optimize asset utilization. Accelerating too hard in your car increases fuel consumption unnecessarily. Overheating the engine on your Caterpillar extraction equipment can result in significant damage and the need for a major overhaul. Yet with remote monitoring (and even intervention equipment) these problems can be avoided.

For use-oriented PSSs the environmental opportunities are obvious. Sharing product and resources, rather than owning individual assets has obvious advantages. Consider libraries—both for books and films—in essence these own a stock of assets and make them available to people for the period they need to use them. Hence, we do not need to consume as much resource in the original production process. Finally, for result-oriented PSS, the service replaces the product. The environmental impact is again obvious—a reduction in resource consumption. Potentially any product that can be digitized can be eliminated. We do not really need to produce books, newspapers, CDs, or DVDs—all of these can be made available digitally. Continued innovation in technology means that we will see increasing numbers of digital assets that exist only in the form of data and computer code.

Bringing it all Together: The Potential of Services

Table 7.1 brings these themes together and illustrates both the nature of the challenges facing society, the implications of these challenges and the potential that the five different forms of PSS offer when addressing these challenges. Clearly, the shift to services is not going to overcome all of these grand challenges, but it may help mitigate some of their impact.

Notes

1. With thanks to my colleagues at Cranfield University who helped to develop the first three of these definitions through the IMRC sponsored Ideas Factories.

References

Cheng, C.Y., Barton, D., and Prabhu, V. (2010). The servitisation of the cutting tool supply chain. *International Journal of Production Research*, **48**, 1–19.

Cracknell, R. (2010). *The Aging Population: key issues for the new Parliament*. London: House of Commons Library Research.

Davies, A. (2004). Moving base into high-value integrated solutions: a value stream approach. *Industrial and Corporate Change*, **13**, 727–756.

Gawer, A. (Ed.). (2009). *Platforms, Markets and Innovation*. Cheltenham: Edward Elgar..

Goedkoop, M., van Halen, C., Te Riele, H., and Rommens, P. (1999). *Product Service Systems: ecological and economic basics*. The Hague: VROM.

Hockerts, K. and Weaver, N. (2002). Towards a theory of sustainable Product Service Systems. INSEAD-CMER Research Workshop on Sustainable Product Service Systems.

Lovelock, C. and Gummesson, E. (2004). Whither services marketing? In search of a new paradigm and fresh perspectives. *Journal of Service Research*, **7**, 20–41.

Mont, O. (Ed.). (2004). Product–Service Systems: panacea or myth. Lund: Lund University.

Mont, O. and Plepys, A. (Ed.) (2003). Customer satisfaction: review of literature and application to the Product–Service Systems. Lund: International Institute for Industrial Environmental Economics, Lund University.

Neely, A.D. (2009). Exploring the financial consequences of the servitization of manufacturing. *Operations Management Research*, **2**, 103–118.

Oliva, R. and Kallenberg, R. (2003). Managing the transition from products to services. *International Journal of Service Industry Management*, **14**, 160–172.

Pisano, G. and Shih, W. (2009). Restoring American competitiveness. *Harvard Business Review*, **July–August**, 114–125.

Porter, M. and Ketels, C. (2003). *UK Competitiveness: moving to the next stage*. London: Department of Trade and Industry.

Sainsbury, D. (2007). *The Race to the Top: a review of Government's science and innovation policies*. London: HM Treasury.

Schmenner, R.W. (2009). Manufacturing, service and their integration: some history and theory. *International Journal of Operations and Production Management*, **29**(5), 431–443.

Slack, N. (2005). Operations strategy: will it ever realise its potential. *Gestão & Produção*, **12**(3), 323–332.

Stern, N. (2006). *Stern Review on the Economics of Climate Change*. London: HM Treasury.

Tukker, A. and Tischner, U. (Ed.). (2006). *New Business for Old Europe: product–service development, competitiveness and sustainability*. Sheffield: Greenleaf.

Vandermerwe, S. and Rada, J. (1988). Servitization of businesses: adding value by adding services. *European Management Journal*, **6**, 314–324.

Wise, R. and Baumgartner, P. (1999). Go downstream: the new profit imperative in manufacturing. *Harvard Business Review*, **7**, 133–141.

8

Reconceptualizing Service through Service-dominant Logic

Irene C.L. Ng, Stephen L. Vargo, and Laura A. Smith

Introduction

Defining the nature of service has been a challenge to researchers. Early work by Baker (1981) argued that, while there seemed to be a widespread consensus on the importance of services, precise definitions were difficult, owing to the varied nature of service industries. Most definitions of service centre upon the idea of 'activities' or 'processes' and the term 'service industry' is widely used to denote an industrial sector that 'do(es) things for you, they don't make things' (Silvestro and Johnston 1990: 206). The current literature on the service sector seems to suggest that the term 'services' is still without a generally accepted definition (Blois 1974; Minter 1982; Lovelock 1983; Drechsler 1990; Vargo and Lusch 2004, 2008).

The American Marketing Association (AMA)'s definition associates services with 'activities' or 'processes' that are performed by the seller. This is similar to the 'deeds, acts or performances' suggested by Berry (1980), Zeithaml and Bitner (1996), and Grönroos (2000). Second, the AMA stresses the characteristics of services, such as the degree of intangibility, heterogeneity, inseparability, and perishability. Or, as Kotler *et al.* (1996: 588) put it, 'a service is any activity or benefits that one party can offer to another which is essentially intangible and does not result in ownership of anything'.

Early researchers such as Rathmell (1966) made a fundamental distinction by considering a good as a thing (noun) and a service as an act (verb). The former was an object, the latter a deed or an effort. In distinguishing between the two Rathmell put forward the idea of a goods–service continuum with pure goods located at one end and pure services at the other; most products, which are a mixture of both good and service would fall between these two extremes (see also Liechty and Churchill 1979; Bell 1981). Whether we choose to follow Rathmell's continuum or not, there is an important interdependence between services and goods, with most services involving physical goods at some stage in the process (Rathmell 1974; Greenfield 2002). As Shostack (1977) argued, there are very few pure goods (which do not involve an element of service) or pure services (that deliver or involve no goods).

An alternative to this continuum is the idea of the goods–service hybrid. Levitt (1981) suggested that there was considerable overlap between services and goods, while Storey and Easingwood (1998) used the term 'service product' to describe the bundle of services and products offered to meet the customer requirements.

Recontextualizing Services

Such characteristics of services have been widely accepted. These are the definitions commonly found in service textbooks, and are collectively known as 'IHIP' from intangibility, heterogeneity, inseparability, and perishability (Lovelock 1999; Zeithaml *et al* 2006; Ng 2007). An acceptance of these characteristics is reinforced by overviews of the field (see, for example, Edgett and Parkinson 1993; and Zeithaml *et al.* 1985). But this is clearly not the whole story as there are service industries that have tangible outputs (such as software), in which production and consumption are not inseparable (car repair) or where outcomes are not fully perishable (recorded lectures) (Johns 1999; Lovelock and Gummesson 2004; Edvardsson *et al.* 2005).

We argue that the inconsistent and fragmented understanding of service is due to the logic inherited from the industrial era where wealth and value were based upon tangible units of exchange. Adam Smith (1776) characterized goods by their exchange value, with that exchange value seen as a characteristic of a good, such that the transfer of a good transferred wealth between nations. Such an understanding places the value of goods high as they embody and represent the tradable form of specialized knowledge (Demsetz 1993). The original manufacturer's responsibility for creating value is considered to have ended once the production unit is exchanged and its ownership transferred to the consumer. In other words, the value reposes in the product itself, that value is attributed to its current owner, and value is realized when products are traded between different parties (Hill 1999). Vargo and Lusch (2004, 2008) labelled this goods-dominant logic, a logic that has pervaded contemporary business thinking.

According to this frame of reference, services were also divided into exchangeable units and the sets of units (information, time, materials) that could be combined and exchanged in varying ways became different service contexts and industries, with each industry developing its own language, systems, structures, and practices. Differences in context, delivery mechanisms, and combinations of the sets of units for exchange have led to the increasing fragmentation of the service sector where the nature of the shared services is obscured by fragmented definitions. This fragmentation also contributes to a lack of knowledge transfer between each individual context. Rather, services and goods, even when combined into one offering, are recontextualized again and again for each new industry, adding to the multiple existing services industries (e.g. transportation, energy, telecoms, hotels, banking). So the boundaries that shape the way services are delivered, configured, and operated, as well as the relationships between customers and firms are established within the structures, language, and practices of each industry. Academic input supports industry-based journals and trade publications (e.g. healthcare, finance, transportation). These often create useful and impactful knowledge, but also endorse and strengthen the boundaries between one area of service and the others.

This mind-set of value as embedded within exchange is what we would term a goods-dominant logic. A dominant logic is the shared mental maps used and developed by groups of individuals as part of their core activities. A dominant logic is represented by a common mind-set or shared perception of how an industry, such as services, works, as well as the accepted tools and approaches used by the 'dominant coalition' in their decision-making (Prahalad and Bettis 1986). Often, contributors to an industry can only work with and apply the logics with which they are familiar, regardless of whether or not they are appropriate (Das 1981).

However, current market changes have put this goods-dominant logic under strain as the boundaries between goods and services are becoming increasingly blurred. Goods are beginning to behave like services and, in return, services behave like goods. E-mailed documents are intangible, but they have been delivered just as surely (and rather more swiftly) than tangible faxes or postal deliveries. The old goods-dominant logic is neither integrative nor robust enough to encompass these changes. Commerce is undergoing a transformation from producer push to networks of multiple agents coming together to meet specific individual needs. In these emerging systems, value is created in use, rather than in exchange (Ng *et al.* 2012). Value-in-use, enabled by technology, is now being co-created between multiple entities through 'value constellations' that are geographically dispersed (Normann 2001), and in multiple partnerships that achieve value unique to individual or customer circumstances. For example, pharmaceutical companies have begun to explore the social and cultural contexts in which medicines are produced, exchanged, and consumed. Each phase has its own particular context, actors, and transactions and is characterized by different sets of values and ideas (Van Der Geest *et al.* 1996).

Reconceptualizing Service

In 2004 Vargo and Lusch reconceptualized service by developing the idea of service-dominant logic (S-D logic), a perspective markedly different from the traditional goods-dominant view (Vargo 2011). Vargo and Lusch (2004) defined service as the application of specialized competences (skills and knowledge), through deeds, processes, and performances for the benefit of another entity or the entity itself (self-service). Following this definition, economic exchange is fundamentally about service provision; in short, everything is a service. In this, S-D logic consolidated a number of observations from earlier work. Storey and Easingwood (1998) pointed out that the ownership of physical products was less important than obtaining services from them; Prahalad and Ramaswamy (2000: 83) described appliances as 'an artifact around which customers have experiences' and Gummesson (1995) proposed that both goods and services render service. It is differentiation between different types of service, rather than between products and services, that has caused some confusion (Bolton 2004; Deighton and Narayandas 2004; O'Shaughnessy and O'Shaughnessy 2011). In S-D logic, service is the value that is being co-created by the customer and the firm through an integration of resources accessible to both parties (Vargo and Lusch 2004). In place of goods and physical resources (termed operand resources) as the basis of economic and social exchange, S-D logic emphasizes knowledge and skills (termed operant resources).

This way of viewing the service sector places emphasis upon the outcomes realized with customers, instead of the processes involved or the act of provision to customers (Vargo and Lusch 2004). S-D logic propounds a set of 10 foundational premises seen in Table 8.1 (Vargo and Lusch 2004, 2006, 2008). The first of these sets service as the fundamental basis of exchange, but S-D logic does not reject the value of goods (Lusch 2011), as the third identifies that goods may be integral to the value-creating process and that their effective integration along with other resources is imperative for economic success (Ballantyne and Varey 2008). In other words, goods are appliances used in service provision, and goods and service have a nested relationship. The seventh foundational premise suggests that the firm can only create a value proposition and further, the customer as part of the system, realizes that value in use.

125

Table 8.1 SD-logic: 10 foundational premises

FP1: Service is the fundamental basis of exchange

FP2: Indirect exchange masks the fundamental basis of exchange

FP3: Goods are a distribution mechanism for service provision

FP4: Operant resources are the fundamental source of competitive advantage

FP5: All economies are service economies

FP6: The customer is always a co-creator of value

FP7: The enterprise cannot deliver value, but only offer value propositions

FP8: A service-centred view is inherently customer oriented and relational

FP9: All social and economic actors are resource integrators

FP10: Value is always uniquely and phenomenologically determined by the beneficiary

Broadening the notion of service to include goods as 'indirect service', means that service scholarship itself now encompasses industries that had not previously regarded themselves as service. In manufacturing and engineering in particular, products were differentiated from services by the transfer of ownership. So the maintenance and support that ensured ongoing functioning, and the education and integration that enhanced that functioning were all considered a separate and distinct set of activities (Ren 2009). Under S-D logic, goods may be 'servitized' with all the various maintenance activities offered by the manufacturer as part of a continuing relationship with the customer in which either party may own the product (see Neely, Chapter 7, this volume).

This chapter argues that such a reconceptualization of service could not have come at a more appropriate time. Advances in manufacturing and technology are achieving greater connectivity between entities than ever before, creating new value constellations and new demand fulfilled through hybrid offerings of physical assets, information, and people. Virtual interaction is playing an increasingly prominent role in the economy and there is a need to better understand virtual worlds as a medium; including virtual companies, brick-and-click delivery, multiple-channels, and web 2.0 in services (van Dijk *et al.* 2007). Leaps in computing power have resulted in newer technologies with greater capability such as the ability to sense facial expressions (Xia *et al.* 2009), and stress levels (Scheirer *et al.* 2002), in addition to moving technology towards a more liberated cyberspace where both autonomous and intelligent entities and virtual objects can act in full interoperability; auto-organizing themselves to co-create value constellations, based on the concept of the 'internet of things' (Dodson 2003) and Cloud computing.[1] Research in the information technological sphere that includes customer behaviours and processes is developing knowledge around service-oriented architectures (e.g. Papazoglou and van den Heuvel 2007; Kounkou *et al.* 2008). Human–computer interaction and interaction design, which views design for and from the user perspective (Parker and Heapy 2006; van Dijk *et al.* 2007), have tried and tested approaches to reflect the structure of user's activities in the design of products and processes (e.g. Engeström 1999; Johnson *et al.* 2000).

Given that orientation, an S-D logic view of service would necessarily evolve its knowledge domain from management and social science, to include manufacturing/engineering ('product') and computer science and information technology (connectivity). There is therefore an urgent need for greater integrative frameworks that are transdisciplinary, and could assist firms in capitalizing on opportunities to create value with customers in different ways that are not hindered by constraining logics. Indeed, Ng *et al.* (2011) suggested that there is a need for service to have better abstraction for the purpose of transferability of knowledge across sectors, and for replicability and scalability of the service so that future service design by firms could be systemic, structured, and yet socially meaningful to ensure sustainable service excellence. In this sense, S-D logic could provide the integrative logic required to unite and progress knowledge.

Vargo and Lusch (2004) draw on several authors who believe that a goods-dominant logic may not help further the understanding of how consumers create value from combinations of 'goods' and 'services' and the interactions between them (Normann and Ramirez 1993; Grönroos 1994; Kotler 1997). Many suggestions have been made for a holistic and systems-based approach to understanding value creation, one that is not constrained by the need to determine the boundaries of either 'product' or 'services' (Ng and Briscoe 2011). Such a perspective views organizations as sites of value creation (Normann 2001; Vargo and Lusch 2004). While customers are not just the recipients of products, but also increasingly, their co-producers and co-designers of value propositions. Such co-creation is gaining greater attention and prominence (Ng *et al.* 2010; Chandler and Vargo 2011). Value is increasingly created within an ecosystem of multiple stakeholders that includes customers and their communities, a dynamic system termed a value constellation by Normann (2001). Normann describes 'density' as the best combination of resources mobilized for a particular context, such as a specific customer at a given time and place. Ultimately, density means that customers could have a whole world of specialist knowledge available when and where they like, with the potential to incorporate knowledge available only to them. Density is increasingly enabled by technology, which liberates the world from the constraints of time (when things can be done), place (where things can be done), actor (who can do what), and constellation (with whom it can be done). Central to the value constellation is the notion of learning communities. Individuals and communities will need to be capable of sharing data, information, and knowledge, and to be able to learn and uniquely apply what has been learned from elsewhere and integrate such resources for their own individualized contextual outcomes. These changes have significant implications for manufacturing, technology, and service organizations, all of which need to develop strategies for understanding, anticipating, and meeting demands through various hybrid offerings of physical assets, information, and people.

S-D logic (Vargo and Lusch 2004, 2008) provides a lens through which we can view the various participants in this value-creating system all applying their competencies for the benefit of others. In co-creating value, each participant renders a service within the system to achieve outcomes for itself, as well as for the wider group. Through it, we may view both the value-creating system communities and organizations, and the detail of the way resources (physical assets, human, and information) may be reconfigured and redesigned. Because this perspective is not confined to either product-based or human activities within the system, it has the potential to demonstrate how the firm can reformulate its value proposition.

Operationalizing Service from a Service-dominant Logic Perspective

We propose that S-D logic is useful when there is a need to have a *complete understanding of the value-creating service system* where all entities, be they products or people, render a 'service' or a 'competency' to that system. By reconceptualizing activities in this way, attention may be directed beyond the design process, the human activities and the supply chain, towards the *design of the equipment* itself, in particular, when there is a need to re-evaluate the role of the product, processes, and technologies in the system. S-D logic can help reconsider the design and configuration of the whole system. Following S-D logic indirect service provision (e.g. tangible objects) within the system may be designed not merely for function (which is acontextual) but also for their capacity to act as resources for co-creation within the system. In other words, an S-D logic approach is useful when there is a *need for tangible objects to be redesigned and re-engineered to improve their relationships with the human co-creators*, with other tangible objects, and with formal processes. Following this, objects within the system become true enablers of value creation.

To understand service from an S-D logic perspective is to understand the role of exchange and use within the firm's value proposition. Traditionally, a firm's value proposition was seen as an exchangeable unit. Here, the first step towards understanding value proposition is to disassociate exchange value from exchangeable units, and to reformulate exchange so that it is aligned with the customer's processes of achieving use-value. This means that the firm's value proposition is no longer exchangeable units, but its *fit* with and contribution to the value-creating activities of the customer in use situations. By viewing the firm's value proposition as a part of the whole value-creating system, the firm's value proposition can be exchanged with customer resources such as money, but parts of the monetary amounts could also be substitutable with other resources (other suppliers and the customers themselves) in the value-creating service system, where other resources could be more effective or efficient in use-contexts.

We argue that operationalizing a firm's value proposition in this manner enables the firm to identify the resources that contribute to specific value propositions, which are aligned to the value realized by customers in use and in context, without the need to be constrained by the boundaries of 'product' and 'service'. Only when a firm is able to visualize its offering as just a part of the value system, can it see how the propositions fit in with the customer's mission. Clearly, such a transition is a challenging one, more so as most firms operate with both internal and external structures developed under a very different logic, such that they see themselves still as manufacturers or service companies. The idea of a hybrid organization with communication between human activities, equipment, and technology demands a re-specification and re-visualization of the firm's offering and the development of a set of value propositional attributes that are aligned to co-create value-in-use. This is likely to require a re-evaluation of a firm's internal structures and boundaries, to enable it to mobilize its resources in a very different way. A difficult challenge at the best of times.

Conclusion

This chapter argues that an S-D logic perspective has the potential to illuminate our understanding of both service and value creation. In addition, it suggests a way to operationalize S-D logic by redrawing a firm's value propositional attributes such that these are aligned with their realization by the customer in use contexts. By doing so, we show that firms' offerings are hybridized between product and service and connected to one another. Together with the customer, value creation becomes a constellation where resources are integrated by all stakeholders. An S-D logic approach shows the complexity of the value-creating system but also provides a framework by which that system can be understood. This chapter shows how the operationalization of a value-creating system through an S-D logic approach could generate new insights in terms of interactions between tangible objects, human activities, and customer resources.

Notes

1. Cloud computing is the development and use of Internet-based (hence, 'cloud') computer technology (hence 'computing'). Cloud computing signifies IT-related capabilities provided 'as a service', allowing users to access technology-enabled services from the internet with little knowledge of, expertise with, or control over the technology infrastructure that supports them.

References

Baker, M.J. (1981). Services—salvation or servitude? *Quarterly Review of Marketing*, **Spring**, 7–18.

Ballantyne, D. and Varey, R.J. (2008). The service-dominant logic and the future of marketing. *Journal of the Academy of Marketing Science*, **36**, 11–14.

Bell, M. (1981). A matrix approach to the classification of marketing: goods and services. In: *Marketing of Services*, Donnelly, J.H. and George, W.R. (Ed.), pp. 208–212. Chicago, IL: American Marketing.

Berry, L.L. (1980). Services marketing is different. *Business*, **30**(May–June), 24–29.

Blois, K.J. (1974). The marketing of services: an approach. *European Journal of Marketing*, **8**, 137–145.

Bolton, R. (2004). Invited commentaries on 'Evolving to a New Dominant Logic for Marketing'. *Journal of Marketing*, **68**, 18–27.

Chandler, J.D. and Vargo, S.L. (2011). Contextualization and value-in-context: how context frames exchange. *Marketing Theory*, **11**, 35–49.

Das, R. (1981). *Managing Diversification: the general management perspective*. New Delhi: Macmillan.

Deighton, J. and Das, N. (2004). Commentary on 'Evolving to a new dominant logic in marketing'. *Journal of Marketing*, **68**, 18–27.

Demsetz, H. (1993). *The Nature of the Firm. Origins, evolution and development*. New York: Oxford University Press.

van Dijk, G., Minocha, S., and Laing, A. (2007). Consumers, channels and communication: online and offline communication in service consumption. *Interacting with Computers*, **19**, 7–19.

Dodson, S. (2003). The internet of things. *Guardian*, 9 October.

Drechsler, L. (1990). A note on the concept of services. *Review of Income and Wealth*, **36**(3), 309–316.

Edget, S. and Parkinson, S. (1993). Marketing for service industries—a review. *The Service Industry Journal*, **13**(3), 19–39.

Edvardsson, B., Gustafsson, A., and Roos, I. (2005). Service portraits in service research: a critical review. *International Journal of Service Industry Management*, **16**, 107–121.

Engeström, Y. (1999). Activity theory as a framework for analyzing and redesigning work. *Ergonomics*, **43**(7), 960–974.

van der Geest, S., Whyte, S. and Hardon, A. (1996). The anthropology of pharmaceuticals: a biographical approach. *Annual Review of Anthropology,* **25,** 153–178.

Greenfield, H.I. (2002). A note on the goods/services dichotomy. *Service Industries Journal,* **22,** 19–21.

Grönroos, C. (1994). From marketing mix to relationship marketing: towards a paradigm shift in marketing. *Asia-Australia Marketing Journal,* **2,** 9–29.

Grönroos, C. (2000). *Services Management and Marketing: a customer relationship approach,* 2nd edn. Chichester: Wiley.

Gummesson, E. (1995). Relationship marketing: its role in the service economy. In: *Understanding Services Management,* Glynn, W.J. and Barnes, J.G. (Ed.), pp. 244–268. New York: John Wiley & Sons.

Hill, P. (1999). Tangibles, intangibles and services: a new taxonomy for the classification of output. *Canadian Journal of Economics—Revue Canadienne D Economique,* **32**(2), 426–446.

Johns, N. (1999). What is this thing called service? *European Journal of Marketing,* **33**(9/10), 958–973.

Johnson, P., Johnson, H., and Hamilton, F. (2000). Getting the knowledge into HCI: theoretical and practical aspects of task knowledge structures. In: *Cognitive Task Analysis,* Schraagen, J.M., Chipman, S.F., and Shalin, V.L. (Ed.), pp. 201–214. Mahwah, NJ: Lawrence Erlbaum and Associates.

Kotler, P. (1997). *Marketing Management: analysis, planning, implementation, and control,* 9th edn. Upper Saddle River, NJ: Prentice Hall.

Kotler, P., Armstrong, G., Saunders, J., and Wong, V. (1996). *Principles of all Marketing: the European edition.* Hemel Hempstead: Prentice-Hall International.

Kounkou, A., Cullinane, A., and Maiden, N. (2008). Using HCI Knowledge in Service-Centric Applications: the S-Cube Network of Excellence. Wild, P.J. (Ed). *HCI2008 Workshop on HCI and the Analysis, Design, and Evaluation of Services,* John Moore's University, Liverpool.

Levitt, T. (1981). Marketing intangible products and products intangibles. *Harvard Business Review,* **59**(3), 94–102.

Liechty, M. and Churchill, G.A., Jr. (1979). Conceptual insights into consumer satisfaction with services. In: *AMA Educator's Conference Proceedings,* pp.509–515. Chicago: American Marketing.

Lovelock, C.H. (1980). Towards a classification of services. In: *Theoretical Developments in Marketing,* Lamb, C.W. and Dunne, P.M. (Ed.), pp. 72–76. Chicago: American Marketing.

Lovelock, C.H. (1983). Classifying services to gain strategic marketing insights. *Journal of Marketing,* **47**(3), 9–20.

Lovelock, C.H. (1999). Developing marketing strategies for transnational service operations. *Journal of Services Marketing,* **13**(4/5), 278–295.

Lovelock, C. and Gummesson, E. (2004). Whither services marketing? In search of a new paradigm and fresh perspectives. *Journal of Service Research,* **7,** 20–41.

Lusch, R.F. (2011). Reframing supply-chain management: a service-dominant logic perspective. *Journal of Supply Chain Management,* **47,** 14–18.

Minter, A. (1982). Why have services been ignored. *The Service Industries Journal*, **2**(3), 65–71.

Ng, I.C.L. (2007). *The Pricing and Revenue Management of Services: a strategic approach. Advances in Management and Business Studies Series*. Abingdon: Routledge, Taylor and Francis Group.

Ng, I.C.L., Badinelli, R., Dinauta, P., Halliday, S., Löbler, H., and Polese, F. (2012). S-D Logic: research directions and opportunities: the perspective of systems, complexity and engineering. *Marketing Theory*, **12**(2), 213–217.

Ng, I.C.L. and Briscoe, G. (2011). Value, variety and viability: designing for co-creation in a complex system of direct and indirect (goods) service value proposition. The 2011 Naples Forum on Service—Service Dominant Logic, Network & Systems Theory and Service Science: Integrating Three Perspectives For A New Service Agenda, 14–17 June, Capri, Italy.

Ng, I.C.L., Maull, R.S., and Smith, L. (2011). Embedding the new discipline of service science. In: *The Science of Service Systems*, Demirkan, H., Spohrer, J.H., and Krishna, V. (Ed.), 2010 volume in Service Science: Research and Innovations (SSRI) in the Service Economy Book Series. Springer.

Ng, I.C.L., Nudurupati, S., and Tasker, P. (2010). Value co-creation in outcome-based contracts for equipment-based service. AIM working paper series, WP No 77-May—2010 http://www.aimresearch.org/index.php?page=wp-no-77 under second review in *Journal of Service Research*.

Normann, R. (2001). *Reframing Business: when the map changes the landscape*. Hoboken, NJ: John Wiley & Sons Inc.

Normann, R. and Ramirez, R. (1993). From value chain to value constellation: designing interactive strategy. *Harvard Business Review*, **71**(4), 65–77.

O'Shaughnessy, J. and O'Shaughnessy, N.J. (2011). Service-dominant logic: a rejoinder to Lusch and Vargos' reply. *European Journal of Marketing*, **45**(7/8), 1310–1318.

Papazoglou, M. and van den Heuvel, W.-J. (2007). Service oriented architectures. *The VLDB Journal*, **16**(3), 389–415.

Parker, S. and Heapy, J. (2006). *The Journey to the Interface*. Report. London: DEMOS.

Prahalad, C.K. and Bettis, R.A. (1986). The dominant logic: a new linkage between diversity and performance. *Strategic Management Journal*, **7**(6), 485–501.

Prahalad, C.K. and Ramaswamy, V. (2000). Co-opting customer competence. *Harvard Business Review*, **78**: 79–87.

Rathmell, J.M. (1966). What is meant by services? *Journal of Marketing*, **30**, 32–36.

Rathmell, J.M. (1974). *Marketing in the Service Sector*, Cambridge, MA: Winthrop Publisher Inc.

Ren, G. (2009). *Service Business Development in Manufacturing Companies: classification, characteristics and implications*. PhD Dissertation, University of Cambridge.

Scheirer, J., Fernandez, R., Klein, J., and Picard, R.W. (2002). Frustrating the user on purpose: a step toward building an affective computer. *Interacting with Computers*, **14**(2), 93–118.

Shostack, L. (1977). Breaking free from product marketing. *Journal of Marketing*, **41**(2), 73–80.

Silvestro, R. and Johnson, R. (1990). The determinations of service quality—enhancing and hygiene factors. In: *Proceedings of the QUIS II Symposium*, July. New York: St John's University.

Smith, A. (1776). *The Wealth of Nations*, Books I–III. Chichester: Wiley.

Storey, C. and Easingwood, C.J. (1998). The augmented service offering: a conceptualization and study of its impact on new service success. *Journal of Product Innovation Management*, **15**, 335–351.

Vargo, S.L. (2011). Market systems, stakeholders and value propositions: toward a service-dominant logic-based theory of the market. *European Journal of Marketing*, **45**(1/2), 217–222.

Vargo, S.L. and Lusch, R.F. (2004). Evolving to a new dominant logic for marketing. *Journal of Marketing*, **68**, 1–17.

Vargo, S.L. and Lusch, R.F. (2006). Service-dominant logic: what it is, what it is not, what it might be. In: *The Service-Dominant Logic of Marketing: Dialog, debate, and directions*, Lusch, R.F. and Vargo, S.L. (Ed.), pp. 43–56. Armonk, NY: ME Sharpe.

Vargo, S.L. and Lusch, R.F. (2008). Service-dominant logic: continuing the evolution. *Journal of the Academy of Marketing Science*, **36**, 1–10.

Xia, M., Zheng, L., and Yuli, X. (2009). Emotional gaze behavior generation in human-agent interaction. In: *Proceedings of the 27th International Conference Extended Abstracts on Human Factors in Computing Systems*. Boston, MA: ACM.

Zeithaml, V.A. and Bitner, M.J. (1996). *Services Marketing*. Boston, MA: McGraw-Hill.

Zeithaml, V.A., Bitner A.J., and Gremler, D.D. (2006). *Services Marketing: integrating Customer Focus Across the Firm*, 4th edn. Boston, MA: McGraw-Hill.

Zeithaml, V.A., Prasuraman, A., and Berry, L.L. (1985). Problems and strategies in services marketing. *Journal of Marketing*, **49**, 33–46.

9

Innovation in Services: An Overview

Ammon Salter and Bruce S. Tether

Introduction

This chapter provides an overview on innovation in services, particularly from the perspective of innovation studies. The study of innovation in services has increased rapidly in recent years, and is now a leading area of inquiry about the nature and sources of growth in advanced economies. At the core of this research area are two questions. The first concerns the *level* of innovation in services, i.e. whether services are less innovative than manufacturing. This is difficult because many of the tools that we have to measure innovation, such as research and development (R&D) expenditures and patenting, are ill-suited to capture innovation in service. While services account for an increasing share of innovative activities, they are also highly diverse. Some services are slow and backward, whereas others are dynamic and open. With the increasing shift to services across advanced economies, the importance of understanding the extent of innovation in services has become imperative, and new tools are needed.

The second question concerns the *nature* of the innovation process within different service industries. This research questions the 'conventional wisdom' of the manufacturing dominated view of innovation, with its emphasis on 'physical' technologies and product life cycles. This research calls attention to the particular features of innovation in services, and how these features may require new thinking about how innovation takes place. It exposes the continuous and open character of much innovation in services. In this area, more is being learnt by combining different research traditions, including innovation studies with research in strategy, organizational development and change, economics, and sociology. This chapter is organized into two main sections. Section 1 examines three different types of services, highlighting some research findings across various studies in this area. Section 2 discusses three key debates concerning innovation in services. The first concerns the measurement of innovative activities in services, and the connection between services and scientific research institutions, including universities. The second explores the protection of innovations, and how firms capture value or the returns to their innovative activities. The third examines the largely organizational character of innovation in services.

Three Types of Services and Their Innovation Dynamics

The study of innovation in services is a relatively recent phenomenon. Until the 1980s, services were essentially neglected and assumed as non-innovators, and 'supplier dominated' (Pavitt 1984), 'merely' adopting technologies developed by manufacturers, whose R&D activities were the primary focus of innovation studies. The first pioneering studies, such as those by Barras (1986), Evangelista (2000), and Miozzo and Soete (2001), initially adapted understandings of innovation in manufacturing to services, and thereby sought to assimilate services into the existing, technology-oriented understanding of innovation. Others, such as Sundbo and Gallouj (2001), took a different road, and emphasized the distinctive nature of services and, by extension, their innovation activities. This placed much greater emphasis on organizational changes, and other 'soft' forms of innovation. Most innovation scholars are now seeking to develop a synthesis approach that can embrace various forms of innovation, which occur in both manufacturing and services.

A considerable challenge that arises when considering innovation in services is the great variety among services activities. Collectively these account for about three-quarters of economic activity in advanced economies. Yet services occupy both the 'top and bottom' of the economy. The best and the worst jobs are in services, and the growth of services has been characterized by growing inequalities in advanced economies, but especially the USA and UK. As Goos and Manning (2003: 77) observe: 'Whichever way you look at it, there is growing polarisation of jobs: . . . there are more good 'MacJobs' and more bad 'McJobs'. . . . Craft and clerical occupations . . . are disappearing while the importance of low and high paid service jobs has increased'. The aim of this section is to emphasize and unpack some of this variety. We do this by exploring three very different service 'sectors' and their innovation activities: traditional services; systemic services; and professional services. This is not intended to be an exhaustive classification, but rather a means of illuminating the variety within services and how they innovate (Tether 2003).

Traditional Services

Even in the most advanced economies, much economic activity remains dominated by small traditional service providers; Evangelista's (2000) 'technology users'. Few of these employ professional staff, and they often lack the absorptive capacity necessary for sustained innovation (Cohen and Levinthal 1990). Survey evidence (National Skills Task Force 2000) indicates that skills gaps and shortages often restrict the ability of these firms to innovate, with weaknesses especially found in 'soft skills', such as communications, problem solving, and team-working. These firms also have high failure rates, operating in sectors characterized by low barriers to entry, and high levels of churn. Many firms choose to remain small, operating within the span of control of their founder (i.e. usually with less than ten employees). Their activities are difficult to scale and are often tied to a particular location, offering niche services to a narrow range of customers.

Many of these businesses therefore operate under extreme organizational liabilities, such as liabilities of smallness and newness (Stinchcombe 1965; Baum 1996), which limit their development. The loss of a key staff member or the decline of their local market can place these firms in a precarious position. They may also lack the ambition necessary to exploit innovative opportunities available to them, and they may be overwhelmed by the entry of large systems firms into their market. For example, the expansion of Tesco, Sainsbury's, and other supermarkets into the local convenience store market has decimated thousands of local retailers in the UK since the 1990s.

Many of these industries are characterized by the use, or potential use, of franchising, although little attention has been placed on this form of organization within innovation studies. By franchising, a small firm can gain access to resources (particularly brand recognition) and the advanced operating routines of a large multi-unit chain, which provides template of practices and technologies that can be used to service a small market (Baden-Fuller and Winter 2005). However, it remains unclear what implications different types of franchise arrangements have for the scope of innovation available to members (Baum and Greve 2001). Some evidence indicates that franchising provides an efficient mechanism for the transfer of learning and therefore these organizational forms may provide a mechanism for the diffusion of advanced practices within traditional service sectors. For example, Banaszak-Holl *et al.* (2002) found that franchised care homes in the USA achieved higher levels of performance than independent operators. They also found that when independent operators joined a franchise their performance increased significantly.

Traditional service firms that are able to exploit locational advantages, capture a lucrative franchise, and/or specialize in a growing market, can generate substantial returns for their owners. Some are also skilled at bricolage—solving problems under severe time and resource constraints. But as yet, we know little about innovation processes in micro firms in traditional services. Innovation research on new and small firms has been highly biased towards high-technology firms in sectors such as biotechnology. These firms are organized around the exploitation of new technologies and/or the provision of knowledge-intensive services. By contrast, there is a dearth of studies on innovation in traditional services, which are widely assumed to be at the tail end of the innovation system, and to be laggards in adopting technological innovations, working practices, and organizational innovations. They are also assumed to lack managerial resources, to have little or no desire to grow, and to be hampered by a lack of demanding customers. Finegold and Soskice identified this as the 'low skills equilibrium', 'in which the majority of enterprises staffed by poorly trained managers and workers produce low quality goods and services' (Finegold and Soskice 1988: 22). They see this as a 'systems failure', in which individuals and employers react rationally to the incentives they face. For example, these firms remain marginally profitable by engaging in risk averse, non-innovative, low product-specification strategies based on low skills, as there is a demand for their goods and services, whereas it might be costly for them to seek to move to high product-specification strategies based on greater innovation and higher skills. Thus a 'low skills equilibrium' is a vicious circle of low value added, low skills, and low wages, with little substantial innovation. Employers do not demand higher skills as they are not necessary for the low specification services they provide, and do not seek to innovate partly because of a lack of demand and partly because they themselves typically have narrow skill sets and are unable to manage innovation. Meanwhile workers have little incentive to gain higher skills because of a lack of demand for these among employers.

More recently, Mason (2005) compared two samples of British companies—those achieving high value added (HVA) and those achieving medium value added (MVA). Mason's aim was to assess the relationship between skill levels and performance. In the *logistics* sector, most HVA firms are foreign owned, and have therefore imported many of their technologies and work practices, while the MVA ones are mainly domestically owned. In this sector, it was the MVA firms that emerged as the more dynamic, as they strived to catch-up with the foreign-owned giants. Logistics may be an exceptional service sector; however, as this shows what can happen when a service sector internationalizes and is exposed to international competition. Many UK service sectors are exposed to little if any foreign competition, and may follow the pattern that Mason found in *plastics, processing,* and *printing.* In these sectors, the gap between HVA and MVA firms in terms of innovation strategies (i.e. product innovation versus cost minimization) and ability to deal with skill problems were substantial. MVA firms struggled to innovate and change their products towards HVA levels, thus displaying a rigid set of capabilities. Indeed, a study by Wilson and Hogarth (2003) on business hotels (and food processing) found similar results. 'In general terms...there was evidence that some of the organizations concerned were firmly embedded in a low-skills equilibrium or on a low-skill trajectory..... Despite the effort of some organizations to innovate and extract themselves from this situation, the most common reaction of respondents was acceptance of their position and of the fact that there was little that they could do to change it' (Wilson and Hogarth 2004: xii). Especially for business hotels, Wilson and Hogarth emphasize that managerial abilities to co-ordinate the innovation process was often the key constraint. More optimistically, there is some evidence that firms in these industries occasionally break out of this locked system. This often requires restructuring the firm, and the use of entrepreneurial resources from outside the existing management team. However, the available evidence suggests that firms in traditional service sectors undertake little substantial innovation.

Systems Firms

While many services industries are dominated by small and micro businesses serving highly-local markets, others, such as banking and insurance, supermarket retailing, and air transport, are dominated by some of the world's largest and most sophisticated businesses. Harvey (1999), for example, argues that supermarkets in the UK (and elsewhere) have been highly innovative, both in themselves and as orchestrators of supply chains. In particular they have developed an ability to consolidate consumer demand and to reorganize supply chains into long-term relationships (with a growing emphasis on 'own label' products), and invested heavily in complex logistics chains with special features dedicated to enabling the provision of a wide range of new fresh and chilled products, which are transported over considerable distances.

In general, systems services typically involve highly developed divisions of labour, sophisticated technologies (including information, communication technologies), complex organizational forms, and professional managers. The airline industry, for example, is largely built on hub-and-spoke networks, which has driven the demand for new aircraft, such as the Airbus A380. Radical innovations in these industries will typically involve changes to more than one of the triumvirate of the division of labour, technologies, and organization, as their complex intertwining can create powerful barriers to innovation among incumbents. Outsiders and newcomers are therefore the main source of more radical innovation. In airlines, for example, it was Southwest Airlines, a 1971 start-up, that pioneered the 'no-frills' model, which has been successfully imitated by easyJet, RyanAir, and many others. Meanwhile in the UK the move to 'direct selling' of retail insurance was pioneered by DirectLine, a start-up backed by a bank which lacked a significant stake in the industry (Channon 1996). When incumbents do initiate change, as Midland Bank did with First Direct, its telephone banking service, this is typically through a new and separate organization.

As in manufacturing, incumbents are often slow to realize and react to the threat of these new players (Henderson and Clark 1990), and often do so unsuccessfully. For example, British Airways sought to respond to Ryan Air and easyJet by establishing Go, its own low cost carrier, but the venture failed and was acquired by easyJet. One reason why large incumbents find it difficult to respond is that they are highly bureaucratic and rule bound. For example, airline pilots have 'scope clauses', which limit the types of aircraft they can fly. These scope clauses effectively reinforce the status quo, and make it difficult for the major airlines to develop new business models using smaller aircraft.

Another powerful influence on the development of these systemic services is regulation. This takes many forms, but one example is IKEA, which has encountered difficulties with the UK's planning authorities in its desire to expand its network of large out-of-town stores. Frustrated by the rejection of planning applications, IKEA decided to move into smaller format, town centre stores, and to start selling its wares on the internet, both of which are forms of organizational/service delivery innovation.

Overall, systems firms tend to be professionally managed and have a significant interest in innovation. With the exception of telecommunications and computer software, innovating through R&D activities and centres is uncommon, and instead firms often rely on ad hoc innovation project teams to develop innovations. Because systems firms are often organized into functional silos it is often vital that these teams bring together people with the capacity to drive change in the various parts of the business. An emerging approach to innovation, which is gaining ground among systems firms, is service design, which is a customer centric approach to developing better service experiences. Virgin Atlantic, for example, has an in-house design team, which collaborates with external service design consultants, to enhance the experience they provide to their customers.

The recent crisis in the financial sector also highlights the interconnected nature of these businesses, and indeed the negative side of innovation, which may be advantageous for individual businesses, but not necessarily society as a whole.

Professional Service Firms

Professional service firms (PSFs), and indeed knowledge-intensive business services more generally, are a particularly dynamic and rapidly growing part of the service sector. Often highly creative and innovative, they also support their clients' innovative activities, and transfer technologies across a wide range of business fields. In short, they are vital creators, shapers, and carriers of technological, managerial, and organizational innovations.

PSFs are characterized by high proportions of professionally qualified staff and frequently use 'traditional' or *ad hoc* organizational structures (Mintzberg and McHugh 1985; Maister 1993). These organizations dominate industries such as law, accountancy, management consulting, architecture, and engineering consulting. Professional services firms survive by the skills and knowledge of their expert labour force, who deliver a range of specialized and often highly customized services to clients (Hitt *et al.* 2001; Teece 2003). PSFs are driven by the requirements of both new and existing clients, and often work through a series of discrete projects (Maister 1993). These projects usually involve direct interaction with clients and other organizations, leading to the co-production of knowledge with clients and other project partners (Gann and Salter 2000; Bettencourt *et al.* 2002; Dougherty 2004).

The ability to perform projects effectively is based on organizational knowledge, and PSFs have developed extensive operating routines to support their work, including project reviews, post-project reviews, team formation procedures, and knowledge management (KM) systems (Hansen *et al.* 1999; Sarvary 1999; Gann and Salter 2000; Lowendhal *et al.* 2001). These operating routines allow PSFs to offer a package of services that draw upon their internal knowledge and experience (Ofek and Sarvary 2001). However, much of the knowledge held by PSFs remains tacit, embedded in uncodified routines, and rooted in the firm's social context (Morris 2001; Dougherty 2004). In most PSFs, particularly those focusing on innovation and creativity, their human capital, which is developed through recruitment and the recursive practice of craft skills over time in different situations (Scott and Brown 1999; Constant 2000), is their key source of competitive advantage: it is unique, rare, and difficult to imitate (Barney 1991). The practice of professional knowledge requires 'artful competence'; learning how to apply the principles of the profession to unique situations, while making do with limited resources (Werr and Stjernberg 2003). Firms often rely on the ability of their employees to develop and nurture their own professional knowledge and networks (Dougherty 2004), and indeed in many PSFs it is the closeness of the interactions between skilled, experienced staff and clients that allows the firm to build what Teece (2002) calls 'relational assets'. Thus, human capital also underlies the two other critical resources of PSFs their reputation and relationships.

Indeed, considerable effort has been made to understand the significance of social capital and networks among professionals and within PSFs (Borgatti and Foster 2003; Brass *et al.* 2004; Cross and Parker 2004; Burt 2005). Obsfteld (2005), for example, explored the role of network position on an individual's involvement in innovation, finding that centrality and density in a network positively affects involvement. Other research has examined the impact of communication, friendship, trust, and hierarchy on shaping patterns of knowledge exchange among professionals (Cross *et al.* 2001; Cross and Sproull 2004; Haas and Hansen 2005). Studies have highlighted the key role of boundary spanners in shaping the performance of teams (Burt 2005), and have demonstrated the effect of individuals' social networks on their professional performance (Cummings and Cross 2003). Meanwhile, Lazega (2001) explores the tensions that exist within PSFs between senior and junior staff, and the often conflicting character of knowledge exchange. Haynes (Chapter 5, this volume) also evaluates the tensions inherent in forms of capital in PSFs.

The often project-based nature of their work can make the activities of PSFs appear highly episodic and ad hoc (Mintzberg and McHugh 1985). Project work involves highly differentiated and customized demands; clients negotiate the services required to meet their specific needs. This negotiation of expectations and the terms of the solution is an essential part of the 'generative dance' that leads to effective projects (Scott and Brown 1999). Thus, the knowledge and skills needed to perform projects can be highly specific and localized. Other projects may require general knowledge that will be applicable across many different projects. The fundamental challenge for these professional organizations is to translate project level learning into organizational capabilities (DeFillippi and Arthur 1998; Davies and Brady 2000, 2004; Gann and Salter 2000; Davies and Hobday 2005). Yet the project-based nature of their activities means organizations often struggle to learn cumulatively through projects, with key lessons rarely being fed back into the organization (Prencipe and Tell 2001).

To increase the effectiveness of their project performance, and to share knowledge across projects, many PSFs have invested substantially in KM (Gault and Foray 2003). Their approach to KM varies, however, with some investing heavily in IT systems to capture knowledge in documents and data, while others have introduced cultural change initiatives to encourage uncodified knowledge sharing within the organization (Nonaka and Takeuchi 1995; Hansen *et al.* 1999; Sarvary 1999; Cross *et al.* 2001; Argote *et al.* 2003). These KM systems are an increasingly important part of the infrastructure supporting innovation in PSFs, allowing them to capture knowledge from past projects and reuse this knowledge in current and future projects.

The work of PFSs spans different degrees of novelty and innovativeness. Much of their work involves projects that entail the relatively routine application of knowledge (e.g. routine conveyancing), whereas other projects may require new solutions. Some large professional services have attempted to develop repeatable solutions (Davies and Brady 2000), creating operating routines and practices that allow them to offer a configurable package of services to a wide range of customers. The development of repeatable solutions often involves the extensive use of KM systems or deliberate efforts to create service platforms.

Yet for many PSFs, repeat solutions offer low margins and uninteresting work, and instead explicitly target complex, non-routine projects that build capability and reputation, and that command higher fees. Arup, for example, a world leading design engineering firm, uses high profile projects to help maintain and enhance its reputation for solving challenging problems (Dodgson *et al.* 2005). These 'magnet' projects demonstrate to existing and prospective clients Arup's problem solving capabilities. They also help the firm attract and retain the best talent. For other PSFs, magnet projects can be millstones, as some clients who perceive that they have less complex problems avoid firms with a reputation for working on risky and difficult projects. They may be attracted instead to organizations with a track record for the effective delivery of less innovative projects. Thus, there is often market segmentation between different subtypes of PSF based on the types of work they engage in.

This discussion highlights the fundamental character of innovation in PSFs, including: the role of highly skilled labour and tacit knowledge in the creation and exploitation of new solutions; the importance of new organizational practices, such as the use of KM systems, in supporting the realization of new innovative opportunities; the 'generative dance' between clients and producers as new solutions are negotiated and co-produced between different actors; the key role of social networks in generating and supporting knowledge creation and exchange through brokerage and closure; and the 'ad hoc' or 'informal' organizational form of most PSFs.

Three Debates Concerning Innovation in Services

Having illustrated some of the variety among services, and innovation in services, we now explore three debates central to a broader understanding of innovation in services. The first concerns the measurement of innovative activities in services, and the connection between services and scientific research institutions, including universities. The second explores the protection of innovations, and how firms capture value or the returns to their innovative activities. The third examines the largely organizational character of innovation in services.

Accounting for Service Innovation, and Services' Links with the Science Base

One of the reasons why services are, or were thought to be innovation laggards is that they do, or at least report doing, relatively little R&D. Despite representing roughly three-quarters of economic activity in advanced economies, services account for less than a fifth of R&D expenditures within the OECD. There is, however, evidence that formal R&D is becoming more important in services. Until the early 1980s, service R&D accounted for less than 5% of total R&D in the USA, but by 2001, this increased to 39% (Howells 2009). The growth of services' R&D in the USA has been concentrated in software, professional, and technical services, and distribution and retail (NSB 2004). In many OECD countries, services R&D accounts for the fastest growing portion of the R&D system.

However, while R&D in services is growing, the significance of R&D for innovation is arguably declining, as innovation is being seen in increasingly broad terms. In the UK, only two-fifths of the firms that responded to the CBI-QinetiQ (2005) innovation survey agreed that investment in R&D is the best indicator of innovation activity, a proportion that fell to a third among service firms.

Overall, services are also relatively weakly connected to the key research institutions such as research-based universities and research institutes. Some services are, however, well connected. Tether and Tajar (2008a), for example, found that R&D enterprises and engineering consultancies are the most likely of all firms to have links with universities and public research organizations. These firms appear to play a significant role in both creating and diffusing knowledge within the national system of innovation. Meanwhile, non-technical services, including financial and business services, were the least likely of all firms to have these links, indicating most service firms are poorly connected to the UK's national system of innovation. There are of course other, indirect links. For example, many physical science graduates have skills that are of immense value in financial services, hence the high number of physicists who work in the City of London. But the limited integration between services and universities is not only evident in the UK. The US National Academy of Engineering (2003a and b) assessed the impact of academic research on performance in five industries, including two service industries: transport, distribution and logistics services, and financial services. They found that despite significant opportunities, the service industries studied were poorly connected to academic research, and that there is 'an underdeveloped interface' between research universities and service industries. The NAE also observed that the contributions of the social and behavioural sciences to industry have been greatly undervalued, and concluded: '[S]ervices industries represent a significant source of opportunity for university-industry inter-action...[but] the academic research enterprise has not focused on or been organized to meet the needs of service businesses' (NAE 2003a: 8). We consider that this remains the case in the UK and elsewhere.

Protecting and Profiting From Innovation in Services

The ability to appropriate or capture the benefits of an innovation is a crucial driver of investments in innovation. Firms can use a variety of mechanisms to protect their innovations, ranging from patents to trade secrets. Research on manufacturing firms has shown that that informal means of protection, such as secrecy, are generally more important than legal mechanisms, such as patents (Levin *et al*. 1987; Cohen *et al*. 2000; Arundel 2001). Service industries are even more strongly oriented to the use of informal methods of protection, such as secrecy, complexity, and lead times, in part because legal mechanisms such as patents cannot be applied.

As they cannot be protected by patents or other formal intellectual property (IP) rights, service innovations are in principal open to being copied, which leads to the argument that if services cannot protect their innovations against copying, they cannot appropriate the returns to innovations, and therefore have little incentive to innovate. In reality, the weakness of IP protection in services may be overemphasized. Overall, it is more likely that the absence of strong IP protection reshapes the pattern of innovation in services rather an inhibiting it. In particular, the weakness of IP protection is likely to: (1) encourage more continuous forms of innovation—rather than innovation in big jumps, which is the archetypal model of innovation in manufacturing; (2) encourage innovation involving 'complementarities' between technologies, skills and organizational competencies, and enhance the significance of controlling complementary assets, such as distribution channels, marketing, and branding (Teece 1986)—for example, an innovation that is easily copied is the 'home delivery' of pizzas or other fast food, yet Domino's Pizza has been able to retain a significant share of this business through its efficient operating routines, reputation, and branding; and (3) encourage innovation in networks, involving customers, suppliers, and competitors. Many service activities are highly complex, involving a wide range of different organizational practices that may span many different organizations. These practices may be very difficult to imitate.

Two areas of huge controversy are the patenting of computer software and of business methods. A review of whether patents should be granted for computer software and for ways of doing business was conducted by the UK Patent Office in 2001. This concluded that business methods should remain unpatentable in the UK. A major fear is that business system patents will become pervasive in the business landscape, creating inefficiencies and dampening effects without a corresponding increase in innovation. In the European Union and Canada business methods have not been patentable, whereas certain business methods can be patented in the USA, Japan, and Australia.

Technological and Organizational Innovation in Services

There can be no question that information and communication technologies (ICT), such as the telephone, computer, electronic data interchange, and the internet have been fundamental to a great deal of innovation in services. Some services firms, notably computer software providers and telecommunications firms are at the forefront of the production of new information technologies. As consumers or users of these technologies, service firms also account for the great majority of all firms' investments in information technologies, with the systems firms such as large banks, airlines, and integrated retailers in the vanguard. As innovation in services is often closely connected with how services are delivered, ICT offers enormous potential for innovation, as the case of Direct Line illustrated earlier. Using German data, Licht and Moch (1999) found investments in ICT to be pervasive across all sectors and all types of innovators. These technologies are not only important for allowing service firms to change their services channels and make their activities more efficient, they also offer the opportunity for existing firms to outsource many functions previously undertaken in-house. Indeed, the expansion of services in the economy is partially explained by firms outsourcing tasks to specialized service businesses. It follows that ICT has been fundamental, not only to technological innovation in services, but also to the organizational innovations that have often accompanied or followed these technological changes.

Notable also is that it has been higher skilled workers who have been able to make the most of computers and other ICT in terms of enhancing their productivity (Bresnahan 1999; Bresnahan *et al.* 2002). And the existence of these hard to replicate complementarities between investments in ICTs and the organizational arrangements through which these are used is the source of sustained performance difference between firms and countries.

Overall, innovation in services is characterized by several patterns, including: a high degree of importance attached to organizational change and an open and distributed model of innovation. The importance of organizational change in services is shown by the results of the European Innobarometer survey of 2002, which asked firms to identify their main 'innovation orientations' (Tether 2005; Tether and Tajar 2008b). Whereas the majority of manufacturing firms claimed to be oriented to product and/or process innovation, service firms were much more likely to be orientated to organizational change. Indeed, more than a third of service firms claimed this was their only innovation orientation. Meanwhile, in terms of their perceived 'strengths at innovation', services with an organizational orientation to innovation placed greater emphasis on the skills of their workforces and their co-operation practices within and beyond the supply chain. By contrast, manufacturers were more likely to emphasize both R&D/technical advancement and the efficiency of production as their strengths at innovation.

These findings support the contention that services emphasize the 'soft-side' of innovation, in which people and co-operative practices are brought to the fore, with less emphasis on 'hard' technology, especially in the form of new or advanced technologies. In other words, they emphasize 'social technologies' rather than 'physical technologies' (Nelson and Sampat 2001). This is not to say that 'physical technologies' are unimportant, only that they need to be combined with skills (including non-technical skills) and organizational practices. This is a point that is highlighted in a study of how close interactive working between airline pilots and air traffic controllers, coupled with the development of organizational arrangements to enhance co-operation, has significantly enhanced the runway capacity at severely congested airports, such as London Heathrow and Frankfurt (Tether and Metcalfe 2003).

The organizational basis of innovation in services is reflected in the intimate connection between the different forms of innovation—product, process, and organizational—in services. The example of Automated Teller Machines in retail banking illustrates this point. What type of innovation was the ATM—a product?, process?, or organizational innovation? The answer is all three. Hipp *et al.* (2000) have argued that in general in services there tends to be a much closer relationship between the various forms of innovation—product, process, and organizational—than is typically the case in manufacturing. This suggests there are often strong complementarities between different types of innovation in services and therefore, to be most effective, innovation requires simultaneous, or near simultaneous changes in many different aspects of the firm (Milgrom and Roberts 1995; Laursen and Mahnke 2001; Laursen and Foss 2003).

Organizational innovation also often stretches beyond individual firms, and much innovation in services is distributed across networks of firms. In recent years, there has been an enormous growth in literature on innovation networks, 'systems of innovation', 'distributed innovation processes', and 'open innovation' (Chesbrough 2003; Coombs *et al.* 2003; Brass *et al.* 2004; Von Hippel 2005). This highlights the interactive character of much contemporary innovation. Much of this research has been spurred by the adoption of a range of new practices by large US firms, such as P&G, IBM, and Intel, and the development of new 'markets for technology', such as Yet2.com or

Innocentive (Arora *et al.* 2001). In addition, the growth of open source software has contributed to an increasing focus on open or distributed forms of innovation (von Hippel and von Krogh 2003).

Arguably, open forms of innovation have long been the norm in many service activities, especially among PSFs, that act as brokers, bringing knowledge and ideas from one place to another (Burt 2005). Bessant and Rush (1995), for example, discussed the significance of consultants as both producers and carriers of knowledge, while Hargadon's (1998) study IDEO shows how that firm draws on knowledge from a whole variety of industries to provide creative solutions based on new combinations of existing knowledge. Many service firms have been leaders in the development of open innovation approaches, effectively harnessing external partners to innovate. However, for many service firms, especially PSFs, there are already tight and overlapping external relations with clients, suppliers, and other professionals. In these environments, projects typically span different organizations to achieve a specific task (DeFillippi and Arthur 1998). The extent and nature of innovation in services, including the extent to which it is open and draws on complementarities between technological and organizational changes, is the subject of ongoing research.

Conclusions

Innovation in services tends to be more continuous rather than occasional, which points to the importance of continuous learning and adaptation. By contrast, radical innovation in manufacturing is associated with occasional periods of retraining and reorganization, with intervening periods of stability based around essentially fixed skills and organizational forms. We should not, however, create the impression that there is a 'services pattern' of innovation, which is distinct from the 'manufacturing pattern'. Neither of these sectors exhibits a single pattern of innovation, and there is a great deal of overlap between the behaviours of service and manufacturing firms. In part this is because many manufacturers have developed service functions, while some services are structured around 'products' and are more akin to manufacturers than highly relational service providers. Ideas are also 'borrowed' back and forth. For example, the Just-in-Time system that was so effectively developed by Toyota and other Japanese manufacturers has its origins in supermarket logistics. What we can say is that there is a mode of innovation that is focused around organizational change, often undertaken in conjunction with technological change, which has a strong emphasis on social technologies and practices, such as teamwork and problem solving. This is especially prominent in services. We are also witnessing the rise of new combinations of services and manufacturing, as firms seek to reposition themselves in the value chain (Davies and Hobday 2005). The blurring boundaries between services and manufacturing makes it difficult to think of two different 'worlds of innovation'.

As we have seen, some service sectors are thought to be 'locked in' to a vicious cycle of low performance and stagnation. These sectors still account for a substantial portion of the service sector and the ability of firms in these activities to break out of this cycle often requires external intervention through regulation and/or competition. At the same time, we see the growing presence of large-scale, systems firms, which are able to combine expertise in operations with extensive adaptation and innovation. These firms often overwhelm traditional service providers. They are able to systematically develop and reshape their practices, to improve the effectiveness and efficiency of their operations, and are responsible for an increasing share of productivity growth. By contrast, PSFs rely on informal or ad hoc organizational forms and expert knowledge to address the often bespoke problems of their clients. These firms play a central role in the innovation system, acting as brokers across different industries and firms. Among PSFs, there are often tensions between repeat and unique solutions, and some firms focus on novelty while others focus on replication.

Although services represent an increasing share of formal R&D, we still have poor measures of innovative activities in services. Moreover, to date little research has explored the mechanisms used by service firms to capture the returns to their innovative efforts. Overall, an empirical toolkit for measuring and mapping innovation is still to be fully developed to completely capture and understand innovation in services. This incomplete understanding also hinders the development of policy towards services, and biases attempts to describe the innovation process in the modern firm, which arguably overemphasizes the importance of physical over social technologies.

References

Arora, A., Fosfuri, A., and Gambardella, A. (2001). *Markets for Technology: the economics of innovation and corporate strategy*. Cambridge, MA: The MIT Press.

Arundel, A. (2001). The relative effectiveness of patents and secrecy for appropriation. *Research Policy*, 30, 611–624.

Baden-Fuller, C. and Winter, S.G. (2005). *Replicating Organizational Knowledge: principles or templates?* Papers on Economics and Evolution 2005-15. Jena: Max Planck Institute of Economics, Evolutionary Economics Group.

Banaszak-Holl, J., Berta, W., Bowman, D., Baum, J.A.C., and Mitchell, W. (2002). The rise of human service chains: antecedents to acquisitions and their effects on the quality of care in U.S. nursing homes. *Managerial and Decision Economics*, **23**, 261–282.

Barney, J. (1991). Firm resources and sustained competitive advantage. *Journal of Management*, **77**, 99–120.

Barras, R. (1986). Towards a theory of innovation in services, *Research Policy*, **15**(4), 161–173.

Baum, J. (1996). Organizational ecology. In: *Handbook of Organizational Studies*, Clegg, S., Hardy, C., and Nord, W. (Ed.), pp. 77–114. London: Sage.

Baum, J. and Greve, H.R. (Ed.). (2001). *Multiunit Organization and Multimarket Strategy*. Oxford: JAI/Elsevier.

Bessant, J. and Rush, H. (1995). Building bridges for innovation—The role of consultants in technology transfer. *Research Policy*, **24**, 97–114.

Bettencourt, L., Ostrom, A., Brown, S.W., and Roundtree, R.I. (2002). Client co-production in knowledge-intensive business services. *California Management Review*, **44**(4): 100–128.

Borgatti, S.P. and Foster, P.C. (2003). The network paradigm in organizational research: a review and typology. *Journal of Management*, **29**, 991–1013.

Brass, D.J., Galaskiewicz, J., Greve, H.R., and Tsai, W.P. (2004). Taking stock of networks and organizations: a multilevel perspective. *Academy of Management Journal*, **47**(6), 795–817.

Bresnahan, T.F. (1999). Computerisation and wage dispersion: an analytical reinterpretation, *Economic Journal*, **109**, 390–415.

Bresnahan, T.F., Brynjolfsson, E., and Hitt, L.M. (2002). Information technology, workplace organization and the demand for skilled labour: firm level evidence. *Quarterly Journal of Economics*, **117**, 339–376.

Burt, R.S. (2005). *Brokerage & Closure: an Introduction to Social Capital*. Oxford: Oxford University Press.

CBI-Qinetiq (2006). *Innovation Survey, 2005*. London: Confederation of British Industry.

Channon, D. (1996). Direct Line Insurance PLC: new approaches to the insurance market. In: *Strategic Innovation*, Baden Fuller, C. and Pitt, M. (Ed.), pp. 55–74. London: Routledge.

Chesbrough, H.W. (2003). *Open Innovation: the new imperative for creating and profiting from technology*. Boston, MA, Harvard Business School Press.

Cohen, W.M. and Levinthal, D.A. (1990). Absorptive capacity: a new perspective on learning and innovation. *Administrative Science Quarterly*, **35**, 128–152.

Cohen, W.M., Nelson, R.R., and Walsh, J.P. (2000). Protecting their intellectual assets: appropriability conditions and why U.S. manufacturing firms patent (or not). NBER Working Paper Series. Cambridge, MA: National Bureau of Economic Research.

Constant, E. (2000). Recursive practice and the evolution of technological knowledge. In: *Technological Innovation as an Evolutionary Process*, Ziman, Z. (Ed.), pp. 219–230. Cambridge: Cambridge University Press.

Coombs, R., Harvey, M., and Tether, B.S. (2003). Analysing distributed processes of provision and innovation. *Industrial and Corporate Change*, **12**, 1125–1155.

Cross, R. and Parker, A. (2004). *The Hidden Power of Social Networks*. Boston, MA: Harvard Business School Press.

Cross, R. and Sproull, L. (2004). More than an answer: information relationships for actionable knowledge. *Organization Science*, 15(4), 446–462.

Cross, R., Parker, A., Prusak, A., and Borgatti, S.P. (2001). Knowing what we know: supporting knowledge creation and sharing in social networks. *Organizational Dynamics*, 30(2), 100–120.

Cummings, J.N. and Cross, R. (2003). Structural properties of work groups and their consequences for performance. *Social Networks*, 25, 197–210.

Davies, A. and Brady, T. (2000). Organizational capabilities and learning in complex product systems: towards repeatable solutions. *Research Policy*, 29(7–8), 931–953.

Davies, A. and Brady, T. (2004). Building project capabilities: from exploratory to exploitative learning. *Organization Studies*, 26(9), 1601–1621.

Davies, A. and Hobday, M. (2005). *The Business of Projects: managing innovation in complex products and systems*. Cambridge: Cambridge University Press.

DeFillippi, R. and Arthur, M. (1998). Paradox in project-based enterprise: the case of film making. *California Management Review*, 40(2), 125–139.

Dodgson, M., Gann, D. and Salter, A. (2005). *Think, Play, Do: markets, technology and organization*. London: Oxford University Press.

Dougherty, D. (2004). Organizing practices in services: capturing practice-based knowledge for innovation. *Strategic Organization*, 2, 35–64.

Evangelista, R. (2000). Sectoral patterns of technological change in services, *Economics of Innovation and New Technology*, 9(3), 183–222.

Finegold, D. and Soskice, D. (1988). The failure of training in Britain: analysis and prescription. *Oxford Review of Economic Policy*, **Autumn**, 21–51.

Gann, D. and Salter, A. (2000). Innovation in project-based, service-enhanced firms: the construction of complex products and systems. *Research Policy*, 29, 955–972.

Gault, F. and Foray, D. (2003). *Measuring Knowledge Management in the Business Sector: First steps*. Paris, OECD.

Goos, M. and Manning, A. (2003). McJobs and MacJobs: the growing polarization of work in Britain. In *The State of Working Britain 2003*, Dickens, R., Gregg, P., and Wadsworth, J. (Ed.) Palgrave-MacMillan, Basingstoke, pp. 71–85.

Haas, M.R. and Hansen, M.T. (2005). When using knowledge can hurt performance: the value of organizational capabilities in a management consultancy company. *Strategic Management Journal*, 26, 1–24.

Hansen, M.T., Nohria, N., and Tierney, T. (1999). Whats your strategy for managing knowledge. *Harvard Business Review*, **March-April**, 106–116.

Hargadon, A. (1998). Firms as knowledge brokers: lessons in pursuing continuous innovation, *California Management Review*, 40, 209–227.

Harvey, M. (1999). Innovation and Competition in UK Supermarkets. CRIC Briefing Paper No. 3. ESRC Centre for Innovation and Competition, University of Manchester, Manchester, UK.

Henderson, R.M. and Clark, K.B. (1990). Architectural innovation—the reconfiguration of product technologies and the failure of established firms. *Administrative Science Quarterly*, **35**, 9–30.

Hipp, C., Tether, B.S., and Miles, I.D. (2000). The incidence and effects of innovation in services: evidence from Germany. *International Journal of Innovation Management*, **4**(4), 417–454.

von Hippel, E. (2005). *Democratizing Innovation*. Cambridge, MA: The MIT Press.

von Hippel, E. and von Krogh, G. (2003). Open source software and the 'private-collective' innovation model: issues for organization science. *Organization Science*, **14**(2), 208–223.

Hitt, M., Bierman, L., Shimizu, K., and Kochhar, K.R. (2001). Direct and moderating effects of human capital on strategy and performance in professional service firms: a resource-based perspective. *Academy of Management Journal*, **44**, 13–28.

Howells, J. (2009). Services R&D. IPTS Working Paper on Corporate R&D and Innovation, No. 05/2005.

Laursen, K. and Foss, N. (2003). New HRM practices, complementarities, and the impact on innovation performance. *Cambridge Journal of Economics*, **27**(2), 243–263.

Laursen, K. and Mahnke, V. (2001). Knowledge strategies, firm types, and complementarity in human-resource practices. *Journal of Management and Governance*, **5**, 1–27.

Lazega, E. (2001). *The Collegial Phenomenon*. Oxford: Oxford University Press.

Levin, R.C., Klevorick, A.K., Nelson, R.R., Winter, S.G., Gilbert, R., and Griliches, Z. (1987). Appropriating the returns from industrial-research and development. *Brookings Papers on Economic Activity*, **3**, 783–831.

Licht, G. and Moch, D. (1999). Innovation and information technology in services. *Canadian Journal of Economics*, **32**(2), 363–383.

Lowendhal, B.R., Revang, O., Fosstenlokken, S.M. (2001). Knowledge and value creation in professional service firms: a framework for analysis. *Human Relations*, **54**(7), 911–931.

Maister, D. (1993). *Managing Professional Service Firms*. New York: Free Press.

Mason, G. (2005). In search of high value added production: are skills the vital ingredient? Report for the Department for Education and Skills Project on Employer Demand for Skills and High Value Added Product Strategies. London: National Institute of Economic and Social Research.

Milgrom, P.R. and Roberts, B.M. (1995). Complementarities and fit: strategy, structure and organizational change in manufacturing. *Journal of Accounting and Economics*, **19**, 179–208.

Mintzberg, H. and McHugh, A. (1985). Strategy formulation in an adhocracy. *Administrative Science Quarterly*, **30**, 160–197.

Miozzo, M. and Soete, L. (2001). Internationalization of services: a technological perspective. *Technological Forecasting and Social Change*, **67**(2/3), 159–185.

Morris, T. (2001). Asserting property rights: knowledge codificiation in the professional service firm. *Human Relations*, **54**, 54–71.

National Academy of Engineering (2003). *The Impact of Academic Research on Industrial Performance*. Washington DC: National Academies Press.

Nelson, R.R. and Sampat, B.N. (2001). Making sense of institutions as a factor shaping economic performance. *Journal of Economic Behavior and Organization*, **44**, 31–54.

Nonaka, I. and Takeuchi, H. (1995). *The Knowledge-Creating Company*. Oxford: Oxford University Press.

NSB (2004). *Science and Technology Indicators 2004*. Washington: National Science Foundation.

Ofek, E. and Sarvary, M. (2001). Leveraging the customer base: creating competitive advantage through knowledge management. *Management Science*, **47**(11), 1441–1456.

Pavitt, K. (1984). Sectoral patterns of technical change: towards a taxonomy and a theory. *Research Policy*, **13**(6), 343–373.

Prencipe, A. and Tell, F. (2001). Inter-project learning: processes and outcomes of knowledge codification in project-based firms. *Research Policy*, **30**(9), 1373–1394.

Sarvary, M. (1999). Knowledge management and competition in the consulting industry. *California Management Review*, **41**(2), 95–107.

Scott, C. and Brown, J.S. (1999). Bridging epistemologies: the generative dance between organizational knowledge and organizational knowing. *Organization Science*, **10**(4), 381–400.

Stinchcombe, A.L. (1965). Social structure and organization. In: *Handbook of Organizations*, March, J. (Ed.), pp. 142–193. Chicago, IL: Rand McNally.

Sundbo, J. and Gallouj, F. (2001). Innovation as a loosely coupled system in services. In: *Innovation Systems in the Service Economy: Measurement and case study analysis*, Metcalfe, J.S. and Miles, I.D. (Ed.), pp. 43–68. Boston, MA: Kluwer Academic Publishers.

Teece, D. (1986). Profitting from technological innovation: implications for integration collaboration, licencing and public policy. *Research Policy*, **15**, 285–305.

Teece, D.J. (2002). *Managing Intellectual Capital*. Oxford: Oxford University Press.

Teece, D.J. (2003). Expert talent and the design of (professional services) firms. *Industrial and Corporate Change*, **12**(4): 895–916.

Tether, B.S. (2003). The sources and aims of innovation in services: variety within and between sectors. *Economics of Innovation and New Technology*, **12**(6), 1051–1081.

Tether, B.S. (2005). Do services innovate (differently)? Insights from the European Innobarometer Survey. *Industry and Innovation*, **12**(2), 153–184.

Tether, B.S. and Metcalfe, J.S. (2003). Horndal at Heathrow? Capacity creation through co-operation and system evolution. *Industrial and Corporate Change*, **12**(3), 437–476.

Tether, B.S. and Tajar, A. (2008a). Beyond industry-university links: sourcing knowledge for innovation from consultants, private research organisations and the public science base. *Research Policy*, **37**(6–7), 1079–1095.

Tether, B.S. and Tajar, A. (2008b). The Organisational cooperation mode of innovation and its prominence amongst European service firms. *Research Policy*, **37**(4), 720–739.

Werr, A. and Stjernberg, T. (2003). Exploring management consulting firms as knowledge systems. *Organization Studies,* **24**(6), 881–908.

Wilson, R. and Hogarth, T. (2004). Skills in England, 2003. Report for the Skills and Learning Council, Institute of Employment Research, Warwick University, Coventry.

10

Offshoring and Outsourcing of Administrative and Technical Services: A Modularity Perspective

Martin Spring, Luis Araujo, and Katy Mason

Introduction: The Service Offshore Outsourcing Phenomenon

The offshore outsourcing of administrative and technical services is rapidly becoming widespread in business practice, 'the newest deepening of globalization', according to Kenney *et al.* (2009: 888). The 2011 World Investment Report (UNCTAD 2011) is devoted to 'non-equity modes of international production', i.e. international production by modes other than foreign direct investment, such as contract manufacturing, services outsourcing, contract farming, franchising, licensing, and management contracts. According to this report, at a conservative estimate, the international trade in IT services and business process outsourcing (BPO) is at least $90–100 billion, or about 5% of total non-equity mode production (about $2 trillion). By way of comparison, as a global sector, it has about half the value of contract manufacturing of automotive parts (UNCTAD 2011: 133). The growth in outsourced models of international production is noted in the preface to the report by Ban Ki-moon, Secretary-General of the United Nations:

> Increasingly, transnational corporations are engaging with developing and transition economies through a broadening array of production and investment models, such as contract manufacturing and farming, service outsourcing, franchising and licensing. (UNCTAD 2011: iii)

As such, service outsourcing is attracting the attention of researchers across the management disciplines, including international business, operations management, information systems management, and general management. The focus on services, and particularly on knowledge-intensive services, adds an extra dimension to well-established analyses of the offshoring of manufacturing. It has become increasingly prevalent for a number of reasons. Perhaps most obvious is the availability of 'commodity bandwidth' (Kenney *et al.* 2009: 891). For example, Metters and Verma (2008) paint a telling historical picture of the striking capacity, speed, and cost improvements in contemporary information and communications technology; between 1996 and 2004, the data-carrying capacity of lines beneath the Atlantic and Pacific Oceans grew by factors of seventy-eight and forty-two, respectively. Even between 2001 and 2002, the capacity of lines from the USA to India grew by a factor of seven (Metters and Verma 2008). More recent data indicate an annual growth rate from 2007 to 2011 of about 50% per year in international internet capacity, and a sixfold increase in that same period, to reach 55 Tbps (i.e. 55×10^{12} bytes per second)[1] (Telegeography 2011). A second important factor has been the growth in availability of highly-skilled and highly-educated labour in relatively low-cost countries (Manning *et al.* 2008; Lewin *et al.* 2009).

From the demand side, organizations in developed economies have increasingly looked for ways to focus their investment and management attention on fewer and fewer activities. Since the early 1990s, approaches such as total quality management and business process re-engineering (Hammer and Champy 1993) have provided a catalyst for large firms to reappraise the efficiency of their internal processes and the scope of their activities. Innovations in performance measurement, such as benchmarking, quality measures, and activity-based costing, provide firms with finer-grained metrics (Zenger and Hesterly 1997), which facilitated and informed radical rethinking of organizational processes. The unbundling of corporate hierarchies prompted by such reappraisals led to the outsourcing of processes considered as inefficient or marginal to success, and, given the opening up of supply markets for technical services and the development of the necessary ICT infrastructure, this outsourcing could increasingly be international. The genesis of offshore outsourcing in techniques such as business process re-engineering is evident in the terminology used, not least by the OECD—BPO.

Some accounts of this process of restructuring seem to suggest that a pre-existing set of activities may simply be 'fine-sliced' and redistributed organizationally and geographically:

> The value chain is no longer divided into large groupings such as R&D, Production, or Marketing. The functions and operations within each category can be sliced into dozens or hundreds of sub-activities. For each sub-activity or operation the

question then asked is where to perform it and whether to perform it within the firm, or outsource it. (Contractor *et al.* 2010: 1419)

A rather subtler treatment is provided by Sako (2006), who reminds us that offshore outsourcing of services is often no simple matter of picking up an existing set of activities and transplanting them to another organization and another location, but may often be part of more fundamental unbundling of administrative and technical work. These efforts have led to a variety of outcomes. In many instances, we have seen the rise of 'shared services' (Merrifield *et al.* 2008), i.e. back-office processes formerly carried out in each division of a large firm, which are aggregated, standardized, and provided to all divisions from one service centre, which remains in-house. Procurement, HR support, and other such services are typically involved. With accurate cost drivers in place, restructured activity centres can be benchmarked against external suppliers. Highly efficient units may be encouraged or required to provide external services, or even be spun off as self-sufficient businesses in their own right. For example, the UK-based outsourced service provider Vertex began in 1996 as a shared service centre within the then newly created United Utilities water and electricity supplier. Many of the large road freight and logistics companies began as in-house logistics operations within manufacturing and retail firms. Alternatively, such unbundling may be undertaken precisely to aggregate and standardize with a view to outsourcing (Kakabadse and Kakabadse 2002). As further codification of productive knowledge takes place and standard ICT enterprise packages become more widely diffused, some writers anticipate that common organizational processes will lose their proprietary character and become commoditized (Davenport 2005).

Against this background, the purpose of this chapter is to outline some of the treatments of offshore outsourcing prevalent across at least some of the management literatures, and to suggest that an approach based on the 'modularity theory of the firm' can shed helpful light on the complexities of offshore outsourcing practice. In some senses, the problem we examine here is the one identified by Graz and Niang (2011):

> The ability to develop a global market of services is not only a matter of technology or economic logic. It also supposes an ability to define the gradual decomposition of complex work into simpler work sequences. The more fragmented the nature of the labour and consumption processes, the more [the] requirements to codify them. (6)

Offshore outsourcing of services is something that, evidently, more and more firms are finding ways to do. However, this does not mean that it is merely a question of 'fine-slicing the firm' (Contractor *et al.* 2010: 1423).

Treatments of Offshore Outsourcing of Services in (Some of) the Management Disciplines

The growing prevalence of offshore outsourcing of services has been reflected in the publication of several special issues in leading journals across various fields: *MIS Quarterly* and *Journal of Operations Management* in 2008, *Journal of International Business Studies* in 2009, and *Journal of Management Studies* in 2010. All these special issues have dealt specifically with administrative, technical, 'professional', or 'high value-added' services.

The dominant theoretical framework for the analysis of outsourcing within management and organization studies over the past thirty years has been transaction cost economics (TCE). Regardless of geography, TCE's project has been to determine the appropriate governance mechanism—market, firm, or 'hybrid'—given characteristics of the activity to be undertaken (Williamson 1979). Moreover, the international business field has based much of its analysis of the appropriate model of production for the multinational firm on TCE, based on the principle that various additional sources of asset specificity, uncertainty, and sources of opportunism arising from the international nature of the production alter the calculation of the most efficient governance structure in transaction cost terms (Buckley and Casson 1976; although see Buckley and Chapman 1997 on the measurement problem). In relatively recent studies of offshore outsourcing of services in, for example, the operations management literature, this view still predominates (Ellram *et al.* 2008; Stratman 2008). Such work draws attention to the risks associated with investment in specific assets and the supposed attendant hold-up problems under the assumption of opportunistic behaviour by suppliers. Services, especially knowledge-intensive or higher value-added services, are presumed to accentuate these problems of risk and opportunism because they are 'intangible' and therefore difficult to monitor in respect of quality. A quotation from a recent paper in this vein illustrates: 'When a firm outsources services it should expect to have significant potential for overpayment and under-servicing' (Ellram *et al.* 2008: 157). Outsourcing internationally and across large distances is understood to add to these risks. Similarly, in the information systems (IS) literature, King and Torkzadeh comment, in their introduction to the recent *MIS Quarterly* special issue that, among the papers presented: 'the most commonly applied theoretical lens was transaction cost economics' (King and Torkzadeh 2008: 205–206).

TCE has, of course, been subjected to sustained critique (e.g. Ghoshal and Moran 1996) and its unproblematized use in international business has waned. Buckley and Lessard (2005), for example, see it as most strongly associated with internalization theory and international joint ventures in the 1970s and 1980s. Furthermore, it seems that the practice of many organizations flies in the face of the predictions made by TCE, in that activities that would appear to be subject to huge potential opportunism are nevertheless outsourced (Lewis and Roehrich 2011). For example, Lewin and Peeters (2006) note that the extent of outsourced offshoring of engineering services in their survey—62% outsourced versus 38% captive (i.e. in-house)—is somewhat surprising, being that engineering might be considered a relatively critical, knowledge-intensive activity. TCE would suggest that only the most 'routinized intellectual labour' (Learner and Storper 2001: 659) would be managed in this way; clearly that is not the case in practice.

As part of the rise of the resource-based view, Kogut and Zander (1992, 1993) demonstrate theoretically and empirically that the internalization decision in the multinational corporation is much less determined by concerns about reducing risks of opportunism, and much more to do with the ease or difficulty with which complex knowledge can be codified and transferred for the market mechanism to be used in place of the firm. This builds on the early work of Teece, who demonstrated the importance of tacit knowledge transfer in such situations (Teece 1976, 1977). Kogut and Zander, therefore, see 'the firm as a repository of social knowledge that structures cooperative action' and this conception 'lies at the foundation of an evolutionary theory of the multinational corporation' (Kogut and Zander 1993: 627)—in particular, a theory of the *boundaries* of the multinational corporation. Of course, the TCE and knowledge-based arguments for the boundaries of the firm can be applied to any firm, multinational or not. However, the social, cultural, political, and geographical distance involved in the international setting heighten the supposed difficulties—difficulties of opportunism under a TCE analysis and of knowledge codification, transfer, and application under an evolutionary analysis such as that advocated by Kogut and Zander (1993).

If the TCE and evolutionary approaches are mainly concerned with different ways of explaining the boundaries of firms, others are more concerned with co-ordination *between* firms. For example, work in the IS offshoring literature examines collaboration and co-ordination mechanisms by which potential difficulties arising from the hierarchical relationship between user and provider (captive or outsourced) may be mitigated (Levina and Vaast 2008; Olsson *et al.* 2008). The focus on inter-firm co-ordination rather than, or at least as well as, opportunism has a strong pedigree in the IS literature (Clemons *et al.* 1993).

Determining the Activities to be Outsourced or Offshored

Many of the themes discussed above—when to outsource/offshore (TCE), how to design the service delivery system (operations management) and how best to co-ordinate with the supplier (IS)—assume an ability to determine *ex ante* what it is that is to be outsourced and or offshored. For example: 'service processes need to be seen as potentially de-coupled' (Metters and Verma 2008: 146); 'the value proposition of these standard services is generally well understood' (Stratman 2008: 278). The fallacy of this type of assumption was evident to Kogut and Zander (1993: 626):

> The question posed above [why economic activity should be organized within a firm] presumes that the underlying knowledge can be packaged and transferred at a cost. It cannot always be.

Much more recently, and with recourse to 'interdependency theory', Kumar *et al.* (2008) suggest that the 'stickiness' of the knowledge involved in a task will determine whether it can be subdivided into work segments that can be carried out independently of one another or transferred 'lock, stock and barrel', 'encapsulated and intact' (Kumar *et al.* 2008: 660), to the offshore site. Even this view presupposes an ability to assess the extent and nature of the 'stickiness' of the knowledge involved.

Our analysis, then, is concerned with ways to understand how and why activities may be broken up for the purposes of offshore outsourcing, and what the implications of this may be for the boundaries of firms and the nature of relationships between them. In particular, we use the notion of modularity, which is now explained.

Approaches to Modularity

Modularity has been studied in operations management and related fields from a variety of perspectives for at least forty-five years. One theme has been that modularity is a way to design products and organize processes so that variety might be achieved in the end product (and the work has been mostly about products, rather than services) without the additional cost associated with high-variety process types such as job shops and small batch manufacturing. Work in this vein includes Starr (1965), Pine (1993), Ulrich (1995), Sanchez and Mahoney (1996), and Forza and Salvador (2002). In the automotive industry, modularity was revealed in greater detail as part of the International Motor Vehicle Project (Womack *et al.* 1990), and has been a theme of subsequent work in the sector (e.g. Doran 2003; Sako 2004). The particular conjunction of modular design, outsourcing, and novel approaches to co-location in the sector (particularly in the Brazilian context) was the subject of a flurry of work in the mid-1990s (Collins *et al.* 1997; Marx 1997).

Others have looked to modular approaches to reveal more general principles at work. With their different emphases, but similar themes, Baldwin and Clark (1997, 2006, 2008) and Langlois (Langlois and Robertson 1995; Langlois 2002, 2006) have developed what Langlois refers to ('lavishly', according to him) as the 'modularity theory of the firm'. This sees modularity not as a rather grossly self-evident approach to product design that may have implications for the organization and management of supply networks, but as a much more general and pervasive principle explaining the organization of productive activity of any sort. As we have discussed at greater length elsewhere (Araujo and Spring 2006; Spring and Araujo 2009), Baldwin and Clark (2006) propose the idea of mundane transaction costs (MTCs) as a way to explain where transactions between organizations, as opposed to transfers *within* organizations, take place in a system of production activities. MTCs are the costs of defining[2] what is to be sold, counting the units to be sold, and compensating the provider. They are termed 'mundane' as a (somewhat mischievous) contrast with Williamson's notion of transaction costs, which are based on 'intriguing…stories about guileful trading partners and expensive assets placed at risk' (Langlois 2006: 1398). Williamson's transaction costs are those arising from efforts to forestall 'hold-up' problems between trading partners in a market transaction, problems that arise in turn because of asset specificity and opportunism. Other more routine or mundane concerns attract less attention. As Kogut and Zander (1993: 626) summarized their critique of TCE (albeit for rather different reasons): 'Hazard of the market need not be consequential in this calculation'.

In effect, this examination of MTCs subjects to closer and more critical scrutiny Williamson's claim that a 'transaction occurs when a good or service is transferred across a technologically separable interface. One stage of activity terminates and another begins.' (Williamson 1985: 1). MTCs are one way of working out why a 'technologically separable interface' occurs at one point but not another: Baldwin and Clark (2006) suggest that transactions occur where MTCs are lowest. This gives rise to a 'thin interface', where what is to be transferred can be relatively fully specified, and hence be subject to a transaction rather than a transfer within the firm. In contrast, a 'thick' interface occurs where a large degree of ambiguity remains over the specification, iteration, and collaboration are required, and, if a transaction is possible at all, it is more likely to be for an expenditure of effort than for a defined and measurable outcome. Baldwin and Clark (2006) also argue that, although to some extent technologically determined, thin(ner) interfaces don't 'just happen'—they can be 'engineered' by the use of modularity principles in the design of both products and organizational processes. Or, as Loasby (1998: 142) puts it: '…what Williamson calls "technological separability" is not a natural given but a human creation'.

Herbert Simon's famous parable of two watchmakers, Hora and Tempus (Simon 1962: 470) also shows that there are strategic choices to be made and that, by adopting what we might (but Simon didn't) call a modular approach, Hora made watches of equal complexity with much greater success. Hora's exploitation of the 'near-decomposability' of the watchmaking process into subprocesses of building subassemblies—in other words, designing techno-logical separability into the product and his process—made his overall strat-egy more successful. Note that, although one can imagine that this strategy could lead to subcontracting of the subassembly stages, benefit accrues even without that step.

Modularity, Cost Structures, and Standards

Langlois (2006) develops this further. Hora's investment in designing his watches so that they could be built in convenient subassemblies saved him from incurring variable cost. Baldwin and Clark's (Baldwin and Clark 2006; Baldwin 2008) case study firms' encapsulation of all the information required to specify a plastic moulding compound for an automobile not only made a transaction possible but also, especially over a number of design projects, replaced the recurring (i.e. variable) costs of *ad hoc* iterative design work with the fixed cost of designing a standard way of communicating and testing designs between the two firms. Langlois (2006) suggests that MTCs are vari-able costs—some variable with time, others with volume of activity—and that it is possible to alter these by, at some level of aggregation, making capi-tal investments in technological and institutional arrangements that make it easier to transact. (See also Spring and Araujo 2009: 459–460.)

The development of the protocol in the Baldwin and Clark example is idi-osyncratic to those two firms or, perhaps, to the assembler and several of its suppliers. However, the development of institutional interfaces of this type can be brought about at higher levels of aggregation—across a sector, or wider still. An extreme case of pan-sector, transnational standardization of this sort is the 'International Commercial Terms' system by which the various distri-butions of responsibilities between buyer and seller for loading, unloading, shipment, insurance, customs clearance, and the like are summarized in thir-teen internationally agreed standard contracts. This comes about through a gigantic collective 'capital investment' through the International Chamber of Commerce, which has the effect of radically reducing the time spent in, and therefore the cost of, any one negotiation and definition of the basis of trading between two firms. In other words, it reduces (variable) MTCs.

Modularity involves other costs. One that is well known is the so-called 'modularity trap', where the sunk costs of investment in one architecture prohibit or inhibit a subsequent shift to another, more appropriate architec-ture (Chesbrough and Kusunoki 2001). As discussed by Henderson and Clark

(1990), architectural innovation—changing the disposition of functions between modules, rather than making self-contained modifications *within* modules—can cause traumatic difficulties for established firms, as their structures are no longer appropriate to the new product architecture. This is an early statement of the so-called 'mirroring hypothesis' (MacCormack *et al.* 2008), which suggests that the structure of firms and industries 'mirrors' the structure (or architecture) of the product or service it produces. Second, in some respects, interfaces in products always involve waste (e.g. space, weight) and over-engineered specifications. Hence we see that desktop PCs are 'more modular' than laptops. The incorporation of bus bars, input–output connections between modules, separate power supplies, and the like is not a problem in the case of a desktop, but these are reduced to a minimum in laptops and netbooks, for which weight and size of the whole are at a premium. This is achieved through more integral architecture and less use of standard, interchangeable modules (for example, a laptop screen cannot be swapped or upgraded in the way that a PC monitor can).

Similarly, Simon (1991/1969) argued that the design of organizations could be regarded as the decomposition of tasks into modules. Highly interdependent tasks should be grouped together while those that do not should belong to separate modules. The role of authority in organizations is to provide an architecture of standards and 'rules of the road' to allow actors to form stable expectations about the behaviour of others (Simon 1991/1969: 39). In markets, co-ordination by adjustment of prices and perhaps more importantly, quantities sustain a modular and decentralized structure of exchange. For example, inventory control systems initiate purchase orders when quantities fall below prespecified levels and adjust aggregate production levels (ibid.: 40).

The Dynamics of Modularity

As noted by Baldwin and Clark (2006: 42), 'for the most part, transaction costs economics and contract theory look at static systems of production'. These authors are concerned, in their wider project, with the interaction between modularity and innovation (Baldwin and Clark 1997), but we wish to draw attention to other aspects of the interplay between MTCs and change. First, technological change, initiated by the parties involved or more widely, alters the MTC structure and hence, according to Baldwin and Clark's reasoning, has the potential to shift transaction points up and down supply chains.[3] A telling recent example of this is RFID[4] technology. Uses such as tracking pallets in warehouses are well known, but some researchers point to a future where RFID chips become so cheap and therefore ubiquitous that they can be used to track and hence charge us for (almost) every move we make (Zipkin 2006); for example, the adoption of 'pay as you throw' for domestic garbage made possible by the use of RFID chips on bins to weigh household waste. In this way MTCs can be reduced to such an extent that transactions may be introduced where none were previously imaginable. It is not difficult to identify other instances in economic history of technologies that have made standardization, counting, and compensating cheaper—for example, shipping containers[5] (Donovan 2004). In sum, technological change can move transaction points in production and distribution chains.

However, technological innovation is not the only source of reduction (or indeed, increase) in MTCs. Institutional innovation or evolution also changes MTCs. At the level of two firms working together, it is likely that they will adapt to one another (Håkansson 1982), and establish routines for standardizing, counting, and compensating. Alternatively, the buyer may become better at drawing up specifications and service-level agreements (Mayer and Argyres 2004), thereby making the use of the market (transaction) more attractive than the use of the firm's own capacity (transfer), all other things being equal. As Langlois (2006) points out, such institutional apparatus may be collectively designed and implemented, for example by the development of sectoral or international standards. Thus, MTCs, as Langlois (2006) puts it, have a 'secret life' (in that they are ignored in comparison to the 'sexy' transaction costs associated with opportunism) and a secret life *cycle*, in that, for the reasons outlined here, they change, they are dynamic. Hence, the point at which transactions can most efficiently take place in a sequence of activities or transfers will change, too.

MTCs as outlined here can explain how transactions are made possible in relatively stable sequences of processes, and how these transactions may move around or multiply as transaction-enabling technologies (e.g. RFID) change. In instances where technological and economic change of a systemic nature are present, a manifestation of these more 'mundane' transaction costs known as 'dynamic transaction costs' (Langlois 1992) can explain periodic shifts toward large-scale vertical integration. Broadly speaking, the argument goes that, faced with such systemic change and the need simultaneously to change several stages in a production or service process, these dynamic transaction costs, 'the costs of persuading, negotiating and coordinating with, and teaching others' (Langlois 1992: 99), are so large that the activities are better brought back within the firm. This principle can be used to explain why, for example, Ford vertically integrated to introduce mass production of automobiles. An alternative, 'fast and loose' definition of dynamic transaction costs is the 'costs of not having the capabilities you need, when you need them' (Langlois 1992: 113), or 'the costs of persuading, negotiating and coordinating with, and teaching others' (Langlois 1992: 99). Again, this is a story of getting things done rather than forestalling opportunistic behaviour by guileful trading counterparts.

This linking of the ability to make transactions with the productive capabilities of firms has subsequently been developed by Langlois and others. In some ways this work begins to treat transactions and capabilities as complementary rather than competing explanations of the boundaries of firms and of industry structure. In this way, the work of Langlois (Langlois 1992, 2004; Langlois and Robertson 1995) and of Jacobides (Jacobides 2005; Jacobides and Winter 2005) has demonstrated, through generic analysis and industry-level case studies, how reconfiguration takes place by the gradual development of more effective markets for particular factors, and of the capabilities of the firms playing various roles in the industry. Markets and capabilities, on this view, are mutually constitutive. And what is clear, especially from Langlois (2006), is that the extent and nature of vertical integration or disintegration is shaped by individual and collective efforts to build market-supporting institutions, such as systems of standards that facilitate trading between firms, and technologies that make transactions easier (cf. Zipkin 2006).

Modularization and the Geography of Production

The modularization of manufacturing and service processes has, then, led to activities formerly carried out *within* organizations being dispersed across organizational boundaries, i.e. outsourced. It has also made it easier and more attractive, in varying degrees, for activities to be dispersed spatially. An extreme example of vertical specialization is provided by the growth of contract manufacturing in electronics (Sturgeon 2002; UNCTAD 2011). In this field, pressures of market volatility and increased international competition coupled with growing outsourcing have led to what Sturgeon (2002: 455) calls the modular production network, because '...distinct breaks in the value chain tend to form at points where information regarding product specifications can be highly formalized.[...] The locus of these value chain break points appear to be largely determined by technical factors, especially the open and de facto standards that determine the protocol for the hand-off of codified specifications'. In other words, the adoption of modular architecture and international standard interfaces between components means that it is easy for components to be manufactured in geographically dispersed production networks and then brought together, by assemblers and or end users, into working systems.

Links based on highly codified knowledge provide speed, flexibility, and access to low cost inputs while allowing for a rich flow of information—but with the rich flow of information embodied in the modules themselves. The pool of these turn-key contract manufacturers provides generic capacity to suppliers and access to external economies of scale. Standards and protocols allow firms to switch contract manufacturers easily while these contractors are able to quickly substitute production locations as well as integrate operations across low- and high-cost locations. Institutional and geographic fragmentation of production (offshoring) go hand in hand in this example. It is notable in this account, however, that, while the globally dispersed network is effective for the repetitive production of modules, once the architecture and standards are established, the process of establishing these architectures, of codifying standards and interfaces, still takes place in certain locales. So, the answer to Sturgeon's question to himself—'What really goes on in Silicon Valley?' is that it is a key location for standard-setting, for turning tacit knowledge and thick interfaces into codified knowledge and thin interfaces.

This interplay between localized, deeply embedded episodes of architectural innovation and standard-setting on the one hand, and dispersed, disembedded (or at least differently embedded) routine production on the other, is summarized as follows by Michael Storper:

> The history of economic geography is thus a story of coordination over space and has been shaped by two opposing forces: (1) the constant transformation of complex and unfamiliar coordination tasks into routine activities that can be successfully accomplished at remote but cheaper locations (e.g. commodification) and thus an ongoing tendency toward deagglomeration or dispersion of production; and (2) bursts of innovations that create new activities requiring high levels of complex and unfamiliar coordination, which, in turn, generate bursts of agglomeration. (Learner and Storper 2001: 641)

Modularity and Services

Modularity is increasingly being used as a basis for designing services within firms, in a manner analogous to the design of modular products (and for many of the same reasons: see Chapter 3). However, in this present chapter, the emphasis is on the more fundamental notion of modularity as an explanation of industry structure—the 'modularity theory of the firm'—as applied to the outsourcing and offshoring of services. The purpose in this section is to examine how readily this approach—also one with its roots in manufacturing and product-based industries—might be applied to services.

The language of modularity in the sense meant here is present in several recent discussions of offshore outsourcing of services (Mithas and Whitaker 2007; Kenney *et al.* 2009; Contractor *et al.* 2010; Mudambi and Tallman 2010; Mudambi and Venzin 2010). Processes or activities are either discussed as 'modules' unproblematically or, with at least some implication that work is required to create modules, are discussed as more or less 'modularizable'. However, there is very little discussion of the reasons for some processes being more or less susceptible to being modularized, of the steps required to achieve modularization, or of any underlying theoretical approach that might inform such an analysis.

The key driver for modularizing and offshoring services is—as in manufacturing—the ability to disaggregate processes, simplify interfaces between processes and reduce MTCs (Baldwin and Clark 2006). Apte and Mason (1995) examined the disaggregation of information-intensive services in response to global competition and the opportunities afforded by information technology and qualified pools of skills in a number of lower-cost locations. They advance a framework for disaggregating services based on the characteristics of service activities, namely information intensity, customer contact, and physical presence needed. Activities that score high on the first attribute and low on the second and third, have a high potential for offshoring. Along similar lines, Blinder (2006) goes as far as saying that impersonally delivered services have more in common with manufactured goods that can be stored in boxes, than they do with personal services. Mithas and Whitaker (2007) invoke modularity as part of their analysis of the susceptibility to global dispersion of various service occupations: in fact, they study the mediating role of three information-related variables—codifiability, standardizability, and modularizability—on the relationship between the information intensity of a service activity and its potential for disaggregation. The results suggested a positive association between information intensity and perceived disaggregation potential, and a negative association between need for physical proximity and disaggregation potential. It is particularly interesting that the 'occupation' was the unit of analysis in this study, rather than the process.

The approach in these and other studies, then, is to identify the types of services that are likely candidates for redesign along modular lines. However, there may be dangers in taking the analogy with redesigning products for modularity too far. Kogut and Bowman (1995: 250), for example, observed that the analogy between modularity in product and organizational design is overdrawn. Interfaces in human systems can rarely be rendered as opaque as in physical systems and the notion of 'information hiding' that underpins modular product designs (Baldwin and Clark 1997) may not translate so readily to organizations and service processes. Human systems have the potential for redesigning interfaces through mutual adjustments and joint learning. As Kogut and Bowman (1995: 251) remark: 'In a product design, it is nonsensical to think of one module "teaching" another. Teaching, cooperation, and joint problem solving are distinctively human activities.' Instead, they propose the notion of permeability as characterized by the communication flows and cooperation among people who nominally have to cross standard interfaces such as those defined by functions, divisions, or ownership boundaries. In summary, while the easy coupling and decoupling of modules in physical systems is locked in place by rigid architectural rules, human systems can evolve through improvements across interfaces that enable cooperation and joint learning.

Furthermore, the line between personal and impersonal services is continuously shifting, as personal services (those involving direct contact with the end customer) become increasingly modularized and elements of them become 'back-office', information-intensive services, thus increasing their chances of being offshored. As an example, consider the case of legal services (*TIME Magazine* 12 May 2008; *Wall Street Journal* 26 November 2008). Forrester Research Inc. has forecasted the offshoring of some 35,000 US legal jobs to India by the end of 2010 and as many as 79,000 by 2015. One US-based firm reckons that reviewing a million litigation e-mails costs less than US$10 per hour in India rather than the US$60–85 per hour that US-based legal staff would cost. In theory, then, even a complex, professional, and highly personal service can be decomposed, codified, and partly standardized so that some service modules can now be offshored and integrated within a total service package offered by US law firms despite obvious concerns about confidentiality, ethical breaches, and security. While these examples show that this is achieved in practice, a recent study of a UK law firm by Lewis and Brown (2012) shows a more nuanced picture, suggesting that professional service operations based in high-wage economies already incorporate varied tasks and occupations (e.g. para-legals) and, interestingly, that genuinely professional staff often find themselves offering rather standard services because their clients lack the knowledge to specify anything more customized.

Sturgeon's (2002) modular production networks could thus be seen to be equally applicable to services where we have begun to witness the same patterns of vertical specialization and transnational production sites. Contract service offshoring flagships in some regions (e.g. Infosys, Tata Consultancy, Wipro in India) are now seeking to internationalize, to fight skills shortages at home, including setting up operations in regions where outsourced work has traditionally come from (*The Guardian* 13 October 2007). Infosys, for example, has been building a multinational network of offices from Mexico to China and has recently acquired the call centre operations of Philips in Poland. Tata Consultancy Services has recently acquired the outsourcing unit of Citigroup Global Services, is running call centres in Britain, and sending some of their banking client's work to Brazil. Some Indian companies are recruiting directly from British and US universities to combat skills shortages at home. The skill of these international contract service providers is the ability to pull apart complex performance requirements from their clients and remodularize them in more efficient ways taking advantage of their network of locations.

However, the modularization and offshoring of services also provide telling examples of the limits to modularity as a design principle. Dibbern *et al.* (2008), in a study of German financial services companies' software offshoring to India found that clients incurred significant post-contractual costs for activities such as requirements' specifications and design and knowledge transfer. The more specific client knowledge required, the higher these costs, as the costs of managing knowledge asymmetries between client and provider tended to be particularly high in these cases. Previous experience of the client would tend to reduce these costs but could not fully offset them in highly client-specific projects. In these cases, it appears as if the attempt to standardize interfaces is not only destined to fail but physical and cultural distance hampers the communication flows and co-operation across permeable boundaries that Kogut and Bowman (1995) argue, are needed to address the rigid divisions brought about by modularity. Given these difficulties, it is perhaps unsurprising that management and other specialist consultancies are often involved in the process of helping their clients analyse and disaggregate processes as well as tap into offshoring opportunities [see, for example, Lampel and Bhalla (2008)]. Olsson *et al.*'s (2008) study focuses on two US companies who used their Irish software development sites as bridges to offshore work to India. The Irish sites were initially set up as low-cost offshore locations but rising Irish labour costs and the development of a pool of technical and managerial skills in India led to pressures to break down tasks further and seek lower cost locations for offshoring work.

In sum, while modular approaches will make progressively more service activities more readily accessible from other firms, the modularity theory of the firm also tells us that in varying degrees, these interfaces are never 'frictionless' or cost-free, and hence that firms must work to become expert at managing them, at orchestrating their network. This will always be to some extent a matter for the firms and their immediate counterparts to work through; but the modularity theory of the firm also tells us that, as in the development of many manufacturing industries over the past 150 years, it is also a matter for 'market-supporting institutions' (Langlois 2004: 360) such as standards. This is an important part of the emerging story in the offshore outsourcing of services. As Graz and Niang (2011) explain, the (huge) Indian BPO industry is increasingly shaped by international quality and security standards—such as the capability maturity model integration, defined by the Software Engineering Institute at Carnegie Mellon University—that are not of the Indian industry's own making. This is a fact much bemoaned by senior managers of leading BPO firms as well as senior standards officials of the Indian government (Graz and Niang 2011: 13). In the consumer electronics industry, Sturgeon (2003) suggests that Silicon Valley's most important role is as a site for the setting of standards and, therefore, determination of the organizational and spatial structure of the industry. It seems that a battle is underway to determine whether the shape of the BPO industry is to be determined in Bangalore or Pittsburgh.

Notes

1. As an illustration, according to SingTel, their SEA-ME-WE 4 cable system, costing some US$500 million, has a capacity of 1.28 terabits per second. This is the equivalent of handling more than one million internet users simultaneously having real-time access to a 1 Mb file. Global capacity in 2011, then, was about forty-two times this: http://home.singtel.com/about_singtel/network_n_infrastructure/submarine_cable_systems/networkinfra_submarinecablesystems.asp).
2. In Baldwin and Clark (2006), it is 'standardizing' rather than 'defining'.
3. As we shall see, other forces are at work, possibly in mitigation of the effect of changing MTCs.
4. Radio Frequency Identification technology.
5. Of course, containerization reduced the costs of handling at ports and the like, but the reduction in MTCs in, say, chartering a ship for transporting goods is a cost less frequently discussed.

References

Apte, U.M. and Mason, R.O. (1995). Global disaggregation of information-intensive services. *Management Science*, **41**(7), 1250–1262.

Araujo, L. and Spring, M. (2006). Services, products, and the institutional structure of production. *Industrial Marketing Management*, **35**(7), 797–805.

Baldwin, C.Y. (2008). Where do transactions come from? Modularity, transactions, and the boundaries of firms. *Industrial and Corporate Change*, **17**, 155–195.

Baldwin, C. and Clark, K.B. (1997). Managing in an age of modularity. *Harvard Business Review*, **Sept/Oct**, 84–93.

Baldwin, C. and Clark, K.B. (2006). *Where do Transactions Come From? A network design perspective on the theory of the firm*. Boston, MA: Harvard Business School.

Blinder, A.S. (2006). Offshoring: the next industrial revolution? *Foreign Affairs*, **85**(2), 113–128.

Buckley, P.J. and Casson, M. (1976). *The Future of the Multinational Enterprise*. London: Macmillan.

Buckley, P.J. and Chapman, M. (1997). The perception and measurement of transaction costs. *Cambridge Journal of Economics*, **21**(2), 127–145.

Buckley, P.J. and Lessard, D.R. (2005). Regaining the edge for international business research. *Journal of International Business Studies*, **36**(6), 595–599.

Chesbrough, H. and Kusunoki, K. (2001). The modularity trap: innovation, technology phase-shifts and the resulting limits of virtual organizations. In: *Managing Industrial Knowledge: creation, transfer and utilization*, Nonaka, I. and Teece, D.J. (Ed.), pp. 202–230. Thousand Oaks, CA: Sage.

Clemons, E.K., Reddi, S.P., and Row, M.C. (1993). The impact of information technology on the organization of economic activity: the 'Move to the middle' hypothesis. *Journal of Management Information Systems*, **10**(2), 9–35.

Collins, R.S., Bechler, K., and Pires, S.I. (1997). Outsourcing in the automobile industry: from JIT to modular consortia. *European Management Journal*, **15**(5), 498–508.

Contractor, F.J., Kumar, V., Kundu, S.K., and Pedersen, T. (2010). Reconceptualizing the firm in a world of outsourcing and offshoring: The organizational and geographical relocation of high-value company functions. *Journal of Management Studies*, **47**(8), 1417–1433.

Davenport, T.H. (2005). The coming commoditization of processes. *Harvard Business Review*, **83**(6), 100–108.

Dibbern, J., Winkler, J., and Heinzl, A. (2008). Explaining variations in client extra costs between software projects offshored to India. *MIS Quarterly*, **32**(2), 333–366.

Donovan, A. (2004). The impact of containerization: from Adam Smith to the 21st century. *Review of Business*, **25**(3), 10–15.

Doran, D. (2003). Supply chain implications of modularization. *International Journal of Operations and Production Management*, **23**(3/4), 316.

Ellram, L.M., Tate, W.L., and Billington, C. (2008). Offshore outsourcing of professional services: a transaction cost economics perspective. *Journal of Operations Management*, **26**(2), 148–163.

Forza, C. and Salvador, F. (2002). Managing for variety in the order acquisition and fulfilment process: the contribution of product configuration systems. *International Journal of Production Economics*, **76**, 87–98.

Ghoshal, S. and Moran, P. (1996). Bad for practice: a critique of the transaction cost theory. *Academy of Management Review*, **21**, 13–47.

Graz, J.-C. and Niang, N. (2011). Connecting India: the rise of standards in service offshoring. *The Service Industries Journal*, **32**(14), 2287–2305.

The Guardian (13 October 2007), India outsources outsourcing.

Håkansson, H. (1982). *International Marketing and Purchasing of Industrial Goods*. Chichester: John Wiley.

Hammer, M. and Champy, J. (1993). *Reengineering the Corporation: a manifesto for business revolution*. London: Nicholas Brealey.

Henderson, R.M. and Clark, K.B. (1990). Architectural innovation: the reconfiguration of existing product technologies and the failure of established firms. *Administrative Science Quarterly*, **35**, 9–30.

Jacobides, M.G. (2005). Industry change through vertical disintegration: how and why markets emerged in mortgage banking. *Academy of Management Journal*, **48**(3), 465–498.

Jacobides, M.G. and Winter, S.G. (2005). The co-evolution of capabilities and transaction costs: explaining the institutional structure of production. *Strategic Management Journal*, **26**(5), 395–413.

Kakabadse, A. and Kakabadse, N. (2002). Trends in outsourcing: contrasting USA and Europe. *European Management Journal*, **20**(2), 189–198.

Kenney, M., Massini, S., and Murtha, T.P. (2009). Offshoring administrative and technical work: new fields for understanding the global enterprise introduction. *Journal of International Business Studies*, **40**(6), 887–900.

King, W.R. and Torkzadeh, G. (2008). Information systems offshoring: research status and issues. *MIS Quarterly*, **32**(2), 205–225.

Kogut, B. and Bowman, E.H. (1995). Modularity and permeability as principles of design. In: *Redesigning the Firm*, Bowman, E.H. and Kogut, B. (Ed.), pp. 243–260. New York: Oxford University Press.

Kogut, B. and Zander, U. (1992). Knowledge of the firm, combinative capabilities and the replication of technology. *Organization Science*, **3**, 383–397.

Kogut, B. and Zander, U. (1993). Knowledge of the firm and the evolutionary theory of the multinational corporation. *Journal of International Business Studies*, **24**(4), 625–645.

Kumar, K., van Fenema, P.C., and von Glinow, M.A. (2008). Offshoring and the global distribution of work: implications for task interdependence theory and practice. *Journal of International Business Studies*, **40**(4), 642–667.

Lampel, J. and Bhalla, A. (2008). Embracing realism and recognizing choice in IT offshoring initiatives. *Business Horizons*, **51**(5), 429–440.

Langlois, R.N. (1992). Transaction-cost economics in real time. *Industrial and Corporate Change*, **1**, 99–127.

Langlois, R.N. (2002). Modularity in technology and organization. *Journal of Economic Behavior and Organization*, **49**, 19–37.

Langlois, R.N. (2004). Chandler in a larger frame: markets, transaction costs, and organizational form in history. *Enterprise and Society*, **5**(3), 355–375.

Langlois, R.N. (2006). The secret life of mundane transaction costs. *Organization Studies*, **27**(9), 1389–1410.

Langlois, R.N. and Robertson, P.L. (1995). *Firms, Markets and Economic Change*. London: Routledge.

Learner, E.E. and Storper, M. (2001). The economic geography of the internet age. *Journal of International Business Studies*, **32**(4), 641–665.

Levina, N. and Vaast, E. (2008). Innovating or doing as told? Status differences and overlapping boundaries in offshore collaboration. *MIS Quarterly*, **32**(2), 307–332.

Lewin, A.Y. and Peeters, C. (2006). Offshoring work: business hype or the onset of fundamental transformation? *Long Range Planning*, **39**(3), 221–239.

Lewin, A.Y., Massini, S., and Peeters, C. (2009). Why are companies offshoring innovation? The emerging global race for talent. *Journal of International Business Studies*, **40**(6), 901–925.

Lewis, M.A. and Brown, A.D. (2012). How different is professional service operations management? *Journal of Operations Management*, **30**(1–2), 1–11.

Lewis, M.A. and Roehrich, J. (2011). Contracts, relationships, integration: towards a model of the procurement of complex performance. In: *Procuring Complex Performance: studies of innovation in product-service management*, Caldwell, N. and Howard, M. (Ed.), pp. 21–40. New York: Routledge.

Loasby, B. (1998). The organisation of capabilities. *Journal of Economic Behaviour and Organization*, 35(2), 139–160.

MacCormack, A., Rusnak, J., and Baldwin, C. (2008). Exploring the duality between product and organizational architectures: a test of the mirroring hypothesis, Version 3.0 edn. *Harvard Business School Working Paper*, No. 08-039.

Manning, S., Massini, S., and Lewin, A.Y. (2008). A dynamic perspective on next-generation offshoring: the global sourcing of science and engineering talent. *Academy of Management Perspectives*, 22(3), 35–54.

Marx, R. (1997). The modular consortium in a new VW truck plant in Brazil: new forms of assembler and supplier relationship. *Integrated Manufacturing Systems*, 8(5), 292–298.

Mayer, K.J. and Argyres, N.S. (2004). Learning to contract: evidence from the personal computer industry. *Organization Science*, 15(4), 394–410.

Merrifield, R., Calhoun, J., and Stevens, D. (2008). The next revolution in productivity. *Harvard Business Review*, 86(6), 72–80.

Metters, R. and Verma, R. (2008). History of offshoring knowledge services. *Journal of Operations Management*, 26(2), 141–147.

Mithas, S. and Whitaker, J. (2007). Is the world flat or spiky? Information intensity, skills, and global service disaggregation. *Information Systems Research*, 18(3), 237–259.

Mudambi, R. and Venzin, M. (2010). The strategic nexus of offshoring and outsourcing decisions. *Journal of Management Studies*, 47(8), 1510–1533.

Mudambi, S.M. and Tallman, S. (2010). Make, buy or ally? Theoretical perspectives on knowledge process outsourcing through alliances. *Journal of Management Studies*, 47(8), 1434–1456.

Olsson, H.H., Conchúir, E.Ó., Ågerfalk, P.J., and Fitzgerald, B. (2008). Two-stage offshoring: an investigation of the Irish bridge. *MIS Quarterly*, 32(2), 257–279.

Pine, B.J. (1993). *Mass Customization*. Boston, MA: HBS Press.

Sako, M. (2004). Modularity and outsourcing: the nature of co-evolution of product architecture and organization architecture in the global automotive industry. In: *The Business of Systems Integration*, Prencipe, A., Davies, A., and Hobday, M. (Ed.), pp. 229–253. Oxford: Oxford University Press.

Sako, M. (2006). Outsourcing and offshoring: implications for productivity of business services. *Oxford Review of Economic Policy*, 22(4), 499–512.

Sanchez, R. and Mahoney, J.T. (1996). Modularity, flexibility, and knowledge management in product and organization design. *Strategic Management Journal*, Winter Special Issue, 17, 63–76.

Simon, H. (1962). The architecture of complexity. *Proceedings of the American Philosophical Society*, 106, 467–482.

Simon, H. (1991/1969). *The Sciences of the Artificial*. Boston, MA: MIT Press.

Spring, M. and Araujo, L. (2009). Service, services and products: re-thinking operations strategy. *International Journal of Operations and Production Management*, 29(5), 444–467.

Starr, M.K. (1965). Modular production: a new concept. *Harvard Business Review*, Nov–Dec, 131–142.

Stratman, J.K. (2008). Facilitating offshoring with enterprise technologies: reducing operational friction in the governance and production of services. *Journal of Operations Management*, **26**(2), 275–287.

Sturgeon, T.J. (2002). Modular production networks: A new American model of industrial organization. *Industrial and Corporate Change*, **11**(3), 451–496.

Sturgeon, T.J. (2003). What really goes on in Silicon Valley? Spatial clustering and dispersal in modular production networks. *Journal of Economic Geography*, **3**(2), 199.

Telegeography. (2011). *Global Internet Geography Executive Summary*. Washington: PriMetrica.

Time Magazine (12 May 2008), Call my lawyer...in India.

Ulrich, K. (1995). The role of product architecture within the manufacturing firm. *Research Policy*, **24**, 419–440.

UNCTAD. (2011). *World Investment Report 2011: non-equity modes of international production and development*. New York: United Nations.

Wall Street Journal (26 November 2008), With times tight, even lawyers get outsourced.

Williamson, O.E. (1979). Transaction-cost economics: The governance of contractual relations. *Journal of Law and Economics*, **22**(2), 233–261.

Williamson, O.E. (1985). *The Economic Instituitons of Capitalism: firms, markets, relational contracting*. New York: The Free Press.

Womack, J.P., Jones, D.T., and Roos, D. (1990). *The Machine that Changed the World*. New York: Rawson Associates.

Zenger, T.R. and Hesterly, W.S. (1997). The disaggregation of corporations: selective intervention, high-powered incentives, and molecular units. *Organization Science*, **8**(3), 209–222.

Zipkin, P. (2006). The best things in life were free: on the technology of transactions. *Manufacturing & Service Operations Management*, **8**(4), 321–329.

11

Service Systems for Value Co-Creation

Laura A. Smith and Irene C.L. Ng

Introduction

Over the last few decades, there has been growing interest from both marketing researchers and practitioners in the creation of value (Eggert and Ulaga 2002). In a series of publications on service-dominant logic (S-D logic), Vargo and Lusch (2004: 2008) reviewed the economic foundations that underpin how value creation is understood. In doing so, they put forward a number of propositions, which have had a significant impact on current management theory and practice. These propositions were reviewed earlier in Chapter 8 (this volume). The central tenet of value creation under S-D logic is that value is always uniquely and phenomenologically determined by the customer. This raises two important issues: first, that the enterprise cannot deliver value itself but only offer value propositions, and second, that the customer is always a co-creator of value, suggesting that a customer's value-creating processes and resources affect the success of a company's value proposition. Given this orientation, and as the context of value creation is not within the firm's control, the management of the customer as a co-creator of value presents itself as a major challenge in the design and management of service systems. This chapter investigates the challenges of a service system for value co-creation through a review and comparative analysis of three widely published cases considered service systems for co-created outcomes. As a result, six challenges of a service system for value co-creation are summarized: determination challenge; measurement challenge; revenue challenge; context challenge; resource challenge; and skills challenge.

Approaches to Customer Value in Management: Value-in-Exchange vs. Value-in-Use

For centuries, the nature of value has been discussed and debated, with the discussion being traced back as far as Aristotle (Vargo *et al.* 2008). The elusive and indefinable nature of value has, in part, been embedded within the foundations of economic theory and the study of market exchange (e.g. Vargo and Morgan 2005; Vargo and Lusch 2004, 2008). From these foundations, two general meanings of value have evolved—'value-in-exchange' and 'value-in-use'—with each reflecting a different way of thinking about value and its creation.

Value-in-exchange is believed to have stemmed from economic thought at the start of the Industrial Revolution. Economists of the time, such as Adam Smith (1776), theorized about the exchange of goods, which were produced simply as a means to acquire other goods. Value creation therefore was equated to the transactions in which these goods were exchanged. In other words, a transaction represented the exchange of *value* between two parties, normally taken to be the exchange of producers' goods and services for their value in money. While within this approach the things of value were not limited to goods, services, and money, but could also include other resources such as time, energy, and feelings (Kotler 1972), they are often equated to monetary value, particularly because of its measureable quality. It can be argued that this is the dominant way in which value has been viewed for centuries and, as such, the management literature and management practice reflects this. Notably, value creation within management literature has primarily taken a transaction-centric approach, which has manifested in two streams of literature. The first stream, found predominantly in the area of customer lifetime value and customer retention, is centred on the appropriation of value by the producer through exchange with the customer; here value creation is often defined as the economic worth of a customer to the company. As such, it focuses on the value outcome that can be derived from providing and delivering superior customer value to the market (Payne and Holt 2001). The second stream from the 'market orientation' literature is on the creation and distribution of value to the customer through the provider's offering. Conventional strategy literature argues that a company's success depends on the extent to which it delivers to the customer what is of value to them, emphasizing the linkages between providing superior customer value and achieving organizational profitability, performance, and competitive advantage (e.g. Naumann 1995; Slater and Narver 1995).

In 2004, Vargo and Lusch's seminal paper on S-D logic claimed that this is a goods-dominant logic (G-D logic), whereby value is considered to be created (manufactured) by the producer and distributed to the consumer. As such, within this prevailing logic, value is generally thought to be created through a series of activities performed by the producer. This view has also been referred to as a 'manufacturing logic' or the 'old enterprise logic' (Normann 2001; Zuboff and Maxmin 2002; Chandler and Vargo 2011).

This prevailing logic is thought to have resulted in a view of value creation, represented in Figure 11.1, in which the producer of a good or service procures resources and activities from a chain of suppliers and constructs an offering through the processing, assembly, and packaging of these activities, parts, and materials. This view of value creation implies that the company's production processes create value for customers through the manufacturing and delivery of an offering. That is, the company embeds value in the offering, be it tangible or intangible, by transforming raw materials and activities into something that customers want. In this sense, value is created by the company in the form of a good or service, and this valuable offering is delivered through an exchange in the marketplace for money. Value is measured by this exchange transaction, and the customer then consumes or destroys this value embedded in the offering they have purchased.

In management literature, this perspective of value creation suggests that superior customer value and therefore competitive advantage, is achieved by the producer 'adding value' to the offering to be exchanged in the market place. Levitt (1969), for example, pointed out that competitive advantage is not created by what companies produce in their factories but by what they add to their factory output in the form of packaging, services, advertising, customer advice, financing, delivery arrangements, warehousing, and other things that people value. Exploring value from this perspective alone may be

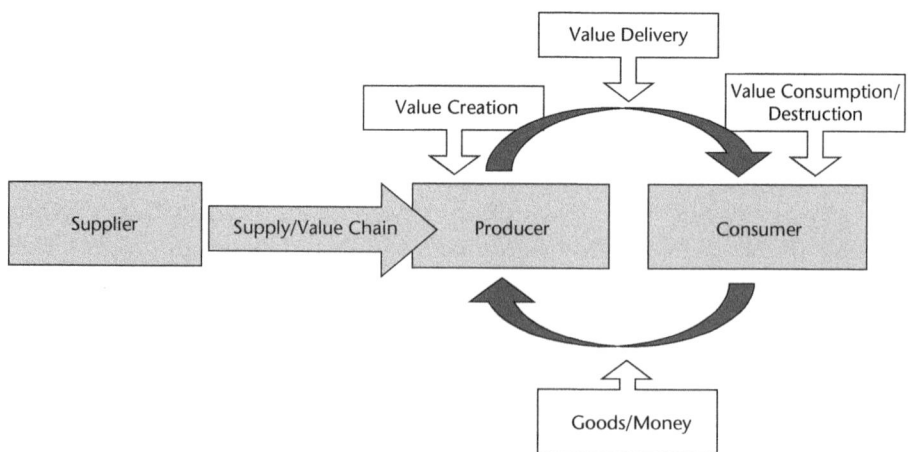

Figure 11.1 Model of value-in-exchange (Vargo 2009)

overemphasizing the exchange transaction in the creation of value for the customer, as it is shown to represent only one level of value for the customer. It has also been shown that value is created after the exchange transaction, in a customer's use of the offering (Lapierre 1997).

As such, much of contemporary marketing literature has moved the discussion of customer value away from the transaction-centric understanding of value-in-exchange, to the concept of value-in-use. Accordingly, most current literature would now describe customer value as that which is experienced by the customer in use situations, rather than what is determined by the producer for exchange. In a comprehensive definition of customer's evaluation of value, Woodruff (1997) defines customer value as the following:

> Customer value is a customer's perceived preference for and evaluation of those product attributes, attribute performances, and consequences arising from use that facilitate (or block) achieving the customer's goals and purposes in use situations. (Woodruff 1997: 142)

This definition captures the dynamic and context-dependent nature of how customers judge value, the criteria they use to do so, and the relative importance they place on such criteria (Parasuraman 1997; Payne and Holt 2001). Thus, it reflects the phenomenological nature of value creation, described by Holbrook (1994, 2006) as 'an interactive relativistic preference experience'. In their 2004 and 2008 articles, Vargo and Lusch similarly contend that value is perceived and determined by the consumer on the basis of 'value-in-use' and that value is contextual, experiential, and idiosyncratic.

Value-in-use, however, is not a new concept, as a customer's perception of value has arguably always been part of the notion of utility (Sawhney 2006). As Drucker (1974: 61) put it, 'what the customer buys and considers as value is never a product; it is always utility—that is—what a product does for him'. Having said this, value-in-use in its modern conceptualization goes beyond simply the utility of an offering. The idea of utility implies that the customer's role in value creation is passive and their activities are limited to evaluating the benefits of the product or service. In contrast, S-D logic proposes that value-in-use is co-created as a phenomenological experience of the beneficiary and as a result, the customer is an active participant in value creation.

Value Co-creation

The customer as an active participant in the provision of service has been a central theme in service literature, as the customer is seen to play an active role in the process of service delivery and as a result, determine the quality of service outcome (see for example, Fitzsimmons 1985; Dabholkar 1990; Schneider and Bowen 1995; Heskett *et al.* 1997; Meuter and Bitner 1998). This active participation in service delivery is related to early service literature on inseparability, whereby the production of service activities cannot be separated from the customer's consumption, or use, of that service and therefore the customer is inextricably involved in the process (Ordanini and Pasini 2008). Of course, it is arguable that this may not be the case in every service context; customer involvement may vary dramatically across services. For example, there may be very little customer involvement in the servicing of a car; the garage does the work with minimal instruction from the customer. However, high levels of customer involvement are required when buying and tailoring a suit. Herein lays a potential key distinction between service co-production and the co-creation of value. Under S-D logic, co-production can be viewed as the customer's involvement in the realization of the company's value proposition, rather than the value outcome. Value co-creation, in contrast, is viewed as the customer's realization of the value proposition to obtain value-in-use (Ng *et al.* 2008). Under this distinction, customers are always co-creators of value while they may not always be co-producers of service.

The customer as an active participant in value creation has been a growing concern in marketing (e.g. Wilkstrom 1996; Prahalad and Ramaswamy 2000, 2004; Grönroos 2008, 2011) and is converged in the S-D logic premise of value co-creation (Vargo and Lusch 2004, 2008). Central to the premise of value co-creation is the notion that companies cannot provide value, but merely offer propositions of value; it is the customer that determines value and co-creates it with the company at a given time and context. Thus, a company's offering, whether it be goods or services, is merely value unrealized, i.e. a 'store of potential value', until the customer realizes it through co-creation in context and gains the benefit (Ng *et al.* 2010). This view raises a number of important implications not dealt with under traditional transaction-centric management practices. First, value realized in context would mean that the social, ecological, and environmental surroundings while not possible to control, are endogenous to the process of value co-creation (Vargo *et al.* 2008). Second, customer's resources to co-create value become central towards realizing a firm's value proposition.

Much of the literature views value co-creating entities, be they individuals, groups, organizations, firms, or governments, as systems, constellations, or networks of resources (e.g. Normann and Ramirez 1994; Normann 2001; Vargo *et al.* 2008; Vargo and Lusch 2011). These systems take action, apply resources, and work with other systems in mutually beneficial ways to co-create value (Vargo *et al.* 2008). Principally then, both the customer and the firm can be considered to be systems, each of which is an arrangement of resources connected by a value proposition (Spohrer *et al.* 2007, 2008; IfM and IBM 2008; Vargo *et al.* 2008). This is illustrated in Figure 11.2.

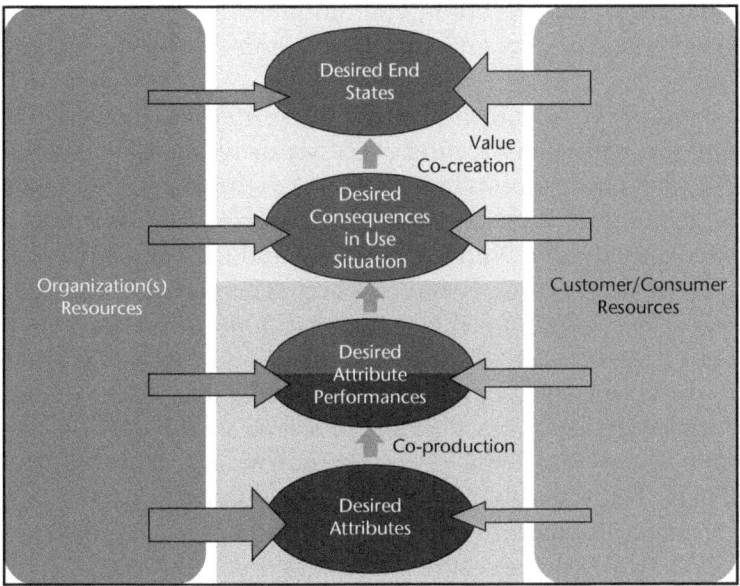

Figure 11.2 Model of value co-creation

Source: (Updated from Ng *et al.* 2011: 441 with kind permission from Springer Science + Business Media B.V.).

From an S-D logic perspective, a system's resources can be classified as either operand or operant (Vargo and Lusch 2004). Operand resources are typically considered tangible resources, including economic resources, goods/materials such as natural resources, which require some action on them to create value. Operant resources, on the other hand, are typically intangible resources, such as knowledge and skills, and cultural and social resources that are capable of acting on operand and other operant resources to create value. Each system has the ability to access resources from their own system and from other systems through exchange. These systems include internal (e.g. own, employees), private (e.g. friends, stockholders), and market-facing (suppliers, other economic exchanges) systems and resources (Vargo *et al.* 2008). This is a developed concept in the case of the organization system and is covered in the field of operations management through service supply chain literature. However, S-D logic and service science suggest that customers also deploy operand and operant resources made available to them by the firm, by other internal, private, and market-facing systems, and by themselves, and in that way realize value-in-use (Arnould *et al.* 2006). This is what is described by the S-D logic as customer resource integration. Arnould *et al.* (2006) go further to suggest that the configuration of customers' operant resources, their family relationships, commercial relationships, brand communities, imaginations, knowledge, skills, and physical powers influence *how* customers will employ their oper-and resources.

These resource systems are thought to be deployed and integrated in the use experience through value-creating processes or resource integration. Payne *et al.* (2008) describe processes in this context as the procedures, tasks, mechanisms, activities, and interactions, which support the co-creation of value, and further contend that both the customer and the company systems have these value-creating processes and practices. The practices and processes of both systems are thought to come together in joint interaction or encounter interactions (Payne *et al.* 2008; Grönroos and Ravald 2009). These interactions may exist at varying levels of co-creation, shown in the centre of Figure 11.2, and it is argued that such practices and processes are the ones that need to be managed to achieve successful co-creation outcomes (Payne *et al.* 2008).

It has been suggested that co-creating contexts may present opportunities for firms to propose offerings that enable better outcomes for customers (e.g. Prahalad and Ramaswamy 2004; Payne *et al.* 2008; Grönroos and Ravald 2009). Payne *et al.* (2008) go as far as to suggest that the firm, through the development of interactions, may create opportunities to engage itself with customers' work and influence their realization practices/processes and therefore the value emerging from these practices/processes. However, as we have depicted through the width of the arrows in Figure 11.2, resource contributed by each system may not be equal throughout the context and therefore there are implications for control and power over the context. This is because the context for achieving end-states for an offering's use holds greater information and visibility for the customer than for the firm, resulting in the customer having access to more contingent resources. For example, a mobile phone company may understand that the use of a mobile phone requires some level of quietness, privacy for the conversation, and good reception for the call, but it can only provide the reception. The customer, at the point of use, would need to harness contextual and in some cases, material resources (e.g. going into a room) to achieve end-states at the point of use. Literature has suggested that service systems for co-creation may not always result in the best outcomes and in some cases, may even result in benefits that are lower than expected or proposed (Yip 2012). For example, some authors have implied that while firms and consumers are able to co-create value, they are also capable of co-destroying value (Plé and Cáceres 2010; Echeverri and Skålén 2011). While it is arguable whether value that has not been realized can be destroyed, it is reasonable to suggest that expected or proposed value may result in negative value if the resources and processes for co-creation between systems are not compatible or aligned. Moreover, as the firm designs and manages its system for co-creation, this may involve a re-evaluation of organizational principles, structures, and processes, and consequently may represent a major managerial challenge (Prahalad and Ramaswamy 2000; Oliva and Kallenberg 2003). For example, the 'DART' model presented by Prahalad and Ramaswamy (2004) highlights dialogue, access, risk assessment, and transparency between customer and organization systems as important building blocks towards a firm understanding how value might be co-created. In this model, it is suggested that co-creation means interactivity, engagement, and equal propensity to act from both systems. As such, it suggests that the firm may have to give customers access to information and data to ensure effective learning and to inform customers of any risks. Companies have traditionally benefited from information asymmetry between the consumer and the firm. If firms strategically manage and design their service system for co-creation, that asymmetry may be diminished and firms can no longer assume opaqueness of prices, costs, processes, and profit margins (Prahalad and Ramaswamy 2004).

As discussed, literature on value co-creation has presented models of value co-creation and suggested benefits and possible implications of an organizational system for co-creation. With the exception of Payne *et al.* (2008), limited research has been conducted into how organizations should manage co-creation. This chapter goes on to address the question of *what challenges do the design and management of a service system for co-creation present?*

Method

To address this question, the chapter reviews and comparatively analyses three case studies, the unit of analysis of which is an individual contract. A case study method is an appropriate approach for improving understanding of operational issues, as it allows an investigation of potential challenges for management and design of service systems for co-creation (Eisenhardt and Graebner 2007). The cases presented have been widely reported in a series of publications[1] (see Ng and Nudurupati 2010; Ng *et al.* 2010, 2011, 2012a and b; Smith *et al.* 2012) and it is proposed that they are representative cases of service systems for co-created outcomes. As previously discussed, service systems are considered a dynamic configuration, or arrangement, of resources that create and deliver value between the provider and the customer through service (IfM and IBM 2008). Each of the cases is explored in terms of the type and configuration of provider and customer resources employed in the delivery of a co-created outcome, which is determined by the contract terms.

All three case studies explore maintenance, repair, and overhaul service contracts in the defence industry and were conducted between 2007 and 2010. The details of each case are provided in Table 11.1. Two of the cases

Table 11.1 Service systems for co-created outcomes–case studies

	Provider organization	Customer organization	Equipment	Primary contract outcome	Contract pricing mechanism	Performance measure	People directly employed on contract
Case 1*	Aerospace Systems (anonymized) (primary contractor)	Western-European Defence Department	Fastjet	To maintain a defined level of available mission-ready flying hours across a fleet of approx. 200 aircraft	10+ year (through-life) contract. Total value of approx. £946m. Charged based on an annual rate (barring exceptions and pain/gain share mechanisms). Incentives against key performance indicators	Measurement of availability of a bank of flying hours of the aircraft. In addition, there was a non-contractual key performance indicator based on GFX (Government furnished materials, including supplying physical facilities, material, data, IT, and labour). This was part of the Defence Department's performance measurement in delivering the necessary assets and labour for the programme.	+1500 people on a joint project team comprising the Defence Department Equipment and Support organization and Aerospace Systems
Case 2*	Western-European Defence Department	Western-European Defence Department	Missile system	To maintain a defined level of percentage availability of the missile system	13+ year (through-life) contract. Approx. £156m firm price contract, including incentives against key performance indicators	The measurement of availability in barracks and the availability in the 'operating theatre' (e.g. in Afghanistan)	+1500 people on a joint project team comprising the Defence Department and Missile Systems

| Case 3** | ABC (anonymized) | Western-European Defence Department | Multipurpose military helicopter engine | To provide engine support on request (including preventative, scheduled, and unscheduled) | Paid on the basis of time and material, including the actual cost of direct labour, materials, and equipment use, and a fixed add-on to cover overheads and profit. | To respond to requests within 24 hours. Measurement against specified overhaul turnaround times. | Provider employees only. Approx. 30 directly incurred on the programme. Over 1000 directly allocated from various departments. |

*Cases 1 and 2 relate to a project consortium funded by the Engineering and Physical Science Research Council (UK). The information for these cases has been reproduced, with author permission, from the following publications: Ng and Nudurupati 2010; Ng et al., 2010, 2011, 2012a.

**Case 3 was made possible through the ESRC/AIM Services Fellowship programme and information for the case has been reproduced, with author permission, from the following publications: Ng et al. 2012b, Smith et al., 2012.

are specifically concerned with contracts on performance-based outcomes in which the company is tasked to deliver specific levels of performance in collaboration with the customer, rather than merely provide assets or activities. It can therefore be argued that these contracts in particular serve as an exemplar for co-created and co-produced value, where both parties are focused on achieving outcomes.

Findings: The Challenges of Service Systems for Co-creation

The Determination Challenge

Payne *et al.* (2008) stated that in managing the co-creation of value, business strategy starts by understanding the customer's value-creating practices and processes and selecting which of these they wish to support. This positioning within the customer's processes thus defines the scope of the firm's value proposition. Evidence from the cases similarly suggests that there may be multiple value propositions for co-created value, upon which a firm may wish to contract. From the cases, four value propositions for co-created systems are found for defence equipment, each representing a different service system for the co-creation of value-in-use of military equipment.

These value propositions are: (1) the potential performance of the asset in use; (2) the minimum disruption to potential use; (3) maximizing potential availability of equipment for use; and (4) supporting capability for a given operational goal (Smith *et al.* 2012, forthcoming). The first of these value propositions is representative of traditional manufacturing of equipment, in which three firms—Aerospace Systems, Missile Systems, and *ABC*—contracted on the transfer of ownership of the equipment. The equipment proposes a certain value to the customer, the Defence Department, in use through its potential performance, but is realized almost solely by the Defence Department's customer system in the context of their own operating environment. As such, the only organizational system resource supplied for integration is the asset itself. Second, it was found that organizations could co-create for minimum disruption to the asset's potential performance in use, through collaborative support of processes and practices for recovery of the asset at the point of failure. This is demonstrated in Case 3, where *ABC* provides unscheduled support through the integration of organizational resources such as time and materials. Third, Cases 1 and 2 contracted on availability for use of equipment determined as the 'readiness' of a fleet of engines or a weapon system for deployment. In these cases, aerospace systems and missile systems not only contractually provide their system resources for integration, but are also responsible for the management and activity of resource integration. Last, while not explicit in any of the case contracts, there was evidence of organizational resources being integrated for the capability of equipment in use towards certain operational outcomes. For example, in Case 3 the firm was found to provide advice and materials for specific military operations:

> You can say right, the serviceable assets—I could take that assembly, that assembly and that assembly and build an (*asset*) good for (*a certain performance*) and send it to (*achieve this goal*) (cited in Smith *et al.*, forthcoming; Table 11.1)

Analysis of the three cases shows that in designing a service system for co-creation, there may be multiple levels of value-creating practice and process upon which the firm can base its value proposition. This is the determination challenge of which value-creating processes contract upon.

The Measurement Challenge

In the design of a service system for co-creation, once a firm has determined the value-creating practices and process it wishes to support, it is faced with a measurement challenge. Payne *et al.* (2008) and Payne and Frow (2005) discuss the difficulty of developing appropriate metrics for value-in-use, stating that metrics to measure and monitor the performance of customer relationships are often not well developed or well communicated. The challenge of developing appropriate measures is illustrated in Case 1, where the contracted performance measure for aerospace systems is a measurable bank of available flying hours. However, Aerospace Systems also adheres to non-contractual GFX metrics, which reflect the measures against which the Defence Department is monitored. Therefore, the contract measures performance against the value of the equipment in use, but this is not necessarily the only measure of value in use for the customer's achievement of its own goals.

The Revenue Challenge

Related to the determination and measurement challenges is the task of how to manage revenues in service systems for value co-creation. As shown in Table 11.1, firms in Cases 1 and 2 both charge based on a firm price annual rate for availability of equipment, barring exceptions and pain/gain share mechanisms. Alternatively, in Case 3, *ABC* charges based on the actual resources consumed. Although Cases 1 and 2 operate to a different level of contracted outcome than Case 3, it does raise the issue of mutuality of value outcomes. If a service system for co-creation is to be viable, it must hold potential value for both the customer and the provider. When considering financial benefits of service systems, it has been reported by the National Audit Office that in Case

1, the Defence Department has saved £1.3bn, reducing the cost per flying hour by 51%. Similarly, in Case 2 the Defence Department has estimated cost savings of £175m over the period of the equipment's lifetime (http://www. defenseindustrydaily.com/). This illustrates potential financial benefit for the customer of a service system for co-creation. However, it has been shown, in the case of servitization, that a shift towards delivering value-in-use is not always profitable for the providing organization, as although it is seen to increase revenue, it is not always profitable for the bottom line (Neely 2008). What is not evidenced in the cases is whether Cases 1 and 2 have both benefited financially from a service system for co-creation. Arguably, a firm price contract holds an element of risk not present in the revenue management mechanism of *ABC,* which guarantees that a loss is not made, as all direct and indirect costs of achieving the outcome are covered. This presents a revenue challenge of service systems for co-creation.

The Context Challenge

An S-D logic perspective of value creation suggests that value created in use is contextual. Therefore, social, ecological, and environmental surroundings at the point of use, while not possible to control, would be endogenous to a service system designed for value co-creation (Vargo *et al.* 2008). As a result, the management of a service system for co-creation could be affected by context. Findings from the cases suggest that use of defence equipment is dependent on context. Indeed, customer's use of equipment, and more specifically their repeat and changing conditions of use, led to uncertainties in achieving outcomes consistently.

In all three cases, it was found that the variety of use situations directly influenced the firm's ability to co-create outcomes. In Case 3, for example, the helicopter engine was designed over thirty years ago for use in European climates. Circumstances and use situations have changed over the lifetime of the engine and now the customer is operating it in hot and sandy conditions in Afghanistan, which affect the engine's performance in use. This is illustrated in the following extract from an interview with a programme manager in Case 3:

> We have deployed equipment out in Afghanistan and then we have other training activities in the UK and in Europe, the conditions are quite different, when they're out in theatre, it's quite a harsh environment for a helicopter, when they come back they tend to require more overhaul of the modules. (ESRC/AIM Services Fellowship programme, unpublished raw data)

This demonstrates a variety in request for organization resources dependent on context of use. In addition, it was also found that over time, with changing use conditions, the firm needed to redesign the equipment or install new technologies so that it could be used more effectively. Concurrently, the firm would also redesign the service and support activities to facilitate use of equipment more efficiently. In Cases 1 and 2, where firms contracted on outcomes, findings showed that the variety of use became a serious issue as contracts required constant amendment to accommodate increasing sets of contextual possibilities. This suggests that contextual variety in use presents a challenge in the management of service systems for co-created outcomes.

The Resource Challenge

It has been argued previously in the chapter that in designing and managing a service system for co-creation, a customer's resources to co-create value become central towards realizing a firm's value proposition. Evidence from the case studies suggests that firms integrate customer operand resources, including material and information resources in the delivery of co-created outcomes. The following extract from a programme manager in Case 3 illustrates use of customer material resources in the firm's practices and processes for co-created outcomes:

> Sometimes we're using his assets as well. So if he's got assets in store then we request that we have those parts to use in his (*assets*). We've also asked our customers whether we can buy some of his stock. (cited in Smith *et al.*, forthcoming)

The following extract from the same case provides an example of information required to co-create outcomes:

> I'd have to know what they're doing with it, how many hours they're running with it and what their plans are for it longer-term and also some records of the history of each of the (*assets*) (cited in Smith *et al.* 2012: 12).

As the case evidence suggests, a service system for co-creation requires integration of customer materials and information in the firm's value-creating processes and practices to achieve outcomes. This may present potential challenges, in terms of gaining access to information and material, if this requirement is not stipulated under contractual agreements. This thus gives rise to a customer resource challenge in managing a service system for co-creation.

The Skills Challenge

Further to integration of operand resources such as material and information, case evidence also suggests that firms may need to transform and align the customers' operant resources (i.e. people behaviours) to achieve contracted outcomes. In fact, analysis of Cases 1 and 2 suggests that both behavioural and information alignment between the two systems provide significant explanatory power on contract performance (see Ng *et al.*, 2012a).

Under availability based contracts such as Cases 1 and 2, the customer's failure to co-create value results in the firm not being able to achieve the outcomes they have been contracted to deliver. Hence, the customer's skills and ability to access resources to co-create value becomes the firm's responsibility. Case evidence suggests that aerospace systems and missile systems put in place structures and processes to ensure expectations are congruent and competencies are complementary between themselves and their customer, the Defence Department. This was partially achieved through becoming fully engaged in the use practices and processes of the customer, to understand the pressures from the use of the equipment, and to recommend how both the firm and the customer resources could be deployed to deliver the outcomes across varying states and varieties of use. Even in Case 3, which was not contracted on availability, there is evidence of customer behaviour transformation. For example, a programme manager states:

> Helicopters have got a lot heavier and the flying has got a lot harder, especially in hot climates. Therefore, we're seeing corrosion. [To prevent injury or damage] we've instructed that they inspect the engines every 1,000 hours and any corrosion witnessed on the blades, they've got to throw them away and replace them. (ESRC/AIM Services Fellowship programme, unpublished raw data)

Given the importance of behavioural alignment in the achievement of outcomes, it can be implied that firms must develop customer management as a core competence, a point echoed by Prahalad and Ramaswamy (2000). The challenge for transforming operant resources, therefore, may present itself as a skills challenge. However, to achieve behavioural transformation is not merely an issue of skill; the firm must be in a position to transform the behaviour of customers as well as be empowered for such behavioural transformation. In Cases 1 and 2, contractual mechanisms ensure a certain degree of power and influence. In Case 3 however, it is likely that *ABC* has less control over customer behaviour in use.

Discussion

A service system for value co-creation, particularly for the delivery of outcomes, changes the boundaries of the firm. In the traditional notion of value creation, the customer system was 'outside the company' and value creation occurred inside the company through its activities, as in Figure 11.1.

The company and the consumer had distinct roles of production and consumption respectively. Aerospace systems produced an aircraft; the Defence Department used that aircraft as part of a system of resources to achieve military operations. Service systems for value co-creation shift the boundaries of value creation, shifting the skills sets and capability of the company to focus on *effects* of what they make/do and the *effects* of what customers do in combination for value-in-use. This redraws a system to focus on joint system capability of customer and company.

The transition from practices under the traditional view of value creation to practices, which are co-created is not a minor change, as the six challenges suggest. Indeed, this chapter proposes that service systems for value co-creation face at least six challenges in design and management: determination challenge; measurement challenge; revenue challenge; context challenge; resource challenge; and skills challenge. These challenges are in part due to the two primary implications of an S-D logic view of value creation, as discussed earlier in the chapter. First, value-in-use is realized in context and therefore would mean that the social, ecological, and environmental surroundings, while not possible to control, are endogenous to the process of value co-creation and therefore to the provider's service system (Vargo *et al.* 2011). This is because value-in-use is context dependent and even when the customer and the company do the exact same thing each time, the state of the world changes and together with it, the way the service is being delivered (Ng *et al.* 2010). Therefore, a service system for co-creation would compel the company to understand customer needs and use requirements better across differing environmental conditions, so that customers are able to realize the company's value proposition through their part in the co-creation process. In doing so, Storbacka and Lehtinen (2001) argue that this may involve: a review of co-creation opportunities; planning, testing, and prototyping value co-creation opportunities with customers; implementing customer solutions and managing customer encounters; and developing metrics to assess whether or not the enterprise is making appropriate value propositions.

Second, an S-D logic view of value creation suggests that customers' resources to co-create value become central towards realizing a firm's value proposition. As Prahalad and Ramaswamy (2004) discuss, the customer as a co-creator does not mean a transfer or outsourcing of activities to customers, a customization of products and services, or a scripting or staging of customer events (see Table 11.2). Rather, it is about collaborative, partnered achievement of outcomes and requires behavioural, information, and process alignment.

Whether or not an organization chooses to contract on the co-creation of customer outcomes, and therefore act as a partner in the value creation process, is a matter of strategy. It may not be viable for all organizations or industries to adopt this type of business model. As Oliva and Kallenberg (2003)

Table 11.2 The concept of co-creation

What co-creation is not	What co-creation is
'Customer focus', 'Customer is king', or 'Customer is always right'	Co-creation is about join creation by the company and the customer. It is not the company trying to please the customer
Delivering good customer service	Facilitating customer co-construction of the service experience to suit their context
Mass customization of offerings that suit the industry's supply chain	Joint problem definition and solving
Transfer of activities from the company to the customer as in self-service	Creating an experience environment in which consumers can have active dialogue and co-construct their individual experiences; product may be the same but customers will realize different experiences
Product variety	Embracing and recognizing variety in experience
Segment of one	Experience of one
Meticulous market research	Experiencing the offering as customers do in real time
Staging experiences	Co-constructing experiences
Demand-side innovation for new products and services	Innovating experience environments from new co-creation experiences

Source: (updated/adapted from Prahalad and Ramaswamy 2004)

discuss, service systems for co-creation incur operating risks because a service system or co-creation takes responsibility for part or all of the end-user's process over which they may have limited control. Moreover, not all customers may prefer the firm to take an active role in the creation of value-in-use. They may indeed prefer to be the sole resource integrator and simply contract with a firm to acquire the necessary resources to achieve value-in-use on their own. However, the latter challenges of co-creation regarding customer context and resources provide opportunities for firms to innovate their offerings to better support a customer's realization of value without necessarily contracting to co-provide them. Through exploration of use, firms can support the processes and practices of integration and provide information on other resources that might improve their use experience.

Conclusion

Service systems for co-creation are gaining a more prominent role within certain industries, not only in defence, but also in industries such as healthcare (with greater customer empowerment in their treatment), mobile telecommunication and the internet (with user generated content), and education (with self-study courses). Some argue that this is the world we are moving towards, a world in which the customer and their resources are a partner in the processes and practices of the firm (Prahalad and Ramaswamy 2000). As we have discussed, it may not be a question of whether customers and their resources are a partner to the provider in the value creation process. Under S-D logic, customers are always considered co-creators of value, as value is phenomenologically determined by them, in use. In this case, it is a question of to what extent, strategically, providers choose to be a partner in the customers' processes and practices of value creation in use. Through a review of three widely published cases, this chapter summarizes six challenges in the design and management of a service system for co-creation: determination challenge; measurement challenge; revenue challenge; context challenge; resource challenge; and skills challenge.

The challenges presented in this chapter have been identified through exploration of the co-production and co-creation of functional or operational outcomes in the context of business-to-business organizations. Future research in co-creation should also investigate service systems for co-creation in business-to-consumer outcomes. It is likely that in these contexts outcomes will not be limited to functional outcomes but may involve layers of functional and social outcomes. Furthermore, the balance of influence, power, and trust in business-to-consumer markets are likely to be different.

Notes

1. This was made possible through two programmes of research: first, the ESRC/AIM Service Fellowship Programme and second, a grant consortium funded by the Engineering and Physical Science Research Council (UK).

References

Arnould, E.J., Price, L.L., and Malshe, A. (2006). Toward a cultural resource-based theory of the customer. In: *The Service-dominant Logic of Marketing: Dialog, debate and directions*, Lusch, R.F. and Vargo, S.L. (Ed.), pp. 320–333. Armonk, NY: ME Sharpe.

Chandler, J. and Vargo, S. L. (2011), Contextualization and value-in-context: how context frames exchange. *Marketing Theory*, 11, 35–49.

Dabholkar, P. (1990). How to improve perceived service quality by improving customer participation. In: *Developments in Marketing Science*, Duniap, B.J. (Ed.), pp. 483–487. Cullowhee, NC: Academy of Marketing Science.

Drucker, P.F. (1974). *Management: tasks, responsibilities, practices*. New York: Harper and Row, Publishers Inc.

Echeverri, P. and Skålén, P. (2011). Co-creation and co-destruction: a practice-theory based study of interactive value formation. *Marketing Theory*, 11(3), 351–373.

Eggert, A. and Ulaga, W. (2002). Customer-perceived value: a substitute for satisfaction in company markets? *Journal of Company and Industrial Marketing*, **17**(2/3), 107–118.

Eisenhardt, K.M. and Graebner, M.E. (2007). Theory building from cases: opportunities and challenges. *Academy of Management Journal*, **50**, 25–32.

Fitzsimmons, J.A. (1985). Consumer participation and productivity in service operations. *Interfaces*, **15**(3), 60–67.

Grönroos, C. (2008). Service logic revisited: who creates value? And who co-creates? *European Management Review*, **20**(4), 298–314.

Grönroos, C. (2011). Value co-creation in service logic: a critical analysis, *Marketing Theory*, **11**(3), 279–301.

Grönroos, C. and Ravald, A. (2009). Marketing and the logic of service: value facilitation, value creation and co-creation, and their marketing implications. Working Paper Hanken School of Economics.

Heskett, J.L., Sasser Jr, W.E., and Schlesinger, L.A. (1997). *The Service Profit Chain: how leading companies link profit and growth to loyalty. Satisfaction, and Value.* New York: The Free Press.

Holbrook, M.B. (1994). The nature of customer value. In: *Service Quality: new directions in theory and practice*, Rust, R.T. and Oliver, R.L. (Ed.), pp. 21–71. Sage, Newbury Park, CA.

Holbrook, M.B. (2006). ROSEPEKICECIVECI versus CCV: the resource-operant, skills-exchanging, performance-experiencing, knowledge-informed, competence-enacting, co-producer-involved, value-emerging, customer-interactive view of marketing versus the concept of customer value: 'I can get it for you wholesale'. In: *The Service Dominant Logic of Marketing: dialog, debate and directions*, Lusch, R.F. and Vargo, S.L. (Ed.), pp. 208–223. Armonk, NY: M.E. Sharpe.

IfM and IBM. (2008). *Succeeding through service innovation: a service perspective for education, research, business and government.* Cambridge: University of Cambridge Institute for Manufacturing.

Kotler, P. (1972). A generic concept of marketing. *Journal of Marketing*, **36**(April), 46–54.

Lapierre, J. (1997). What does value mean in business-to-business professional services? *International Journal of Service Industry Management*, **8**(5), 377–397.

Levitt, T. (1969). *The Marketing Mode: pathways to corporate growth.* New York: McGraw-Hill.

Meuter, M.L. and Bitner, M.J. (1998). Self-service technologies: extending service frameworks and identifying issues for research. In: *AMA Winter Educators Conference*, Grewal, D. and Pechmann, C. (Ed.), pp. 12–19. Chicago, IL: American Marketing Association.

Naumann, E. (1995). *Creating Customer Value. The Path to Sustainable Competitive Advantage.* Cincinnati, OH: Thompson Executive Press.

Neely, A. (2008). Exploring the financial consequences of the servitization of manufacturing. *Operations Management Research,* **1**(2), 103–118.

Ng, I.C.L. and Nudurupati, S. (2010). Outcome-based service contracts in the defence industry—mitigating the challenges. *Journal of Service Management*, 2, 656–674.

Ng, I., Ding, X., and Yip, N. (2012a). Outcome-based contracts as new business model: the role of partnership and value-driven relational assets. WMG Service Systems Research Group Working Paper Series, paper no. 04/12.

Ng, I.C.L., Guo, L., Scott, J., and Yip, N. (2008). Towards a benefit-based framework for understanding B2B services and its impact on contract and capability. *Proceedings of the 10th International Research Seminar in Services Management*, 27–30 May 2008, La Londe, France.

Ng, I.C.L., Nudurupati, S., and Tasker, P. (2010). Value co-creation in outcome-based contracts for equipment-based service. AIM Working Paper Series, WP No. 77—May (http://www.aimresearch.org/index.php?page=wp-no-77).

Ng, I.C.L., Nudurupati, S., and Williams, J. (2011). Redefining organizational capability for value co-creation in complex engineering service systems. In: *Complex Engineering Service Systems: concepts and research*, Ng, I.C.L., Parry, G., Wild, P., MacFarlane, D., and Tasker, P. (Ed.), pp. 109–128. London: Springer.

Ng, I.C.L., Parry, G., Smith, L., Maull, R., and Briscoe, G. (2012b). Transitioning from a goods-dominant to a service-dominant logic: visualising the value proposition of Rolls-Royce. *Journal of Service Management*, **23** (3), 416–439.

Normann, R. (2001). *Reframing Company: when the map changes the landscape*. Chichester: John Wiley.

Normann, R. and Ramírez, R. (1994). *Designing Interactive Strategy: from value chain to value constellation*. Chichester: John Wiley and Sons.

Oliva, R. and Kallenberg, R. (2003). Managing the transition from products to services. *International Journal of Service Industry Management*, 14(2), 160–172.

Ordanini, A. and Pasini, P. (2008). Service co-production and value co-creation: the case for a service-oriented architecture (SOA). *European Management Journal*, 26, 289–297.

Parasuraman, A. (1997). Reflections on gaining competitive advantage through customer value. *Journal of the Academy of Marketing Science*, **25**(2) 154–161.

Payne, A. and Frow, P. (2005). A strategic framework for customer relationship management. *Journal of Marketing*, **69**, 167–176.

Payne, A. and Holt, S. (2001). Diagnosing customer value: integrating the value process and relationship marketing. *British Journal of Management*, **12**, 159–182.

Payne, A., Storbacka, K., and Frow, P. (2008). Managing the co-creation of value. *Academy of Marketing Science*, **36**, 83–96.

Plé, L. and Cáceres, R.C. (2010). Not always co-creation: introducing interactional co-destruction of value in service-dominant logic. *Journal of Services Marketing*, **24**(6), 430–437.

Prahalad, C.K. and Ramaswamy, V. (2000). Co-opting customer competence. *Harvard Business Review*, **78**, 79–87.

Prahalad, C.K. and Ramaswamy, V. (2004). Co-creation experiences: the next practice in value creation. *Journal of Interactive Marketing*, **18**(3), 5–14.

Sawhney, M. (2006). Going beyond the product: defining, designing and delivering customer solutions In: *The Service Dominant Logic of Marketing: Dialog, debate and directions*, Lusch, R.F. and Vargo, S.L. (Ed.), pp. 365–380. New York: M.E. Sharpe, Inc.

Schneider, B. and Bowen, D.E. (1995). *Winning the Service Game*. Boston, MA: Harvard Business School Press.

Slater, S.F. and Narver, J.C. (1995). Market orientation and the learning organization. *Journal of Marketing*, **59**(3), 63–74.

Smith, Adam. (1776/1904). *An Inquiry into the Nature and Causes of the Wealth of Nations*. London: W. Strahan and T. Cadell.

Smith, L., Maull, R.M. and I.C.L. Ng, (forthcoming) Servitization and operations management: a service dominant logic approach, *International Journal of Operations and Production Management*.

Smith, L., Ng, I.C.L., and Maull, R. (2012). The three value proposition cycles of equipment-based service. *Production Planning and Control*, **23**(7), 553–570.

Spohrer, J., Maglio, P.P., Bailey, J., and Gruhl, D. (2007). Steps toward a science of service systems. *Computer*, **40**, 71–77.

Spohrer, J., Vargo, S.L., Caswell, N., and Maglio, P.P. (2008). The service system is the basic abstraction of service science. In: Proceedings of the 41st Annual Hawaii International Conference on System Science, January, p. 104.

Storbacka, K. and Lehtinen, J. R. (2001). *Customer Relationship Management: creating competitive advantage through win–win relationship strategies*. Singapore: McGraw-Hill.

Vargo, S.L. (2009). Doing research in service: a research meeting on the Service-Dominant Logic. Advanced Institute for Management (AIM) Research Workshop, 19 March 2009, London (http://www.aimresearch.org).

Vargo, S.L. and Lusch, R.F. (2004). Evolving to a new dominant logic in marketing. *Journal of Marketing*, **68**, 1–17.

Vargo, S.L. and Lusch R.F. (2008). Service-dominant logic: continuing the evolution. *Journal of the Academy of Marketing Science*, **36**, 1–10.

Vargo, S.L. and Lusch, R.F. (2011). Its all B2B...and beyond: toward a systems perspective of the market. *Industrial Marketing Management*, **40**, 181–187.

Vargo, S.L. and Morgan, F.W. (2005). Services in society and academic thought: a historical analysis. *Journal of Macromarketing*, **25**, 42–53.

Vargo, S.L., Maglio, P.P., and Akaka, M.A. (2008). On value and value co-creation: a service systems and service logic perspective. *European Management Journal*, **26**, 145–152.

Wilkstrom, S. (1996). Value creation by company-consumer interaction. *Journal of Marketing Management*, **12**, 359–374.

Woodruff R. B. (1997). Customer value: the next source of competitive advantage. *Journal of the Academy of Marketing Science*, **25**(2), 139–153.

Yip, K.T. (2012). What are the attributes of value co-creation and how may they impact on the customers willingness to pay? Observations from three service industries. PhD Thesis, University of Exeter.

Zuboff, S. and Maxmin, J. (2002). *The Support Economy*. New York: Penguin.

Index

Index